Translanguaging, Coloniality and Decolonial Cracks

TRANSLANGUAGING IN THEORY AND PRACTICE

Series Editors: **Li Wei**, *University College London*, **Angel Lin**, *Simon Fraser University*, **Yuen Yi Lo**, *The University of Hong Kong* and **Saskia Van Viegen**, *York University*.

Translanguaging in Theory and Practice aims to publish work that highlights the dynamic use of an individual's linguistic repertoire and challenges the socially and politically defined boundaries of languages and their hierarchy. We invite research from across disciplines by both established and emergent researchers in multifarious settings, including everyday use, educational, digital and workplace contexts. We also actively welcome and solicit studies on translanguaging in contexts where English is not the mainstream language and where other modalities and semiotic resources take prominence over speech and writing. The series is transdisciplinary and encourages scholars to publish empirical research on translanguaging, especially that which aims to disrupt power relations, to create new identities and communities, to engage in the discussion of translanguaging theories and pedagogies, and/or to help the field of translanguaging consolidate its scholarship.

Topics to be covered by the series include:

- Theoretical underpinnings of Translanguaging.
- Translanguaging Pedagogies.
- Translanguaging in Assessment.
- Translanguaging and Language Policy.
- Translanguaging in Everyday Social Practices in Different Contexts and Communities, including Digital/ Social/ Media.

All books in this series are externally peer-reviewed.

Full details of all the books in this series and of all our other publications can be found on http://www.multilingual-matters.com, or by writing to Multilingual Matters, St Nicholas House, 31–34 High Street, Bristol, BS1 2AW, UK.

TRANSLANGUAGING IN THEORY AND PRACTICE: 4

Translanguaging, Coloniality and Decolonial Cracks

Bilingual Science Learning in South Africa

Robyn Tyler

MULTILINGUAL MATTERS
Bristol • Jackson

DOI https://doi.org/10.21832/TYLER1982
Library of Congress Cataloging in Publication Data
A catalog record for this book is available from the Library of Congress.
Names: Tyler, Robyn, author.
Title: Translanguaging, Coloniality and Decolonial Cracks: Bilingual Science Learning in South Africa/Robyn Tyler.
Description: Bristol, UK; Jackson, TN: Multilingual Matters, 2023. | Series: Translanguaging in Theory and Practice: 4 | Includes bibliographical references and index. | Summary: "In this ethnography of bilingual science learning, the author connects microanalyses of classroom discourse to broader themes of de/coloniality in education. The author examines the linguistic landscape of the school and the attitudes of staff and students which produce both coloniality and cracks in the edifice of coloniality"—Provided by publisher.
Identifiers: LCCN 2022039345 (print) | LCCN 2022039346 (ebook) | ISBN 9781800411982 (hardback) | ISBN 9781800413566 (paperback) | ISBN 9781800411999 (pdf) | ISBN 9781800412002 (epub)
Subjects: LCSH: Multilingual education—South Africa. | Translanguaging (Linguistics) | Science—Study and teaching (Secondary)—South Africa. | Language policy—South Africa.
Classification: LCC LC3738.S6 T95 2023 (print) | LCC LC3738.S6 (ebook) | DDC 370.117/50968—dc23/eng/20220824
LC record available at https://lccn.loc.gov/2022039345
LC ebook record available at https://lccn.loc.gov/2022039346

British Library Cataloguing in Publication Data
A catalogue entry for this book is available from the British Library.

ISBN-13: 978-1-80041-198-2 (hbk)
ISBN-13: 978-1-80041-356-6 (pbk)

Multilingual Matters
UK: St Nicholas House, 31–34 High Street, Bristol, BS1 2AW, UK.
USA: Ingram, Jackson, TN, USA.

Website: www.multilingual-matters.com
Twitter: Multi_Ling_Mat
Facebook: https://www.facebook.com/multilingualmatters
Blog: www.channelviewpublications.wordpress.com

Copyright © 2023 Robyn Tyler.

All rights reserved. No part of this work may be reproduced in any form or by any means without permission in writing from the publisher.

The policy of Multilingual Matters/Channel View Publications is to use papers that are natural, renewable and recyclable products, made from wood grown in sustainable forests. In the manufacturing process of our books, and to further support our policy, preference is given to printers that have FSC and PEFC Chain of Custody certification. The FSC and/or PEFC logos will appear on those books where full certification has been granted to the printer concerned.

Typeset by SAN Publishing Services.

For my parents, Christine and Campbell.
And to the young people of Grade 9B, 2016: Nibahle!

Contents

	Acknowledgements	ix
1	De/coloniality and Language in South African Schooling	1
2	Language, the Body and Identity in Learning	22
3	Language at Success High: Ideologies and Practices	41
4	Constraint in Curriculum, Assessment and Classroom Discourse	69
5	Decolonial Cracks Introduced by Students	84
6	Decolonial Cracks in Pedagogy: Freedom and Resistance	109
7	Conclusion: Widening the Cracks	135
	Appendix 1: A Multilingual Science Resources List	147
	Appendix 2: Grade 9 Chemical Reactions Tests and Worksheets: English, isiXhosa and Translingual	149
	Appendix 3: Transcription Convention	154
	References	155
	Index	166

Acknowledgements

It is a generous and brave teacher who allows a researcher access to her classroom. I am very grateful to Ms B for her vulnerability and willingness to help me. Ndiyabulela titshalakazi. Also, to the students of 9B: you took a chance on me and shared your vibrant selves with me. Thank you very much. Ndavuya ndahamba nani.

I would like to thank those people who have encouraged and supported me in completing this book. I am grateful to colleagues and graduate students at the Centre for Multilingualism and Diversities Research for your support and interest along this journey. Your engagement in seminars and discussions on my research has shaped my thinking deeply. Thank you to one of the series editors, Angel Lin, who encouraged me to write the book in the first place. I owe a huge debt of gratitude to my doctoral supervisor, Carolyn McKinney, for her intellectual and personal support beginning during my PhD and extending into this book project. Your encouragement, reading of drafts and insightful critique are invaluable. Thank you, too, for reminding me why we write books and keeping my vision lifted always towards social justice through language and literacy education. I would also like to thank Pam Christie for her very helpful comments on an early draft as well as the two anonymous reviewers of the manuscript who were exceptionally engaged readers. All shortcomings are now solely my own.

Transcribing noisy classroom video data is laborious and painstaking. Thank you to the transcribers and translators who worked with me on the data: Babalwayashe Molate and Juliette Manitshana. I would like to thank the artists who so beautifully transformed a suite of data into the cartoons included here: Zachary Stewart and Julia Davies. I so value your drawing skills. Thank you to Babalwayashe Molate and Lara Krause who worked with me to produce the multilingual Science tests in Appendix 2 which are based on a test developed at Success High.

Lastly, a very warm thank you to my friends and family. In particular, thank you to Mark, Georgia and Erin. Your love keeps me going.

I gratefully acknowledge the permission granted to re-use material from the following publications:

McKinney, C. and Tyler, R. (2018) Disinventing and reconstituting language for learning in school Science. *Language and Education* 33 (2), 141–158.

Tyler, R. (2021) Transcribing whole-body sense-making by non-dominant students in multilingual classrooms. *Classroom Discourse* 12 (4), 386–402. https://doi.org/10.1080/19463014.2021.1896563

Tyler, R. (2022) Identity meshing in learning Science bilingually: Tales of a 'coconuty nerd.' In C. McKinney and P. Christie (eds) *Decoloniality, Language and Literacy: Conversations with Teacher Educators* (pp. 63–77). Bristol: Multilingual Matters.

1 De/coloniality and Language in South African Schooling

Introduction

It is April 2016 and Ms B is teaching her Grade 9 Science class in Khayelitsha, South Africa. Her students are wrestling with understanding how atoms gain and lose electrons during reactions. The topic has been covered in the previous year, and this is the fourth hour that Ms B has spent teaching chemical reactions. Finally, understanding dawns for most of the young people in the room. When Ms B expresses her frustration that it took so long for them to understand, Onke, 15, rocks back on his chair and cries out: '*We were bhided by George!*' ('We were confused by English!').

In this exclamation, Onke meshes features of English and isiXhosa,[1] combined with a wide smile and a glance at his desk mate while rocking back on his chair to create an innovative, multimodal and irreverent performance. The performance is at the same time shot through with the precarity of this particular experience of language for learning Science in school. 'George' is a popular nickname for the English language among isiXhosa speakers, taken from George VI who was king of England at the time when the formal education of isiXhosa speakers in the colonial language was in its ascendancy in Southern Africa. Onke expresses in bald terms the deleterious effects of learning Science exclusively through a colonial language in which he is not yet fully proficient.

Onke's performance reverberates with the de/coloniality (Quijano, 2017) of language and identity for learning which goes to the heart of this book. Both ongoing coloniality and decolonial disruptions to this status quo are salient features of learning in Southern, post-colonial schools serving speakers of non-dominant languages. The study presented in this book focuses on black[2] bilingual teenage students studying Science in a high school – here called Success High – on the outskirts of Cape Town in 2016. As a doctoral researcher, I joined Ms B,[3] Onke, Khethiwe, Thandile, Mbulelo and the other students of Grade 9B for every Science lesson on the topic of chemical reactions over a six-week period. I also facilitated a voluntary Science study group which met in the library two afternoons a week. These teaching and learning activities in which I was a participant observer took place as part of the linguistic ethnography I conducted over nine months in the school. In this book, data will be presented which was collected in the form of photographs, documents, interviews and fieldnotes taken around the school premises, but the focus is on the multi-semiotic learning activities of the students, captured through audio- and video- recordings and photographs of exercise books.

The central argument of this book is that in studying key moments (Li, 2011) in the grittiness of getting learning done at school every day, processes of de/coloniality are revealed, and decolonial options begin to come into view. Data will be presented in the following chapters that demonstrate both the coloniality of language (Ndhlovu & Makalela, 2021; Veronelli, 2015), which frames much of the South African education system, and decolonial cracks (Mignolo & Walsh, 2018; Walsh, 2014), which emerge in this system. The particular focus of this de/colonial lens in the research is language and identity as part of learning. The interpretive approach and eclectic data collection of linguistic ethnography (Copland & Creese, 2015) enabled me to drill down into the detail of microinteractional practices while retaining an eye on the macrolevel of ideologies and policy and pulling these together. This provides fertile ground for bedding down decolonial theory in empirical and fine-grained examples within a particular context. The South African case is intended to resonate with efforts to apply a decolonial lens to bi/multilingual teaching and learning in contexts of coloniality elsewhere.

De/coloniality

Two key concerns in this book are coloniality and decoloniality. Anibal Quijano (2000) proposed the 'coloniality of power' as a way of explaining ongoing unequal and racialised conditions of living for post-colonial peoples worldwide. Quijano argued that at its heart, the inequality and subalternity that is observed among peoples globally is due to structures of power which have outlived colonial administrative regimes. An alternative to coloniality is decoloniality. Mignolo and Walsh (2018: 17) define decoloniality as a 'struggle', a 'response' and a 'practice' *against* the colonial matrix of power and *for* the possibilities of an 'otherwise'. Decoloniality has been inscribed in the literature variously as 'decoloniality', 'de-coloniality', '(de)coloniality' and 'de/coloniality'. It is the last iteration which I take up in this book. Quijano (2017) proposed the vision of the 'de/coloniality of power' as a transformed global reality where the decolonial emerges within a context of coloniality. Within Quijano's rendering is the acceptance that the colonial will continue to exist entangled with the decolonial, at least for some time to come, as asserted by Mignolo and Walsh (2018) in their definition of decoloniality above. The continuation of coloniality even while that coloniality is cracked open by decolonial actions and options (denoted by the slash) is a strong feature of the data presented in this book. I will argue that processes of coloniality and decoloniality are constantly operating and grating against each other in post-colonial schooling.

Coloniality of Language for Learning

Building on Quijano's proposal of the coloniality of power, Veronelli (2015) posited the 'coloniality of language' which she describes as a process of racialising colonised people as communicative agents. Two moves ensued from this racialisation. First, colonised people were found to be lacking in full languaging ability and therefore needing remediation by means of a colonial language; and second, the communication (not quite 'language' in the European sense) of colonised people could only be understood through the lens of European language theory. The first move was part of the invention of race and the inclusion of language (or lack of language) as a defining feature of a race within a racial hierarchy which positioned colonised peoples, and therefore their languaging, as inferior and deficient. The second move resulted in colonised people's languaging being codified, or 'invented' (Makoni & Pennycook, 2005), according to the pattern of European language theory at the time of colonisation, i.e. languages as bounded, countable entities (Ndhlovu & Makalela, 2021). Equally, viewed through the lens of European language theory, much of colonised people's languaging has been invisibilised.

Within education, the removal of the language of the colonised and its replacement by the colonial language has been poignantly described by Ngũgĩ Wa'Thiongo (1986) who wrote:

> Language was the most important vehicle through which that (colonial) power fascinated and held the soul prisoner. The bullet was the means of physical subjugation. Language was the means of spiritual subjugation. (1986: 9)

> Colonial alienation ... starts with a deliberate disassociation of the language of conceptualisation, of thinking, of formal education, of mental development, from the language of daily interaction in the home and in the community. It is like separating the mind from the body so that they are occupying two unrelated linguistic spheres in the same person. (1986: 28)

Ngũgĩ' brings home the violence of the coloniality of language through enforced education through a colonial language. Ngũgĩ's comments about the separating of the mind from the body are significant for the argument I am making here about the prominence of the coloniality of language in the African education context. It is not only an alien linguistic entity which must be occupied by the colonised subject, but it is a form of personhood disassociated from the body. I will return to this point.

Long-established patterns of the coloniality of language have a dominating and over-determining influence on what counts as knowledge, what counts as 'good' language in school and what counts as a resource for learning in South African education today. Within the logic of the coloniality of language, it is unthinkable that the language of non-dominant/racialised/colonised people can communicate the kinds of meanings that a colonial education system requires. As Veronelli (2015: 114) explains: 'to find in colonized peoples the ability to express complex cosmological, social, scientific, erotic, economic meaning is at odds with their reduction to inferior, animal-like beings'. Educated discourse being at odds with black language use was recently problematised by both school and university students in South Africa during the #RhodesMustFall movement and concomitant protests in high schools beginning in 2015. While the protests began as demands for the removal of colonial-era statues, language in learning was also a focus of protesters. University of Cape Town (UCT) student, Mjoli, expressed how she experienced coloniality on campus:

> The UCT I envision is the one that won't propel me to speak English all week long just to be accepted as intellectually equal to everybody. I envision a decolonised UCT that will not laugh at me when I present my research paper in isiZulu. (Mjoli, 2015: 7)

The coloniality of language is further evident in definitions of 'bilingual' or 'multilingual' education or speakers. In South Africa, 'bilingual education' has traditionally referred to education for white children in English and Afrikaans, using a parallel- or dual-medium model (Malherbe, 1946[4]). English-Afrikaans bilingualism in the 20th century was part of a political strategy to unite the white population, recently divided in the Anglo-Boer Wars, against 'die swart gevaar' (the black threat). However, there are no studies of classroom discourse in Afrikaans-English bilingual Science classrooms. This is testament to the accepted, normalised nature of Afrikaans-English bilingualism in South Africa that these classrooms have not garnered interest from South African discourse analysts. The formalising and resourcing of English/Afrikaans bilingualism to the exclusion of multilingualism in African languages and English is part of the racialised language hierarchies in operation in South Africa. Multilingual black South African children such as those in this study are typically construed in the public imagination as either deficient English monolinguals (McKinney, 2017) or as African language monolinguals. Each incorrect assumption leads to a different singular remedy for the teaching and learning problems related to language faced in our schooling system. The first leads to a call for more English and the second to a call for more of whichever standardised African language is deemed to be the 'home language' of the child. Both assumptions are based on language ideologies which this study seeks to expose and critique.

Language ideologies have been defined as:

> the sets of beliefs, values and cultural frames that continually circulate in society, informing the way in which language is conceptualised and represented as well as how it is used. (Makoe & McKinney, 2014: 659)

Three powerful language ideologies that are part of the coloniality of language and circulate in the education sphere in South Africa are a monoglossic ideology, raciolinguistic ideologies and Anglonormativity. A monoglossic ideology constructs one named language as being naturally associated with one nation and monolingual proficiency in the language of the nation as a characteristic of an ideal citizen and the global norm. This ideology leads to the construction of academic subjects such as 'Home Language' and 'Additional Language' which are two of the three compulsory subjects required to earn a National Senior Certificate (the final school exit examination in Year 12) in South Africa. The analysis of a monoglossic language ideology has been taken up by scholars of African multilingualism who have pointed out that the naming, codifying and transliteration of African languages by missionaries and other colonial administrators amounts to the 'colonial invention' (Makoni & Pennycook, 2005; Ndhlovu & Makalela, 2021) of discrete African languages. The colonial invention of African languages is theorised as forming part of a colonial strategy of divide and rule. In South Africa, for example, the nine official African languages enshrined in the constitution of democratic South Africa stemmed from the language ascribed to each of the nine 'native homelands' to which black South Africans were restricted under Apartheid. Raciolinguistic ideologies construct racialised bodies – i.e. all people not considered to be white – as engaging in deficient linguistic practices as appraised through the gaze of the white listening subject (Flores & Rosa, 2015). In multilingual former British colonies such as India, Zimbabwe, South Africa, Singapore and Australia, as well as in the US, arguably the strongest form of coloniality in schooling is what McKinney (2017) describes as Anglonormativity: the assumption that people will be and should be proficient in English and are deficient, or even deviant, if they are not (McKinney, 2017: 80). Anglonormativity positions African language speakers as deficient as they enter the schooling system, and their language resources are re-cast by policymakers and practitioners as a problem that needs to be fixed. Anglonormativity dominates admissions, curricula, staff appointments, learning and teaching materials, classroom practices and the linguistic landscape in schooling contexts such as Success High. The normalisation of English as the only appropriate language for learning is part of the coloniality of language that Ngũgĩ (2018: 125) refers to as 'normalizing the abnormal'. As McKinney (2017) argues, Anglonormativity is not only the insistence upon 'English', but a certain prestigious type of English: one that often adheres to the ethnolinguistic repertoires of whiteness. I would add, along with Ngũgĩ (1986), that it is not only a narrowed form of 'English' which dominates in school, but also a form of 'English' which is stripped of multimodality, in particular, bodily modes of expression.

While South Africa is described as a post-colonial country in political and administrative terms, coloniality persists in all aspects of society, including education. Post-colonial policy and practice in education may be seen as a palimpsest (Christie, 2021) where revisions are made on top of colonial patterns which have been laid down over centuries and persist despite changes. In South Africa, as in most of Africa, the history of schooling is intertwined with the history of colonialism and the imposition of colonial languages on the indigenous people as part of a 'civilizing' mission (Christie, 2020; Guzula, 2022). At the same time colonists and missionaries were engaged in a process of entextualising African languages according to a European theory of language (Makoni & Pennycook, 2005). The first schools were set up by the Dutch and then the British when they settled in the Cape. These schools were opened to serve the white settler population and were not intended for the indigenous or slave populations whom the colonists had subjugated. Schools for white children were started by one or other denomination of the church or departments of education. The few Indigenous African children who received formal education did so at mission schools. It was at one such school where the world icon, Nelson Mandela, began his formal education. In the Cape Colony (now comprised of the Northern, Western and Eastern Cape provinces), the medium of instruction was English, with Afrikaans being added after the union of South Africa in 1910 (Christie, 2020). African languages, while used in the education of indigenous people, were under-developed as languages of Science and Technology. This under-development of African languages for higher status functions has continued to the present day (Alexander, 2001; Prah, 2017). Under-development and under-use of languages forms part of a vicious cycle of language attrition in academic settings (Mohanty, 2019). The less African languages are used in education, the less they will be seen to be useful for academic pursuits.

By the time Apartheid was formalised into a political system, the children of white settlers and the indigenous children were schooled separately, with the indigenous African children receiving a far inferior education to their white peers in terms of resource allocation and curriculum. This inferior schooling system for black children was known as Bantu Education under Apartheid. In this system, schools for black African children were designated with spare facilities and a curriculum which aimed to prepare them for a life of servitude to their white masters. The state mandated language policy of these schools was indigenous African languages as languages of instruction until Standard 6 (approximately 13 years old or seven years of primary plus one year of secondary schooling) with the official languages of the Apartheid state, English and Afrikaans, being studied as language subjects. After Standard 6, subjects were taught in English and

Afrikaans until the last year of high school. Black children as young as 13 protested against the use of Afrikaans in their schooling in the infamous Soweto uprising of 1976 after which the state relented and scrapped Afrikaans-medium education for black South Africans. White children received their schooling in their home language throughout their school years and tertiary studies: Afrikaans for Afrikaans speakers and English for English speakers, with a strong emphasis on English/Afrikaans bilingualism through the teaching of the other language as a subject in all years. A significant minority received bilingual Afrikaans/English education in one form or another (Malherbe, 1946). The situation continues mostly unchanged for white children today (Christie & McKinney, 2017).

With the dawn of democracy in 1994, the writers of the new constitution were tasked with creating new language policies. The most pertinent for this study is the Language in Education Policy (Department of Education, 1997). While viewed as progressive and enabling of multilingualism (Heugh, 2002; Probyn *et al.*, 2002), the policy was flexible enough with the inclusion of practicability clauses that in most schools the status quo of language policy remained unchanged. The policy requires that the language of instruction be any official language of South Africa and that each student should take two languages as a minimum as subjects. For white children, through the School Governing Bodies tasked with drawing up the policy, this meant that they were not compelled to learn an indigenous African language as they opted for their home language and the other dominant language of the white community (i.e. English and Afrikaans). For black speakers of indigenous languages, this meant that in most cases they studied their home language and English, with English being offered as language of instruction from Grade 4 for the majority of students. This has meant that in effect African languages are not developed as academic languages for learning in the disciplines beyond Grade 3. African home language instruction to the exclusion of English is not palatable for parents given the association of 'mother tongue instruction' with inferior Bantu Education (Heugh, 2002). An exception to the ubiquitous policy of English-only education is the recent piloting of a formal bilingual English–isiXhosa model in a rural district in the Eastern Cape Province (Mbude, 2019) which saw selected school-leaving examinations papers being available in isiXhosa for the first time in 2020. Based upon the successes of this pilot, Basic Education Minister Angie Motshekga announced in March 2022 that her department will introduce African languages as languages of learning and teaching beyond Grade 3. Although the plan does not rule out a bilingual approach, the message that has been taken up in the popular media is that the Department of Basic Education will introduce 'mother-tongue instruction'. This announcement has been met with mixed reactions, and the practical implications will take a while to unfold and will no doubt be contentious. However, the proposal is very good news for the improved use of African languages in schooling.

The dominance of English-medium education was entrenched by the new curriculum in 2011. The English Additional Language curriculum assumes a switch to English medium in Grade 4 and argues from this basis for the development of good English literacy in the Foundation Phase (Department of Basic Education, 2011: 8). Preferential resourcing of English to the exclusion of African languages has placed the speakers of African languages at a distinct disadvantage to their white English-speaking counterparts given that research has attested to the importance of using children's most familiar languages as media of instruction for at least the first six years of formal schooling (Bamgbose, 2000; Thomas & Collier, 1997; UNESCO, 1953). Not only this, but African language-speaking children are also severely limited in their exposure to English at school before they make the switch to English medium in Grade 4. The subject English Additional Language is allocated 2/3 hours per week in Grade 1 and 2 and 3/4 hours per week in Grade 3. Scholars such as Macdonald (1990) and McKinney (2017, 2020) have argued that this is far too little to prepare children for coping with the content subject demand and accompanying vocabulary and academic language structures in English from Grade 4. These disadvantages meted out to black children have caused the language in schooling policies in South Africa to be described as racist (bua-lit, 2018; McKinney, 2017). Indeed, the conflation of race and language as a tool of subjugation has been a pernicious feature of coloniality (Kubota, 2021) such that race and language are often inseparable constructs which need to be tackled simultaneously in any decolonising project.

The continuities with South Africa's Apartheid past are visible especially in the lack of materials development and assessments in African languages and a lack of teacher education in multilingual methods. These absences constrain the policy choices that the School Governing Bodies can make (McKinney, 2020) and perpetuate the vicious cycle of African language under-development for academic purposes (Mohanty, 2019). School language policies tend to be simple, brief and not widely consultative if they exist in writing at all (Probyn *et al.*, 2002) with little care given to the exhortation in the Language in Education Policy to 'stipulate how the school will promote multilingualism' (Department of Education, 1997: 3). The majority of schools opt for one language of instruction which is usually English. Schools sometimes argue that they are merely following parent preferences for English-medium education. However, Heugh (2002) found that when black parents were offered their home language instruction alongside English instruction as a bilingual model, they were much more in favour of including their home language than if they had to choose between English and the home language. Another continuity with the past is how practice in classrooms flouts monolingual policy. Scholars have written about code-switching, translanguaging, 'smuggling in the vernacular' and many other creative and productive language practices in South African classrooms. While these practices have been lauded by researchers as important for conceptual and identity development (Guzula *et al.*, 2016; Krause, 2022; Tyler, 2016), they remain illicit and dilemma-filled concessions, with their users often expressing guilt in relation to their practice. The majority of South African classrooms function as 'adaptive translanguaging spaces' (García & Li, 2014: 133) in which translingual practices are used spontaneously (and often guiltily) without systemic supports or connections being made between the more familiar ways of using language and the academic registers to which the school is ostensibly giving the children access.

A further stratification of language policy for black South Africans occurs along class lines. Children with African language backgrounds who attend elite schools surrounded by home language speakers of English find themselves in an immersion language learning situation and often learn English quite quickly, although their home languages are rarely supported at school. Children in rural areas or peri-urban townships do not have such ready access to English and therefore labour more than their middle-class counterparts under an English-medium policy with the goals of their schooling being 'reduced to learning English and memorisation' (Christie & McKinney, 2017: 172). These limited goals of education for racialised bilinguals are echoed by scholars in the US who reflect on their experiences at school as 'a remedial education that focused on perfecting our English rather than pushing us to think critically' (García *et al.*, 2021: 4).

The language policy pertaining to language of instruction, with the recommendations that all children switch to English language of instruction in Grade 4, has had implications for learning materials, most notably textbooks. For content subjects, the textbooks from Grade 4 onwards are still only available in either English or Afrikaans. An exception to this is textbooks in isiXhosa up to Grade 6 produced as part of the Language Transformation Plan in the Western Cape province in 2007. Due to political change in the province, this plan was not sustained and the textbooks are now out of print.

The widespread, innovative practice of the oral use of African languages in schools is mostly characterised by national and provincial education departments pejoratively as 'code-switching'. It has recently been explicitly discouraged and the sole use of English after Grade 3 promoted in official communication to schools (Western Cape Education Department, 2017a, 2017b). The education department's imperative ignores the research on the cognitive and affective benefits of trans- and multilingual language use (reviewed in Chapter 2) and positions as deficient an innovative teaching and learning practice born out of a constraining language environment in schools where coloniality persists. At the same time, apart from demanding 'maximum exposure' to the language of instruction (Western Cape Education Department, 2017b: 1), the education department communication does not offer teachers detailed support in negotiating a curriculum in what for most students is a language only used in school.

The coloniality of language in South African schooling is summarised by McKinney (2020):

> Language in education is thus a space in which the long shadow of Coloniality (and its offshoot Apartheid) is cast with dire consequences for African language speaking children and speakers of non-standardised varieties. (McKinney, 2020: 14)

The consequences of the coloniality of language for the majority of South African children in schools are:

- Their strongest language resources are not recognised for learning or as knowledge-bearing systems.
- They experience a rupture between home and school ways of knowing.
- Their epistemic access to the disciplines of Science is constrained.
- They participate in predominantly teacher-centred discourse structures in class and rely heavily on memorisation as a learning strategy.
- Their innovative languaging-for-learning (Guzula *et al.*, 2016) practices are disparaged.

Decolonial Cracks

Despite the dominance of the coloniality of language in South African education, resistance to it emerges and takes many decolonial forms. Arising predominantly in Latin America, decolonial theory refers to a delinking (Mignolo, 2000) from the ways of thinking and acting delimited by colonialism and coloniality in order to make visible peoples, cultures and languages previously invisibilised by coloniality. Scholars in South America have articulated a richly theorised concept of decoloniality so much so that Grosfoguel (2007) announced a 'decolonial turn' in social studies. Decoloniality calls for new forms of knowledge-making and a centring of peoples, knowledges, places and languages previously oppressed, eradicated or mis-invented within the colonial project (Anzaldúa, 1987; de Sousa Santos, 2012; Maldonado-Torres, 2007; Menezes de Souza, 2019; Mignolo, 2009). Decolonial thought has built upon work by African scholars such as Frantz Fanon, Achille Mbembe, Mahmood Mamdani, Ngũgĩ Wa Thiong'o and Steve Biko who have worked with the concept of *decolonisation*. The African decolonial tradition has been picked up by contemporary African scholars (for example, Alexander, 2009; Bock & Stroud, 2021; McKinney & Christie, 2022; Ndhlovu & Makalela, 2021; Ndlovu-Gatsheni, 2015) and woven together with post-colonial scholarship to form a strong research agenda emanating from Africa.

Two strands of decolonial theory will be traced through this book as lenses that bring the decolonial cracks into focus in the case study. The first is *border thinking*. As Fanon observed in 1961, 'the colonial world is a compartmentalised world' (Fanon, 1961/1990). Between compartments, there are borders. Decolonial thinking necessarily takes place within 'borderlands' (Anzaldúa, 1987; Mignolo, 2000). Anzaldúa (1987) talks about the physical region near the Mexico/US border as a metaphor for an epistemological border which is a productive, although painful, space for knowledge production/learning. Border regions become important 'loc(i) of enunciation' (Mignolo, 2009) or historical, geographical, personal and political places from which we speak or write. An example of how border thinking is manifest in conceptions of language comes from Makoni and Pennycook (2005) who argue that just as African languages have been invented by colonial linguists, so they can also be 'disinvented' and 'reconstituted' in new ways. Processes of disinvention and reconstitution in language, such as different instantiations of translanguaging, are part of the 'serious translinguistic work' envisaged as an essential tool of decolonisation by Pratt (2019). This work, she argues, 'becomes a source of the new social visions that can and must come only out of the conflicting but intersecting histories that produced the colonial encounter' (Pratt, 2019: 121). Pratt's assertion is echoed by Veronelli (2015) who proposes Maturana's (1990) concept of 'languaging' to provide an account of languages from outside the logic of coloniality. It is from Maturana's concept that the terms used to analyse non-dominant students' Science learning described in Chapter 2 have arisen.

The second strand of decolonial theory traced through the book is the *embodied nature of knowledge-making*. Decolonial scholars have argued for a greater emphasis to be placed on the body as locus of enunciation, or the place from which we speak. bell hooks offers a response to Ngũgĩ's (1986) lament of the colonial separation of body and mind:

> To heal the splitting of mind and body, we marginalized and oppressed people attempt to recover ourselves and our experiences in language. (hooks, 1994: 175)

In a decolonial reckoning, language – especially understandings of language from the global South (Ndhlovu & Makalela, 2021) – becomes a vehicle for recovering embodied experience and selves. This includes the body becoming more prominent in pedagogies and knowledge production (Menezes de Souza, 2021, 2019). Accounting for the speaking body located in space and time works against the negation of the situatedness of knowledge and the negation of the colonised body in academic discourse (Menezes de Souza, 2019: 10). Bringing the body into account happens in two ways in the present volume: first, the body is studied as part of a whole semiotic performance which students engage in when learning new content. The focus on the body has connections with the developing understanding of multilingual learning as multi-semiotic (Kusters *et al.*, 2017; Lin, 2019; Lin *et al.*, 2020) in which bodily modes, such as gesture and proxemics, as well as linguistic and graphic modes, shape learning. This in turn connects to the recognition that space and the co-presence of students shapes learning in a dynamic flow of meaning-making (Lin *et al.*, 2020). Returning to Onke whose utterance opened the book, we see that observing his bodily expression as it merged with the linguistic mode of expression can assist in figuring a decolonial reading of his meaning. Second, where possible, the body is represented in data presentations. Interactional data was collected in the class lessons and study group in the form of audio and video recordings. This allowed me to use multiple sources of data to inform the creation of transcripts. Transcript making and digitisation of the data was the first stage in data analysis. A broad transcript was first made of all the recordings and then a second more detailed transcript was made of key episodes for microethnographic analysis. The second stage involved coding the transcripts and formulating the themes of each data chapter. Transcripts in this book include traditional linguistic-only transcripts (marked as extracts); transcripts including action modes (also marked as extracts); and transvisuals in the form of cartoons (marked as figures). The privileging of bodily modes in understanding multilingual learning has implications for data presentation and the use of translations in transcription, which has long been considered a political act (Bucholtz, 2000).

Within the ambit of decolonial theory, decolonial cracks (Walsh, 2014) are places within the edifice of coloniality/modernity that come about as a result of resistance. A crack is a productive metaphor if one accepts the impossibility of destroying or replacing the colonial system (Andreotti & Stein, 2022). The notion of a decolonial crack as a place from which to think and speak is emphasised by Walsh as she determines to develop a 'praxis of fissure' (Mignolo & Walsh, 2018) from a particular localisation and not from disembodied universality or rationality. Walsh draws on Anzaldúa's (2015) notion of las rajaduras/cracks as places between or beyond borders within which to reconfigure subjectivities and to construct paths forward into action. Cracks are inconspicuous but hold potential for thinking and acting 'otherwise' (Walsh, 2014), or interrupting the colonial pattern (Andreotti & Stein, 2022). Thinking and acting 'otherwise' is transgressive and not always possible. In the context of learning at school, practices may form in the underlife of the classroom (Gutierrez *et al.*, 1995) which are more like score marks on the surface of coloniality that require highlighting before they can become cracks. Indeed, Walsh suggests that cracks are in need of constant maintenance and expansion so that they remain open as the forces of coloniality work to seal and cover them as they appear. Walsh argues as follows about the genesis of decolonial cracks:

> The decolonial comes not from above but below, from the margins and borders, from the people, communities, movements, collectives who challenge, interrupt, and transgress the matrices of colonial power in their practices of being, action, existence, creation and thought. (Walsh, 2014)

It is precisely the beliefs and practices that occur on the margins within one Southern school setting that are positioned as decolonial cracks and constitute the focus of this book.

Methods and Positionality

The linguistic ethnographic study upon which this book is based had two main components. The first was a participant-observation of a class of Grade 9 students and their teacher at Success High completing a topic of Natural Science called 'chemical reactions' which lasted for six weeks. The focus of my investigation was on the meaning-making practices of the bi/multilingual participants in the Science lessons, although I also collected data on the linguistic landscape of the school and its official and tacit language policy. Becoming part of Grade 9B early on in the year provided me with many advantages. I was able to build rapport with the teacher and the students and also make the kinds of impressionistic observations which Merriam states characterises the early stages of research (Merriam, 1991: 89). I was particularly interested in bilingual learning practices; however, one of the most important early observations I made in the class lessons was Ms B's extremely rare use of isiXhosa. I expected the teacher to use English predominantly in the early lessons I observed due to my presence as a white, English-speaking researcher – thus powerfully positioned in multiple ways in the classroom. However, as other researchers in South African bilingual classrooms have found, this monolingual use of English, considered 'best practice', usually falls away after the first few lessons with an observer present and the more usual practices of using features from different named languages settles in again (Probyn, 2015). This was not the case in this class as throughout the research project Ms B used English almost exclusively inside the classroom, whether speaking to the whole class or to individuals. This prompted me to consider an intervention element to the project. I got permission from the principal to run a Science study group for Grade 9s. As the group facilitator, I designed, critiqued and maintained the established translanguaging space (García & Li, 2014), and I introduced alternative pedagogical activities that drew upon semiotic resources that were not prominent in the classroom space. It offered a different space to the classroom: less formal and lower stakes with no formal assessment. I introduced YouTube videos to consolidate concepts and used students' questions as a basis for inquiry. As the group was intended to support and extend the curriculum being followed in the classroom, I focused on following the interests of the students, even when these diverged from the topic at hand. This was a privilege I enjoyed because I was free from the constraints of curriculum and paced work plans that were a constant pressure for Ms B in the classroom. Furthermore, owing to my identity as an outsider – in particular, a white student from a prestigious university – the transgressive multilingual and multimodal pedagogies I employed gained a measure of legitimacy, although they were still resisted by students as I will show.

Students could sign up voluntarily to attend the study group and signed a consent form allowing data collected in the group to form part of the research. Students who attended the eight study group sessions consisted of some of those who indicated initial interest, plus others in the class and four students from the other two Grade 9 classes who heard about the group. Attendance varied from session to session, with the smallest group comprising myself and two students and the largest a total of 10 people. The most regular attender at the study groups was Khethiwe. She was an engaged and proactive member of the group. She also freely shared her feelings about the activities we undertook and is therefore a key participant in the study.

I negotiated the use of a table in the school library as the venue for the study group meetings. We sat around the table in a group, surrounded by bookshelves. The students left their school bags outside the library and entered with stationery and sometimes a textbook and notebook. Sitting on the same level, in close proximity to one another, created a convivial and egalitarian space. This assisted me in positioning the young people as legitimate students and knowers (McKinney, 2017). The gap between the students and myself was highlighted at times by the guileless teenagers. When I gave the example of the element gold by showing the students my wedding ring, Asanda retorted: 'We don't have gold here, miss'.

Most activities were organised and initiated by me as teacher-student, but unlike their regular class, some were initiated by the students. I took seriously the exhortation by Reinsmith (1993) that in order for real learning to occur 'time must be wasted, tangents pursued, and side-shoots followed' (Reinsmith, 1993, in Yager, 2004). I was intentionally trying to offer approaches to learning a Science topic that weren't offered in the classroom. Hence, the study group became a research intervention, a co-learning space and a traditional teaching space. Following Kell (2006) who described her study as 'an ethnographic project with an intervention component', I located my intervention within the broader project in what Yin calls an 'embedded single-case design' (Yin, 2009). The embedded units were the different sites of the classroom and the study group within the learning context of the Grade 9s as a whole.

In what follows, I describe something of my locus of enunciation (Mignolo, 2009) in this study as author-researcher-participant. On official forms, I identify as white and a home language English speaker. These identity positions were pre-eminently salient during my fieldwork as the data will bear out. Both put me in a minority position when compared to the school's population, but in a majority position in terms of power and recognition due to the colonial and Apartheid history I have outlined. In informal settings, I like to use the personal descriptor I learned in township speech: 'mixed masala', a term that captures the spiciness of a blend of ethnolinguistic identities. I have tried to capture this in a poem I wrote in 2019:

Home language

My daughter asked me, mama, what language do we speak?

I wish I'd said
my child we speak the language of our home.

That's why we say Ja because our home is in South Africa
That's why we know that a smiley is something on your phone
but also something you can eat
because we live eKapa.

That's why we can read picturesque and know what it means
because the roots of our home language are in Europe and people there
like people everywhere
make language from a pinch of this and an egg borrowed from a buurvrou.

That's why we say flibber flabber flob
and only those who have sat kwiziko lethu for many nights
will know what we mean.

but what I said was -
English

and she replied
Oh ja, we do a lot of English at school.
Yes, mtwanam, everyone does a lot of English at school.

Glossary:
Ja – yes
Smiley – a cooked sheep's head
eKapa – in Cape Town
buurvrou – female neighbour
kwiziko lethu – at our hearth
mtwanam – my child

I was motivated to enact the 'mixed masala' identity through my language use at Success High. I have substantial knowledge of Afrikaans and good productive and receptive ability in oral and written modes. I currently use Afrikaans less often than I do isiXhosa. I have a fair knowledge of an urban variety of isiXhosa and use it conversationally, in teaching, and to read isiXhosa children's books and listen to radio programmes for my own language learning. I have very limited knowledge of any other language. I used isiXhosa at Success High as much as possible. I conversed with administrative staff and students in isiXhosa outside the classroom and used it in a limited capacity in the study group. Despite these efforts, my embodiment at Success High as a white woman with a White South African English accent meant that certain doors were opened and others were firmly closed for me. I was also probably perceived as more of a burden and more of an authority than I would have liked.

Case study scholars have highlighted the different roles that researchers play in their sites (cf. Merriam, 1991; Stake, 1995). Not only did I begin to recognise myself as a student and a mentor to the teacher, but I embarked on the study group and was asked to supervise student teachers at the school by my university. These visible roles helped me to recognise the other more invisible roles I was playing too: those of advocate and community participant. I settled into the 'schizophrenic activity' (Merriam, 1991: 94) of participant observation in which 'one usually participates but not to the extent of becoming totally absorbed in the activity' and 'one (tries) to stay sufficiently detached to observe and analyse' (Merriam, 1991). The balance between participation and observation shifted at different times during my fieldwork when I experienced one or the other as predominant. During the class lessons, for example, I felt more like an 'observer as participant', and in the study group, I felt like a 'participant as observer' (Junker, 1960, as cited in Merriam, 1991: 92).

In a classroom setting, the advantage of participant observation is that you gain access to events or groups that would otherwise be inaccessible to a non-participant observer. Young people's unguardedness means that a classroom researcher is likely to be drawn into the social fabric of the setting whether she wants to be or not. Non-participant observation also has distinct disadvantages. Young people soon lose patience with a detached adult. Teachers may feel threatened if the researcher's detachment is experienced as judgement of their ability. Accepting that participant observation was my only option, I needed to become critically aware of how I was a key participant in the research.

Apart from balancing the roles I played at school, I found the transition between 'fieldwork' and 'other' sites jarring at times and sought to ameliorate this by marking the transition in some practical way. I found satisfaction in the affordances of radio. When I was driving towards a site in my car, I would play the radio station which I associated with that site. So, when driving from the Southern suburbs of Cape Town to Khayelitsha in the morning, I would listen to Umhlobo Wenene, an isiXhosa language station which is popular in Khayelitsha. This also facilitated my isiXhosa learning, and I would ask people at the school to help me understand what I had heard. When returning home in the afternoon, I would listen to Cape Talk, an English language station popular with the middle classes of the suburbs. As I was often tired in the afternoons, this also functioned as 'easy listening' as the language was familiar. In this way, I would prepare for the respective site I was anticipating entering.

As for all linguistic ethnographers, I needed to establish legitimacy in my research site. I needed to be seen as a community participant, although a transient one. I worked on this much in the same way all ethnographers do. I learned community members' names; I offered people cups of tea in the staffroom; I brought the Natural Science teacher the odd box of juice; I engaged in conversations on topics that teachers initiated; I brought the fruit-loving secretarial staff guavas from my fruit tree at home; I arranged a farewell to the Grade 9B and Ms B which included a gift and the screening of a video montage of my data set to music. In short, I came to care about the people at the school. Since the end of my fieldwork, I have continued to supervise teaching students at the school.

Taking on the identity of 'student' was surprising and invigorating. Two of the subjects I engaged in learning which were preordained by my choice of topic were chemical reactions and isiXhosa. In and out of the research site, I threw myself into the learning of these subjects, and this had benefits for my research. Hammersley and Atkinson (1995) quote educational ethnographers Olesen and Whittaker's description of how, in order to provoke the least response in the class tutor, she '(became) a student' by participating in the listening and writing that the students did (Hammersley & Atkinson, 1995: 177). I experienced how my participation as a student in the classroom lent validity to the teacher's activities, given my authority as an adult in the classroom. I deferred to her authority publicly in class and privately in interviews. In my role as isiXhosa student, I was able to defer to staff members' and student teachers' authority in this regard and retain a humble position as a student. How much this managed to off-set the imposing position I occupied as a white, English-speaking postgraduate student at a prestigious university is debatable. As the facilitator of the study group, I often took up the discursive position of 'teacher' and the students supported this through their use of 'miss' as a term of address for me. This is unsurprising in a school environment where ground rules of discourse with adults conventionally delimit formal terms of address. However, I also cultivated the position of 'student' in the study group through explicitly discussing my own Natural Science learning process and adopting inclusive language such as 'we' when discussing learning challenges. Also, observing my own meaning-making in learning about chemical reactions helped me to identify with the students who were my key participants and gain insight into the theory which I was attempting to build.

A role that I was largely unaware of constructing during my fieldwork was that of advocate for multilingualism in education. *Post hoc*, I find the label to be helpful in explaining much of my behaviour during my fieldwork. Interviews are particularly suited to advocacy. While it is the responsibility of an interviewer not to unduly influence the responses of the interviewee, she cannot but exercise influence through the choice of questions asked, and which responses are probed. Dörnyei (2007) holds that 'some delicate balancing act is needed here between non-judgemental neutrality and empathetic understanding and approval' (Dörnyei, 2007: 141). An interview is an advocacy tool in that it presents an opportunity for the interviewee to consider aspects of social reality previously unconsidered, or to consider them in a new light. I also modelled natural translanguaging in my social interactions with the students. Due to the association of white speakers with a specific variety of monolingual English speech, my translanguaging was disruptive and offered another way of seeing white speakers for these students. Finally, the exposure of the participants in my study to academic and business registers in isiXhosa constituted advocacy. The consent letter to parents was translated into isiXhosa from English by a colleague of mine. This formal business register in isiXhosa provoked much interest in the students. Thandile read the expression 'udliwano ndlebe' as a translation of 'interview'. He quickly made a literal translation of 'the eating of the ears' which he found highly amusing and consequently had the opportunity of learning a new expression. Equally the use of a scientific written register in isiXhosa during one study group provided the students with exposure to a register which they had not encountered before.

Outline of the Book

The central questions that this book seeks to answer are:

(1) How is the coloniality of language present in a Southern bilingual Science learning context?
(2) What decolonial cracks in language and identity for learning are observed?
(3) How can these decolonial cracks be widened?

These questions will be explored through presenting analyses of interaction and meaning-making in the case study at Success High using the tools of linguistic ethnography (Copland & Creese, 2015). Linguistic ethnography is able to connect the macro to the micro in a way that enables the application of theoretical concepts such as coloniality and decolonial cracks to concrete and specific social moments. One such moment is Onke's embodied exclamation, '*We were bhided by George!*' which forms part of his learning of Science in school. Tools such as multimodal critical discourse analysis (Machin & Mayr, 2012) enable a rich description of these moments, tracing the roots of their multi-voicedness.

The book proposes decolonial cracks appearing within the colonial edifice of language for content learning. At the mesolevel of the school, cracks in the edifice of coloniality appear as doubts and ambivalences expressed by principals, teachers and students with regards to language policy and practice, and in environmental text and social language use around the school grounds (see Chapter 3). At the microlevel of classroom discourse, cracks appear through the spontaneous practices of students which flout the official dominance of colonial languages (see Chapter 6) and pedagogic interventions which introduce new practices into the main teaching and learning spaces of school (see Chapter 7). In both spontaneous and planned learning practices, the interdependence between language use and identity work is central. The theoretical underpinnings of classroom languaging and classroom identity work in this study are found in post-structuralist applied linguistics and articulate with decolonial theory more broadly. Furthermore, through exploring continuities between recent innovations in applied- and sociolinguistic theory and decolonial theory, the book aims to contribute to the debates about how applied linguistics as a discipline might embrace decoloniality (Despagne, 2020; Ndhlovu & Makalela, 2021; Pennycook & Makoni, 2020; Phipps, 2019; Tyler, 2021).

In this first chapter, I have sketched the framework of de/coloniality within which the South African case study is situated. An outline of the remaining chapters follows.

Chapter 2 theorises key areas underpinning the study: language, the body and identity in learning. Attention is drawn to how the study resists the deficit view of non-dominant multilinguals in academic disciplines such as Science and traces the evolution of concepts to describe multilingual and multimodal classroom discourse, especially as they have been applied in South African Science classroom discourse studies.

Chapter 3 describes the language environment of Success High in Cape Town – in terms of language policy, ideologies and linguistic landscapes. The language profiles of the principal, the students and the teacher are described. While the context is highly ordered by coloniality/Anglonormativity, decolonial cracks, such as ambivalent attitudes and doubt, and multilingual signage also come to the fore.

Chapter 4 introduces the activities and the topic under study in the traditional Science class. The dominant patterns of discourse in the classroom resulting from a language in learning context of coloniality are outlined. Restricted triadic discourse and standardised seatwork (including testing) are the dominant activities described in this chapter. The effect of the English-only whole-class dialogue constrained the depth to which the Ms B and the students could engage in the concepts. The standardised seatwork that was low in linguistic demand meant the students were ill-prepared for the complexities of the scientific register present on the test. However, this same extended seatwork enabled students to have discussions about the topic in their most familiar languages even though this learning was rarely entered into by Ms B.

Chapter 5 offers the proposition of grassroots practices as decolonial cracks. These are learning practices that were undertaken spontaneously by students as they grappled with the topic at hand during the activities of student-questioning dialogue, groupwork, siding, seatwork and cross-discussion (Lemke, 1990). An argument is made that the trans-semiotising and whole-body sense-making on which these practices depend should be better understood and leveraged by teachers and education policymakers in multilingual contexts.

Chapter 6 describes decolonial cracks in learning design and pedagogies. Learning activities are described which were intentionally designed for the study group drawing on a wider range of semiotic resources than were enlisted within the classroom space. These include critical true dialogue, trans-semiotising in seatwork and translation.

Chapter 7 concludes the book by summarising the findings and offering directions for further research and teacher education in bilingual learning contexts of de/coloniality. Here, I turn to Walsh's question: 'How do we, and can we, move within the cracks, open cracks, and extend the fissures?' (Mignolo & Walsh, 2018: 83) to offer suggestions with regards to harnessing students' spontaneous decolonial practices; orientating towards the goal of an expanded repertoire in learning; the requirement for pedagogical translanguaging in classrooms and embracing decolonial research methodologies.

The appendices consist of examples of multilingual Science resources in African languages from South Africa (Appendix 1); examples of multilingual Science worksheets and tests (Appendix 2); and the transcription conventions employed in the book (Appendix 3).

Conclusion

This book takes a close look at the coloniality of language as well as decolonial cracks which were observed in a case study of two Science learning sites in a Cape Town high school. The goal in describing the existing and emergent language and identity practices of the teenagers in this study is to deepen an understanding of non-dominant students' learning of new content in all contexts. Most importantly, I aim to provoke a shift in the assumptions that educators and policymakers have about the meaning-making capacities of non-dominant students and to point to a fuller and more inspiring perspective on these students centred in the global South. In particular, I will argue that the students' translanguaging, trans-semiotising and whole-body sense-making provides a vehicle for the development of useful meshed registers to learn Science. Also, that these meaning-making processes enable productive identity meshing (Tyler, 2022) in which students inhabit a border region of becoming a scientist – a position that holds potential for decolonising Science as a discipline.

South Africa's particular colonial and Apartheid history and contemporary social movements such as #RhodesMustFall and #FeesMustFall produce a rich context for studying de/coloniality in language in education. In particular, through an in-depth linguistic ethnography, this book seeks to explore what a decolonial approach to the study and practice of language and identity in content classrooms might look like, both in South Africa and beyond. The aim is to go beyond either romanticising or vilifying the use of African languages in content learning in order to promote their use as part of an expanded repertoire (Lin, 2015) for learning. In this way, the multilingual turn (May, 2014) and decolonial turn (Grosfoguel, 2007) will be brought into conversation in the book. The book also offers a further theorisation of decolonial cracks, drawing on multilingual and multimodal concepts from applied linguistics, in a content subject learning context such as a Science classroom.

Notes

(1) '-bhida' (isiXhosa) means 'confuse' in English. Onke combines the English past tense suffix '-ed' and the isiXhosa 'bhida' to create a heteroglossic term equating to 'confused'.
(2) I recognise race as a social construct with profound material effects. Apartheid categories of 'black' and 'white' are used in this book as they describe the social positioning of the students and are used in South African society as levers for redress for the injustices of the past.
(3) All names are pseudonyms.
(4) Malherbe (1946) studied monolingual Afrikaans and English medium and different models of bilingual education to explore its consequences for academic achievement and social cohesion between the two linguistically-defined white populations in South Africa. His data included questionnaires for pupils and teachers and intelligence and scholastic tests for 18,773 school-going children.

2 Language, the Body and Identity in Learning

Introduction

Broadly speaking, this research proceeded from a sociocultural frame for understanding learning practices. The key concepts used have been distilled from a wide span of applied linguistic theory on language and identity in learning. The process of this distillation is the topic of this chapter. I will also provide an overview of the evolution of research in bi/multilingual classroom discourse studies, with a focus on South Africa. This overview includes a discussion of the conceptual tools scholars have developed through these studies and follows a trajectory from concepts describing distinct and separate resources to concepts evoking a multi-faceted sense-making performance. The concepts that I have distilled help me to analyse the *border* as it is emphasised in decolonial thought. In the main, I am talking about the border between named languages but also between semiotic systems such as the body and natural language. Border thinking, as well as making the body salient in analysis, surfaces the coloniality of language as well as decolonial cracks in learning.

Code-Switching and Bilingual Learning in African Classrooms

As is true in all applied linguistic research, the terminology used to describe language users in South African studies of bi/multilingual classroom discourse reveals the ideological framing of the objects of study, and this has changed over time. As Probyn (2021) notes, English-medium schooling for African language speakers beyond Grade 4 is so naturalised and invisibilised, that there is no literature on 'English Medium Instruction' (EMI) in South Africa, just as there are no English Additional Language (EAL) or English for Speakers of Other Languages (ESOL) teachers employed in state schools in South Africa (besides for mainstream English language lessons) and little teacher education for teaching through the medium of an unfamiliar language. The tacit assumption is that teachers must teach in English – a language that is often experienced as a foreign language for students – and that they will find ways through the difficulties of this. The most common solution employed by teachers is to switch regularly from English to the most familiar African language of the students if this is a language they share with the students. Apart from its formal linguistic meanings (Myers-Scotton, 1993), code-switching is a widely used term in South Africa to refer to switching from English to an African language in oral classroom language use, especially on the part of the teacher to aid understanding. Indeed, unsolicited, the principal of Success High refers to it during her interview as we shall see in Chapter 3. In layman's parlance, code-switching retains traces of a pejorative meaning as a necessary evil, an uneasy concession, or as one of Probyn's (2009) teachers called it 'smuggling in the vernacular'. However, early studies of classroom discourse in South Africa used the lens of code-switching to describe productive bi/multilingual practices. A prominent example is the study by Ralph Adendorff (1993) on teachers' code-switching practices from English to isiZulu in secondary school English, Biology and Geography lessons. Adendorff found that teachers switched to the students' home language for social as well as academic reasons. Chick (1996) added the insight that when English was used exclusively in a classroom of isiZulu-speaking students, the communication between teacher and students amounted to 'safe-talk' which had as its goal saving face through performing the activity of teaching-and-learning, rather than the development of real conceptual understanding.

After Adendorff's (1993) study, Cleghorn and Rollnick (2002) present the first South African study focusing on multilingual discourse in the Science classroom. While the majority of their data extracts are presented already translated into English, they show how teachers and students use code-switching from English into the African home languages for a number of cognitive purposes such as metalinguistic awareness and deepening understanding. Setati and Adler (2000) and Setati *et al.* (2002) use their analysis of code-switching moves in Mathematics, Science and English classroom discourse to show a possible flexible movement between 'English LoLT' (English medium) and the 'main language' at different points in the learning journey. Later, code-switching moves in a Mathematics classroom were shown to be multi-directional from English to the main language and vice versa (Tyler, 2016). Probyn (2006) also draws on the concept of code-switching by Science teachers, but argues for the development of a 'coherent bilingual approach for teaching Science' (Probyn, 2006: 391) which positions the use of African languages as learning resources. Msimanga and Lelliott (2014) found that Grade 10 students spent more than 90% of time in small group discussions talking in their familiar African languages about the Chemistry tasks. The focus in this study was on the use of African languages in Science discussions. In contrast to the other studies reviewed in this section, they recorded students' discussions with each other rather than focusing on the teacher's speech. They found that students made and supported claims, challenged each other's ideas and questioned each other's thinking by drawing on their multilingual resources in these small group discussions.

Intervention Studies

Activist researchers have recognised the need to demonstrate the efficacy of the use of African languages in education in South Africa due to the pervasive Anglonormativity in the system which positions only English as a marker of intelligence and learning. In the light of this, some studies have either focused on the existing use of African languages in the classroom or have designed an intervention to test or prove its efficacy. Working on the Language of Instruction in Tanzania and South Africa (LOITASA) project in collaboration with colleagues in Tanzania and Sweden, Vuyokazi Nomlomo (2007, 2010) undertook a study in Cape Town focusing on English and isiXhosa Science teaching with a quasi-experimental design. In her study, control groups in Grade 4, 5 and 6 were taught Science in English, and experimental groups were taught Science with learning materials printed in isiXhosa. She found that there was a positive correlation between the use of the students' most familiar language as a medium of instruction and students' conceptual development, academic performance and self-esteem in Science. Indeed, the class of students who were taught in isiXhosa performed better than those who were taught in English. While the study could be seen to promote a monolingual African language approach to teaching Science, the children in the experimental (isiXhosa) group were issued with English textbooks as well as isiXhosa textbooks and therefore experienced some degree of bilingual learning. Nomlomo also found that parents had positive attitudes to English and isiXhosa being used to study science. These results were aligned with what Bamgbose found in Nigeria (Bamgbose, 2000) where children who were introduced to a bilingual Yoruba/English model in Grade 4 made reading gains in both Yoruba and English. In Rwanda, an intervention project was initiated which employed language-supportive pedagogy and language-supportive bilingual textbooks in English and Kinyarwanda in primary schools. Milligan *et al.* (2016) found that the experimental textbooks were popular among teachers, students and head teachers due to their accessibility, and in all eight intervention schools, there was a statistically significant advantage gained by the experimental group in comprehension tests.

Intervention studies using translation in Science learning have also recently been undertaken. Zuma (2006) studied the translation of standardised Grade 8 Science test questions from English into isiZulu (the home language of students) and found that there was very little difference in performance between those tested in English and those in isiZulu. However, when Charamba and Zano (2019) used secondary school Science teaching materials translated from English into Sesotho (the home language of students) and subsequently tested students in these languages, they found a statistically significant higher achievement in those tested in Sesotho. This indicates that using the students' most familiar language is important through all stages of learning not just in assessment. Charamba (2021) studied the effects of bilingual Science assessments which included students' home language in a primary school in Zimbabwe and found a positive effect on tests results when a bilingual Shona-English test was used as opposed to a monolingual English test. In the Western Cape, Heugh *et al.* (2017) found that Grade 8 students who answered Mathematics test questions posed in English, Afrikaans and isiXhosa used more than one version to assist them in their answers.

Despite the persistence of monolingual English education policies in Southern African countries, the classroom practices reviewed in this chapter which flout this policy are beneficial for learning. All of the studies reviewed above proceed from a theoretical framing of discrete named languages or 'nomolanguages' (Krause, 2022) in teaching, learning and assessment. In the next section, a conceptual shift is described from named languages to the resources and repertoires held by speakers.

Resource and Repertoire in Bilingual Learning

Recent shifts in the conceptualisation of language in applied and sociolinguistics have influenced the descriptors attributed to students by some scholars. Whereas a structuralist view of language and traditional linguistics has conceived of named languages as a linguistic fact, this shift recognises that named languages are socially and discursively constructed rather than being recognisable linguistic objects with a defined beginning and end. The emphasis in the 'multilingual turn' (May, 2014) is on what speakers actually do with language, rather than on a set of structures imagined to exist statically in individual speakers' minds. The concept of 'linguistic repertoire' (Blommaert, 2010) has become the focus of analysis of multilingual communication and refers to the totality of features which a speaker may draw upon in generating any utterance. 'Repertoire' is a term that has been in use since Gumperz and Hymes' (1972) foundational sociolinguistic work. Blommaert and Backus (2011) describe linguistic repertoires as being shaped by use:

> Repertoires are the real 'language' we have and can deploy in social life: biographically assembled patchworks of functionally distributed communicative resources, constantly exhibiting variation and change. (Blommaert & Backus, 2011: 23)

Blommaert and Backus point out that these features, or 'resources', making up our repertoires are diverse in origin and are deployed in different ways according to interlocutor and situation. Scholars of multimodality and multilingualism have extended the concept of repertoire to include modes other than the linguistic, arguing that a comprehensive description of meaning-making must take into account all modes and not privilege the linguistic (Blackledge & Creese, 2017; Kusters *et al.*, 2017). Kusters *et al.* (2017) use the term 'semiotic repertoire' to make this point. A repertoire approach to the study of the language use of bilinguals makes it impossible to take named languages as the object of study. As Cummins (2008) has shown, the 'two solitudes assumption' in bilingual education where two named languages are taken to be existing in separate compartments in the mind and not interacting with each other does not hold up to empirical scrutiny and may be restrictive of bilingual learning.

Blommaert and Dong (2010) make the argument that the term 'resource' brings a necessary criticality to the study of language in society:

> Looking at issues of resources makes sure that any instance of language use would be deeply and fundamentally socially contextualised; connections between talk and social structure would be intrinsic. (Blommaert & Dong, 2010: 194)

Considering semiotic features as resources is an approach taken by scholars working on bi/multilingual education with a social justice imperative (Genishi & Dyson, 2009; Stein, 2000) in order to show the potential for meaning-making which children have. Originating in Economics, the metaphor of a resource helps to show that language abilities, like material things, only become resources when value is placed upon them in the social world (Lo Bianco, 1996). Embracing the terms 'repertoire' and 'resource' has implications for the naming and description of multilingual students. Some scholars working in English-dominant post-colonial environments describe their students as 'English Second Language' (ESL) or 'English Additional Language' (EAL) students. This reinforces the hegemony of English and identifies the students according to resources they do not have rather than those they do have. A term such as 'mother tongue education' also subscribes to a monoglossic orientation which has its roots in the coloniality of language, and sometimes ignores the multilingual repertoires of black children which often do not match the standard version of an African language taught in schools. An example of such a multilingual repertoire is well described by Guzula (2022) who writes about her own repertoire acquired at home and at school in South Africa.

Describing the resources that students have in contexts such as the one in this study results in terms such as 'bilingual' and 'multilingual' which point both to their current repertoires (including and superseding features of isiXhosa and English), but also to a hope that these will be recognised as resources in education. While 'multilingual' might seem more aligned with a repertoire view of students meaning-making resources, 'bilingual' allows an African-language-plus-English model to be imagined through employing strategic essentialism (Spivak, 1985) of two named languages. Currently, there are very few examples in South African schools of official bilingual African language/English models.[1] The use of 'bilingual' as a descriptor therefore is a practical and political strategy, following Alexander (2009) to demand recognition of African language plus English at minimum in the schooling of the non-dominant majority of black South African children. This practical strategy echoes the lobbies for bilingual Spanish/English education for Latinx children in the US. A term used in the US which has equal resonance in South Africa is 'emergent bilingual' (García, 2009). This term is future-focused and process-focused recognising even those proficiencies which children are only beginning to develop.

Translanguaging

Since Bakhtin's proposal of the notion of 'heteroglossia' (Bakhtin, 1981) or multi-voicedness as a core characteristic of all speech, a plethora of terms have come into existence to describe the heterogenous, flexible dynamics of multilingual communication. The broadest term in use – languaging – originates in biology (Maturana, 1990) and has been taken up in psycholinguistics (Swain & Lapkin, 2013) and sociolinguistics (Jørgensen *et al.*, 2011). Languaging refers to the process by which humans make meaning using verbal language. The term's emphasis on process and dynamism sets it up as an alternative to the nomolanguages which are so salient within the coloniality of language (Veronelli, 2015). Three terms that are productive for rethinking language in content subject classrooms are 'translanguaging' (García & Li, 2014), 'trans-semiotizing' (Lin, 2015; Lin *et al.*, 2020; McKinney & Tyler, 2018) and 'whole-body sense-making' (Lin, 2019; Tyler, 2021; Wu & Lin, 2019). These terms refer to the employment by multilinguals of features of different named languages in communication and learning. All three terms broaden the lens on multilingual meaning-making to pay close attention to modes and registers beyond only the linguistic. They enable the theoretical reconstitution of empirically observed meaning-making practices for learning. Whether the context is considered 'monolingual' or multilingual, these concepts offer productive languages of description for meaning-making practices. The terms are expanded upon in the sections below.

The term translanguaging has undergone a contextual journey from the field of language education (Baker, 2011; Williams, 1996) to sociolinguistics more broadly (García & Li, 2014; Li, 2017; Oteheguy *et al.*, 2015) while being further refined within education (García, 2009). Oteheguy *et al.* (2015: 281) defined translanguaging as:

> the deployment of a speaker's full linguistic repertoire without regard for watchful adherence to the socially and politically defined boundaries of named (and usually national and state) languages.

Oteheguy *et al.*'s definition positions translanguaging as a transgressive act in which speakers employ their full linguistic repertoire. Elsewhere, these scholars have pointed out that translanguaging does not exclude other meaning-making modes in the speaker's repertoire (García & Li, 2014). I concur with the potential for transgression (and therefore transformation) that employment of a full multilingual repertoire offers, especially within education, but agree with Jaspers (2017) that this is not universally guaranteed with translanguaging:

> Working from the principles of linguistic ethnography (Copland & Creese, 2015) convinces us that no communicative practice is by definition transformative (or constraining). Translanguaging, rather, has the potential to liberate multilinguals from the tyranny of monoglossic and monomodal conceptions of communicative practice as the norm. But in order for translanguaging to be transformative and to be productive for learning, translanguaging as pedagogy must be deliberately designed. (McKinney & Tyler, 2018: 6)

Translanguaging is enacted in a wide variety of practices and contexts, and these influence the effects of the use of diverse semiotic resources in meaning-making. Scholars have taken up translanguaging to refer to a variety of practices in education and the assumptions about language which underpin the term are a matter of some debate (see Bhatt & Bolonyai, 2019; Jaspers, 2017; Turner & Lin, 2020) and usually need explicating in reference to the context of the study in question. Within a South African context, Leketi Makalela has employed the term to describe the nature of indigenous African multilingualism. Makalela interprets translanguaging from within the African value system of interdependence, Ubuntu, and coins the term 'ubuntu translanguaging' (Makalela, 2016; Ndhlovu & Makalela, 2021). Ubuntu translanguaging refers at once to the interdependence between languages and the interdependence between speakers in linguistic encounters of difference, such as those occurring in the Limpopo Valley in pre-colonial times and in post-colonial urban settings in South Africa. The term 'ubuntu translanguaging' can be interpreted as a decolonial lens for studying languaging in that it centres African epistemologies but also draws in applied linguistic theorising from other contexts enabling border thinking.

In the field of bilingual education, the term 'translanguaging' has been widely taken up and is currently being expanded to describe bilinguals' 'languaging-for-learning' (Guzula *et al.*, 2016). Translanguaging is used to describe a variety of practices in bilingual classrooms, including what has been described as code-switching and translation, but challenges the assumption of traditional bilingual education programmes which try to maintain languages in silos, or one language at a time.[2] García and Li (2014) emphasise the creative, innovative and transgressive nature of translanguaging which they hold sets it apart from code-switching, although other scholars disagree (e.g. Bhatt & Bolonyai, 2019). Makalela shows how in African classrooms, multilingualism comes about as a result of indigenous multilingualism rather than the migration-driven multilingualism of Northern contexts (Makalela, 2018). In Southern African education, translanguaging has been used to describe a variety of teaching and learning practices. McKinney describes a lecturer's fluid use of multiple languages to teach early literacy to pre-service teachers (McKinney, 2021). Makalela (2015) describes how ubuntu translanguaging in a senior primary classroom aids epistemic access. Antia and Dyers (2019) describe the use of translanguaging in Linguistics course materials at university for concept development. Guzula (2022) describes a plethora of translanguaging practices employed by facilitators and children in an out-of-school literacy club in Cape Town. These practices included children moving flexibly between languages orally, and facilitators providing written notes on the board in two languages. Antia (2017) describes the use of translanguaged siding by students in a lecture hall in order to make sense of a monolingual English lecture. In Mozambique, Chimbutane (2013) studied a mandated bilingual Changana/Portuguese programme and found that some primary school-age students colluded with the language separation rule in Portuguese Science lessons, while others flouted it, employing translanguaging. Chimbutane found that teachers had to model the use of Changana in Portuguese Science classes; otherwise, the students would not use it. In a Namibian Grade 4 Science classroom, Set (2020) describes the translanguaging of the teacher to enable conceptual understanding while using a monolingual English textbook. Probyn (2021) provides an overview of research into translanguaging in South African classrooms. She reviews studies of both spontaneous and planned translanguaging practice but notes that these practices are not supported in official education policy.

    The variety of uses to which the term translanguaging is put has been criticised as a weakness of the term (Bhatt & Bolonyai, 2019; Jaspers, 2017; Lin *et al.*, 2020). Certainly, in analyses of classroom discourse, more precise terms are required to do the necessary explanatory work. In an educational setting, García and Li Wei distinguished between natural and official translanguaging (García & Li, 2014). Natural translanguaging refers to the spontaneous use of resources belonging to languages regarded as separate in order to accomplish learning; while official translanguaging refers to the planned use of more than one named language in activities and is usually set up by the teacher. Cenoz and Gorter (2017, 2021) use the terms 'spontaneous' and 'pedagogical' translanguaging to make a similar distinction. More recently, Probyn (2015, 2019) has described the use of what she terms 'pedagogical translanguaging' in Science teaching. In using this term, Probyn draws attention to the 'systematic and purposeful' use of both English and isiXhosa, which aligns with the use of 'official translanguaging' in García and Li (2014).

García and Li Wei also point to different positionings of the practice of translanguaging in schools when they describe a learning space as either an *adaptive* or an *established* translanguaging space (García & Li, 2014: 133). In an adaptive space, translanguaging practices occur but may not be sanctioned and are certainly not valorised or planned. An established translanguaging space, on the other hand, is set up to enable translanguaging and may even insist on it at times, for example, in translation activities that form part of translanguaging. In an established translanguaging space, the teacher adopts a 'translanguaging stance' – an attitudinal position that welcomes different forms of translanguaging (García *et al.*, 2017). An established translanguaging space therefore operates as a pedagogical 'third space' (Bhabha, 1990; Guzula, 2022) where new learning opportunities emerge.

Trans-Semiotising

While translanguaging has broadened and deepened the view of multilingualism, Kusters *et al.* (2017) have argued that too often multilingual studies ignore the multimodal aspects of the communication and vice versa:

> There is therefore a lack of transaction between research that focuses on gestures, signs and multimodality on the one hand, and research into linguistic diversity or multilingualism on the other hand. (Kusters *et al.*, 2017: 221)

Recent exceptions to the established multilingual research which Kusters *et al.* criticise are the paper 'Translanguaging and the body' (Blackledge & Creese, 2017) which includes a thorough analysis of the multimodal communication of multilinguals in a United Kingdom market setting; a special issue of the journal Linguistics and Education which presents papers demonstrating children's multimodal and multilingual collaborations in learning (Kyratzis & Johnson, 2017) and the work of Angel Lin (2007, 2015, 2016, 2019). Lin has furthered the understanding of multilingualism in Science education by broadening her analysis of multilingual classroom talk to include other semiotic modes. First, Lin proposes 'trans-semiotizing' as a term that goes beyond translanguaging (He *et al.*, 2017; Lin, 2015; Lin & Wu, 2014):

> The proposal of trans-semiotizing as a communicative strategy broadens our horizon about bi/multilingual communication, since languages (as a central semiotic) not only interact with each other but also intertwine with other semiotics (e.g., visual images, gestures, sound and music) in human communication practices during which the common semiotic repertoire expands under the contributions of communicators. (He *et al.*, 2017: 5)

While translanguaging can also describe moves between modalities (García & Li, 2014), trans-semiotising presses researchers of multilingualism to attend more explicitly to the modes Lin lists. While most applications of trans-semiotising have been made in studies in Hong Kong, it is a term taken up in analyses of the Success High study group in South Africa (McKinney & Tyler, 2018) and in the study of actional modes and language in a Grade 4 Science classroom in Namibia (Set, 2020).

Whole-Body Sense-Making

In both translanguaging and trans-semiotising, the prefix can imply two separate entities between which the actor is moving. 'Trans' can, in one sense, keep scholars stuck in the language of separateness and boundedness which we are trying to avoid (Jaspers, 2017). A term offered by Lin which avoids this conundrum in multilingual education is 'expanded repertoire' (Lin, 2015). While referring to 'what we have', this term indexes a process of expansion which offers an egalitarian and growth-focused vision of using and mastering multiple resources in bilingual learning contexts. This is an important departure from the view too often expressed in South Africa which has the goal of learning being the development of written academic English only. More recently, drawing on the work of Thibault (2011) on the first-order languaging dynamics, Lin (2019) accounts for the co-construal of content meaning in a multilingual Science classroom as 'whole-body sense-making'. She characterises this sense-making by students as being a shared experience; as being directed by their own interests; as having an affective quality; and of course, as drawing on many modes and registers to make meaning (Lin, 2019: 10). Lin shows how short episodes of co-construal of content meaning can reveal rich processes of agentic identity development as part of initiation into a discipline such as Science. The name for this process, whole-*body* sense-making, emphasises the body as a sense-making resource. Harré (1991) has suggested that the body is in fact the locus of human identity, and therefore, Lin's emphasis is welcome in helping researchers more fully understanding identity processes in learning. Whole-body sense-making casts a vision of multilingual content learning as dependent on the meshing of registers (Gibbons, 2006; Lemke, 1990) and identity positions (Ballenger, 1997; Tyler, 2022) while also producing an understanding of the academic subject of science as existing 'in an ongoing connection/interanimation between the everyday world and the scientific world' (Wu & Lin, 2019: 264). Also central to Lin's understanding of whole-body sense-making is the notion of *flow* as a part of translanguaging dynamics (Lin *et al.*, 2020). Sense-making occurs in flows between actors as well as in flows across time.

The term 'whole-body sense-making' privileges the bodily modes of sense-making which intentionally upends the established mode hierarchy in a school setting which holds natural languages (and specifically standard versions of these languages) to be the pinnacle of sense-making resources and other modes to be simply auxiliary. Whole-body sense-making offers an analytical lens on sense-making in learning which can be applied both in 'monolingual' as well as multilingual educational settings. It works against the romanticising as well as the vilifying of multilingual practices in school settings in that the features of different named languages become just one more resource in the repertoire that a student can employ to engage with new academic content. In this way, whole-body sense-making offers a decolonial de-linking (Mignolo, 2011) from the language hierarchies which are a feature of coloniality. Lastly, the descriptor, 'whole', highlights the cohesion and simultaneity of the sense-making that can be achieved while many seemingly conflicting resources are in play.

Trans-Registering, Code-Meshing and Register Meshing

In learning within a discipline such as Science, a new discourse is being co-constructed between teacher and students and among students. The nature of this discourse has been the subject of much theorising and is the focus of this section. I will begin by outlining the concept of register and its particular instantiation in Science and trace a cluster of concepts which have coalesced into binary pairs in analysis of classroom or learning discourse. Thereafter, I will review new work which problematises these binaries when used to analyse learning and show how new propositions of trans-registering, code-meshing and register meshing enable the decolonial cracks in classroom discourse to emerge.

The origin of the notion of register in social semiotics is attributed to Michael Halliday who defines register as 'the clustering of semantic features according to situation type' (Halliday, 1978: 68). Further, a variety of a language can be identified, and recognised, by certain syndromes or patterns of co-occurrence among features at one or another linguistic level (Halliday & Martin, 1993). Scholarship on the language of Science in Western philosophy and linguistics has a long history which is traced by Halliday and Martin from its origins in the 16th century when there existed a project to define a 'philosophical language' (1993: 5) to serve the needs of scientific research. Construing this language as a language for structuring knowledge, Halliday and Martin state that 'the language of Science has become the language of literacy' (Halliday & Martin, 1993: 11). Certainly, the history of these two 'languages' are intertwined, but perhaps more and more they are diverging as the purposes they serve diverge. For example, the language of literacy in school lags behind the innovations made in the social practices of literacy outside of school (such as those in use on social media). The language of the Natural Sciences has particular features in its lexico-grammar which have been identified by scholars such as Gee (2004) and Halliday and Martin (1993). Some of these features include technical vocabulary, a high degree of nominalisation and the use of the passive voice. The clustering of these features in (particularly) written Science language is what is known as the 'scientific register', and it is this register that students of Science need to master and produce for summative, standardised assessments.

The 'scientific register' is a multimodal register, as Lemke describes:

> The language of science is a unique hybrid: It is natural language as linguists define it, extended by the meaning repertoire of mathematics (the set of possible meanings that can be made with mathematical symbols and the conventions for interpreting them), contextualized by visual representations of many sorts, and embedded in a language (or, more properly, a semiotic) of meaningful, specialized actions afforded by the technological environments in which science is done. (Lemke, 2004: 33)

Lemke describes four different modes in this explanation: the linguistic, mathematical symbols, the visual and actions supported by physical tools. Similarly, in their study of rhetoric in the Science classroom, Kress *et al.* (2014) analysed speech/writing, action and visual modes. Lemke, along with many others such as Stein (2000) and Archer (2014), argues that all students' meaning-making modes should be incorporated in the learning journey. While this acknowledgement is important, scholars of multimodality have argued that a critical perspective is also important: the acknowledgement that while all modes have rich meaning-making potential, they are not all valued equally (Kress *et al.*, 2014), especially in the constraints of standardised testing, where the monolingual written mode dominates.

Since the development of the concept of register, however, theorists have asserted that registers are not hermetically sealed linguistic objects. Halliday and Martin argue that registers:

> are best thought of as spaces within which the speakers and writers are moving; spaces that may be defined with varying depth of focus, and whose boundaries are in any case permeable, hence constantly changing and evolving. (Halliday & Martin, 1993: 87)

This dynamic view of the nature of register is also presented by the linguistic anthropologist, Asif Agha who defines a 'semiotic register' as 'a repertoire of performable signs linked to stereotypic pragmatic effects by a sociohistorical process of enregisterment' (Agha, 2006: 80). While the reification of a 'science register' can also over-emphasise its linguistic features, Agha's term 'semiotic register' draws attention to the multimodal realisation of register. Agha's term 'enregisterment' captures the dynamism and evolution of registers as they are used in cultural action. He defines enregisterment as:

> processes and practices whereby performable signs become recognised (and re-grouped) as belonging to distinct, differentially valorized semiotic registers by a population. (Agha, 2006: 81)

By pointing out that registers are 'differentially valorised', Agha emphasises the dimension of power inherent in a register. It is the action of power at work through linguistic ideologies present in the context of school Science that (re)produces registers for Science as bounded and static and includes or excludes particular utterances as belonging to a Science register. Teachers are advised to encourage their students to pay attention to this register in order to appropriate it (Gibbons, 2006; Lemke, 1990). Equally the naming of different registers by discourse analysts can reinforce the reification of discrete registers which, in learning theories, tend to coalesce into register binaries (see Table 2.1).

The first register binary used in discourse analysis is that of 'academic' versus 'everyday' registers (Agha, 2006; Lin, 2016). Academic registers are described in terms similar to how scientific register is described by Halliday and Martin (1993) with 'everyday' registers coming into being when languagers use lexicogrammar to invoke interpersonal meanings. Making a very similar distinction, Lemke (1990) proposed 'colloquial' and 'technical' registers for learning Science (1990: 173). Focusing on how the mode of communication shapes the register, Gibbons (2006) coined the terms 'spoken-like discourse' (less explicit) and 'written-like discourse' (more explicit) in relation to how teachers and students spoke about Science content.

Added to these binaries which refer explicitly to register are those which use other words which have similar meanings to 'register'. Gee proposes 'social languages' (Gee, 2004) which he describes as 'a way of using language to enact a particular socially situated identity and carry out a

Table 2.1 Register binaries

Types more aligned with students' lifeworlds	Types more aligned with the academic world	Associated theorist
Lifeworld social languages	Academic social languages	Gee (2004)
Everyday registers	Scientific/academic registers	Lin (2016); Agha (2006); Halliday & Martin (1993)
Basic Interpersonal Communication Skills (BICS)	Cognitive Academic Language Proficiency (CALP)	Cummins (2008)
Primary discourses	Secondary discourses	Gee (2002)
Colloquial registers	Technical registers	Lemke (1990)
Spoken-like discourse	Written-like discourse	Gibbons (2006)

particular socially situated activity' (2004: 14). In reference to Science learning in particular, Gee distinguishes between 'academic social languages' and 'lifeworld social languages' (2004). Similarly, Jim Cummins (2008) describes in binary terms the difference between basic interpersonal communication skills (BICS, later called conversational language) and cognitive academic language proficiency (CALP, later called academic language) in order to detail what is involved in learning the two language types for bilinguals.

The binaries which the above table sets out are brought into existence when they come to be used as analytical tools for classroom discourse. However, some of these same classroom discourse scholars have recently articulated a 'process-based ontology' to the study of register (Lin *et al.*, 2020: 13). In this understanding, register formation and use for learning is taken to be a fluid and flexible process, characterised by dynamism and shift. An important shift in academic discourse was identified by Barnes (1992) who distinguished between 'exploratory talk' and 'presentational talk' for learning. Barnes described exploratory talk as spoken discourse which is hesitant and incomplete, where ideas are tested as the student is becoming familiar with them. Presentational talk, on the other hand, is spoken discourse which has been well polished as the student has become familiar with the concepts and presents them in an organised sequence in order to communicate understanding. In developing a framework for understanding multilingual students' Science learning in Australia, Pauline Gibbons proposed 'register-meshing' (Gibbons, 2006) as a way of understanding the exploratory discourse used by teachers and students to build a bridge towards the new Science discourse. In moving along a 'mode continuum', Gibbons noted how her participants would employ features of more spoken-like and more written-like English discourse in the same utterance. This kind of language use is commensurable with a broad definition of translanguaging which encompasses both monolingual and multilingual languaging. In this case, it is registers rather than named languages which are shown to be interwoven in the same meaning-making moment. The dynamic and fluid nature of register is thoroughly argued for by Lin *et al.* (2020). They propose trans-registering as a logical extension of the notion of translanguaging where it is not only named languages which are at play in an interactional moment, but registers as well. Wu and Lin (2019) show how in a Biology class in Hong Kong trans-registering occurs through an 'intimate entanglement' of different linguistic and modal features (Wu & Lin, 2019: 261).

Similarly to Gibbons, Lemke conducted his classroom discourse studies in 'monolingual' English classrooms in the US (Lemke, 1990). Even though teaching and learning takes place in one named language, English, Lemke identifies a variety of language resources being used by the students in the form of registers. He describes students languaging-for-learning as a 'version of scientific language' which is a 'hybrid of colloquial and technical registers' (Lemke, 1990: 173). In a bilingual context such as that of Success High in the present study, the number of distinct potential 'colloquial' and 'technical' registers multiplies. Canagarajah has shown even established research scientists employ a diverse semiotic and spatial repertoire while doing their professional work (Canagarajah, 2021). His earlier work has also drawn attention to code-meshing performed by students in the social sciences (Canagarajah, 2011). Therefore, hybridising/mixing/meshing is a core part of meaning-making in scientific endeavours. Scholars have also probed the perceived fixity of academic registers and genres. Paris and Alim introduced a register of affect into their scholarly paper (Paris & Alim, 2014), challenging a genre of writing associated with objectivity and a lack of feeling. Blackledge and Creese (2019) used a play script genre to present their linguistic ethnography of a United Kingdom market. Phipps (2019) included poetry in her monograph, and an edited volume by McKinney and Christie (2022) includes personal reflections by the authors, some of which include code-meshing/translanguaging.

The proposals of register-meshing, 'bilingual' register use, code-meshing and trans-registering do not ignore the importance of students being able to also understand and produce utterances in a tightly defined or 'standardized' register for Science. Lemke avers that one of the roles of a Science teacher is to 'use these different varieties of language and keep them straight for the students' (Lemke, 1990: 173), and Lin argues that teachers and policymakers need to:

> Counterbalance...the need for dialogic meaning making via translanguaging and trans-semiotizing with the need for a space for students to entextualize their understanding of content meaning in target language academic genres. (Lin, 2019: 14)

The point to emphasise here is that previous scholarship on register for science learning has over-emphasised the use of a tightly defined 'science register' and under-emphasised the productive benefit of a meshed register for students, and especially for bi/multilinguals. Hornberger and Link (2012) posited the valorisation of bilingual students' language and literacy practices in their notion of the continua of biliteracy. In the model, binaries such as the register binaries in Table 2.1 are seen as 'theoretical endpoints on what is in reality a continuum of features' (2012: 264). The ends of each continuum represent differences in power within an educational setting between languages that bilinguals use and between modes (written vs oral). Processes of trans-registering and register meshing occur along the continua of biliteracy, rather than at one end or the other, and disrupt the binaries by 'intentionally opening up implementational and ideological spaces for fluid, multilingual, oral, contextualized practices, and voices at the local level' (Hornberger & Link: 265).

Identity Meshing and Conflict in Appropriation

In grappling with a new discourse, students are also negotiating and constructing new versions of themselves. In the same way as the new applied linguistics terms which describe languaging reviewed above unsettle the notion of fixed languages and registers, this study problematises a fixed understanding of identities. Multimodality scholar, Gunther Kress and colleagues articulated the close relationship between semiotic work and identity work in learning as follows:

> The sign-maker remakes the resources of representation available, thereby remaking their potential for self-representation, and their conceptual, cognitive, affective 'inner' world. This, we believe, is the process which we describe as 'learning', though it is also the process whereby the individual constantly remakes her or himself. (Kress *et al.*, 2014: 7)

Implicit in the constant remaking of self through the semiotic resources available to a student is a post-structuralist understanding of identity (Blommaert & De Fina, 2016; García & Li, 2014; Lin, 2015; Norton, 2013; Rampton, 1995). In this understanding, the student of Science references, draws upon and moves between different identity positions in the learning process – 'constantly', as Kress *et al.* (2014) express. This is a particularly important understanding for scholars of identity work in speakers of non-dominant languages. Lin argues that powerful groups in society engage in processes of fixing/essentialising identity positions for non-dominant others, while constructing multiple/fluid positions for themselves (Lin, 2008: 3). Fixing and essentialising are activities of the colonial encounter, whereas recognising multiplicity and fluidity enables a decolonial perspective. To recognise fluidity and multiplicity is not to infer that identity work with regard to learning new discourses is without tension and conflict. As a well-known passage by Bakhtin shows powerfully, in appropriating new discourses as science students do, words and speakers interanimate one another, and words bear traces of other times and other speakers, often uncomfortably:

> Language is not a neutral medium that passes freely and easily into the private property of the speaker's intentions; it is populated – overpopulated – with the intentions of others. Expropriating it, forcing it to submit to one's own intentions and accents, is a difficult and complicated process. (Bakhtin, 1981: 293–294)

Bakhtin here uses the metaphor of struggle to describe the process ('forcing it to submit', 'difficult and complicated') in which language users make 'words', or Discourses (Gee, 2008), their own. And as Kress *et al.* (2014) propose, it is not a static self which appropriates new words but rather the self is dynamic and subject to the words that are appropriated.

This is some of the complication which Bakhtin expresses. The interaction between 'words' and intentions/accents indexes identity work which Gee (2004) argues is integral to learning a new academic discourse:

> Acquisition of a social language is heavily tied at the outset to identity issues. It is tied to the student's willingness and trust to leave (for a time and place) the lifeworld and participate in another identity, one that, for anyone, represents a certain loss. For some people, it (acquisition of a social language) represents a more significant loss in terms of a disassociation from, and even opposition to, their lifeworlds because their lifeworlds are not the type of middle-class ones that historically have built up a sense of shared interests and values with some academic specialist domains. (Gee, 2004: 18)

Gee picks up Bakhtin's notion of an identity struggle involved in learning a new 'academic social language' (Gee, 2004) or register. For some, the struggle is more intense than for others. Scholars have documented examples of some more outspoken students struggling to accept these losses. For example, Brown (2006) studied teenage Science students in an urban California school and reported on their alienation from the discourse of science captured in one student's cry, 'It isn't no slang that can be said about this stuff' (Brown, 2006: 96). Of course, students are often forced to accept the loss of their everyday registers in the Science classroom, through punishment of their use or through the reinforcement of test scores. But if these are the only conditions for students accepting this loss, then their use of the new scientific registers will most likely be limited to what Lemke (1990: 91) calls 'fixed words', the rote learning of phrases with or without understanding them.

The idea of identity 'loss', however, presupposes sealed and pre existing identities. In order to 'participate' in a new identity, a student must 'leave' another identity. In contrast, a post-structuralist view of identity/subjectivity draws attention to the dynamic nature of identity work and refers to 'positioning' as a key discursive process (Davies & Harré, 1990). Post-structuralist understandings of identity propose that for learning to be successful, it may be necessary for students to perform more than one identity position simultaneously or for students to shuttle between identity positions. Makoe and McKinney (2009) showed how a multilingual Grade 1 student in South Africa was able to shuttle between identity positions of sub-teacher and peer facilitator in 'hybrid discursive practices' in order to create a successful classroom community. Makalela (2014) described university students who created an 'identity matrix' and 'merged identities' for learning through Kasi-taal – a mixed language form. In a bilingual Haitian Creole/English senior primary science class, Ballenger (1997: 10) noted how students engaged both social and academic identity positions simultaneously during science debates: 'the social intentions remain enmeshed in the arguing and theorising'. Hanrahan

(2006) describes a science teacher in Australia who presented a 'hybrid identity' as she taught her class using tales of herself as a science student and engaged her students. McKinney (2010), also, describes black teenage girls in Johannesburg as having 'hybrid identities' as their subversive multilingual and embodied performances stand out against the assimilationist discourses of their previously whites-only school. Emphasising how some identity performances require the drawing together of different cultural time periods, Masola (2020) used the term 'ukuzilanda'. Ukuzilanda (to fetch oneself) is a process of connecting a pre-colonial African identity with a contemporary identity in a dynamic flow.

In my own work with the Success High students, I have noted how students draw on social and academic identity positions simultaneously through the use of different modes and registers. I have termed this 'identity meshing' – a term that builds upon Gibbons' (2006) notion of register meshing outlined above in which different linguistic registers are meshed in one utterance during learning. Identity meshing is 'drawing together two or more identity positions previously considered to be distinct and enacting these simultaneously in order to create a new voice' (Tyler, 2022: 69).

Tied to identity positioning in learning is a teacher's communicative approach (Mortimer & Scott, 2003). An authoritative communicative approach centres the teacher's understanding of a topic and canonical Science knowledge, whereas a dialogic approach engages the student's interest in the topic and uses this as a starting point. Rosebery *et al.* (1992) connect the dialogic approach to serving the students' sense-making purposes or interest:

> Students must not simply acquire scientific ways of doing, reasoning, talking, and valuing; they must also find ways of appropriating scientific discourse so that it can serve their own sense-making purposes. (Rosebery *et al.*, 1992: 67)

Scientific discourse serving students' own sense-making purposes is akin to Freire's (1996) 'problem-posing education' in which the starting point for inquiry is a locally found and articulated problem. This re-orientation is articulated in my study as a decolonial crack in pedagogical design. Like the discomfort and struggle attendant to the identity shifts in appropriating a new discourse (Bakhtin, 1981), being open to inquiry-driven learning can be challenging, but necessary. Tolentino describes inquiry-driven learning as a pedagogical crack:

> Learning comes in the cracks when we are open and willing to deal with the uncomfortable conversations, the unpredictable questions, and the spontaneous outbursts. (Tolentino, 2007: 50)

Examples of inquiry-driven learning as decolonial cracks can be found in Chapter 6.

Conclusion

There is an applied linguistics research trajectory on bi/multilingual practice which begins with studies employing the lens of code-switching. In Africa, current scholars employing recently coined terms build upon the work of earlier scholars who have used the code-switching paradigm to uncover multilingual learning strategies. The recently coined applied linguistic concepts reviewed in this chapter, when applied to non-dominant bilingual students such as those attending Success High, evoke a decolonial borderland as described by Anzaldúa (1987). Concepts using the prefix '*trans*' evoke movement across borders, which is productive when considering pedagogical translanguaging learning activities such as translation. *Meshing* of languages, registers or identity positions and *whole*-body sense-making enables a vision of dwelling and thinking *within* the border regions between previously considered distinct objects of meaning-making. Mignolo (2000) espouses border thinking as an essential position from which new visions of the decolonial will emerge. Therefore, attending seriously to the processes of translanguaging, trans-semiotising and trans-registering as well as meshing of languages, registers and identity positions in science learning is construed here as a decolonial endeavour (Pratt, 2019). All these concepts will be brought to bear on the data presented in this book.

In the next chapter, I will introduce the language environment of Success High, detailing ideologies, language profiles, reported practices and the linguistic landscape of the school.

Notes

(1) Although see https://molomhlaba.org/wp-content/uploads/2019/09/LANGUAGE-POLICY.pdf and Mbude, 2019, for hopeful examples.
(2) For a South African example which points to the futility of trying to keep languages separate in a parallel medium setting, see Banda (2010).

3 Language at Success High: Ideologies and Practices

Introduction

Building on the conceptual framing and background to the study in Chapters 1 and 2, I aim to highlight in this chapter both the coloniality/Anglonormativity of the language environment of the school and the decolonial cracks appearing in the linguistic landscape, language attitudes and multilingual practices of the community. The language environment of a school is conceived of in this study as the tangible and intangible, visible and invisible instances of languaging and discourse about language. This chapter examines the school language policy; interviews with the principal and the Grade 9B Science teacher; questionnaire data gathered from teachers and students; as well as photographic and fieldnote data collected around the school grounds during the nine month ethnography at the school. In this way, the chapter also provides a frame for understanding the classroom and study group interaction in Chapters 4–6. The overarching language ideologies and practices within the school community have bearing on the practices within the two focus sites.

Khayelitsha is a township situated 25 minutes' drive east of Cape Town city centre. In South Africa, a township refers to an area comprising both formal and informal housing designated by the Apartheid government as a residential area for black Africans in order to provide cheap labour for the urban economy. While many people have always lived permanently in Khayelitsha ('our new home'), under Apartheid residents were viewed by the state as migrants from the 'black homelands', predominantly those located in the Eastern Cape, and had no citizenship status in Cape Town. Up to today, many Khayelitshans live in conditions of precarity typical of denizenship (Ndhlovu & Makalela, 2021) worldwide. Another feature of denizenship as identified by Ndhlovu and Makalela is the opportunities made available due to the multilingual language features acquired in a township setting. The richness and complexity of multilingual languaging in township settings in Cape Town has been well documented (Dowling *et al.*, 2019; Krause, 2022; Stroud & Mpendukana, 2009), and Khayelitsha is no exception. Success High is in many respects a typical South African township school. It draws students largely from the local area and is a no-fee school. The school has a homogenous student-body: students are black, dominantly isiXhosa-speaking and from majority working-class backgrounds. But Success High is also atypical as it is selective (prospective students must write an entrance test in Mathematics, Science and English prior to admission); it receives donor funding for specific projects; and its staff is multiracial. The school was started as a Mathematics and Science intervention project to improve the uptake of these subjects in Khayelitsha high schools. In 1999, a programme was being run within a teachers' training college for matriculants to redo Mathematics and Science in one year post-matric in order to prepare them for university. When the programme's directors saw that Mathematics and Science intervention needed to happen earlier in the school career, they began offering Grade 10–12 curricula specialising in Mathematics and Science funded by the Western Cape Education Department. In 2011, the programme moved to its own campus and became a fully-fledged state school, and Grade 8 and 9 were included. Mathematics, Physical Science, Life Science and Computer Science are compulsory subjects. The school has several teaching and learning development programmes running in conjunction with one of Cape Town's universities. The selection of Success High as a research site was, in brief, due to its isiXhosa-dominant emergent bilingual student body; its reputation as the top-achieving academic school in Khayelitsha; and my personal contacts at the school.

School Language Policy

As outlined in Chapter 1, the state devolves the formation of language policy to the local school level, and it is the responsibility of the School Governing Body (SGB), of which the school principal is a member, to form the policy. My exploration of Success High's language policy began during my interview with the principal. The policy is a replication of a proforma school language policy designed by a non-governmental organisation set up to support school governing bodies with issues of school governance predominantly in ex-whites-only schools. The wholesale adoption of the proforma policy supports Probyn et al.'s (2002) finding that SGBs are not well equipped to form school-specific language policy. In this case, the proforma policy does not suit the linguistic makeup of the school at all. In her interview, the principal began to talk about the policy by minimising its significance describing it as 'basically a very short policy'. This low-priority status of the school language policy aligns with Kgobe and Mbele's (2001) nationwide South African study which found that only five out of 27 schools participating in the study had developed language policies (as cited in Probyn et al., 2002). The history of the Success High policy reveals the lack of interrogation of the low-profile policy within the school community. It serves to fulfil a legal requirement that the school has an official policy, but it has not undergone much consultation. The principal informed me that the policy was written in 2015, has been 'seen by the staff', 'adopted by the SGB' and 'kept on file' (fieldnotes, 030216). She indicated that she was the primary author of the policy but was informed by other schools' policies and a book on school leadership and management that she had been given. She reported that the students have not read the policy and allowed that this was 'a shortcoming that we don't involve students more' (fieldnotes, 150416). Tacit language policies are however adopted by all members of the school community, and some of these will be discussed in the next section.

In the summary of the school language policy in her interview, the principal frames the cornerstone of the policy as being the stipulation of the language of instruction: 'although the home language of the teacher and the students may be...but the language of learning and teaching will be English' (Principal interview). The principal leaves a pause, a blank space where one would expect a description of the largely homogenous isiXhosa-speaking teachers and students. Initially, a concession is given towards the home language of the teacher and students; however, the home language of the teacher and students is framed as an absence. In fact, this mirrors the written policy where the home languages of the students remain invisible in the written policy:

Extract 3.1 Success High language policy – students
While Success High is an institution in which the medium of instruction and language of office is English, it nevertheless enrols students with *divergent linguistic capacities*. (emphasis mine)

The emphasis of the policy is on English: its hegemonic position in school life and the capacities of the students in this language. 'Divergent linguistic capacities' amounts to a deficit positioning of the students at the school. The phrase indicates that there are at least some students whose English proficiency is lacking. Table 3.2 (see p. 64) reveals that the students of Grade 9B, the focal class, share the linguistic capacities of isiXhosa as a home language and are strongly multilingual in the languages of South Africa. The descriptor 'divergent' hides both the commonality of students' repertoires and their richness. It also perpetuates the invisibility of isiXhosa as a main language among the student body in the language policy. Indeed, there is only one reference to isiXhosa in the policy as a whole, and this is in stating that it will be offered as a subject, only at Home Language level. In this way, the language abilities of the students as isiXhosa-English dominant multilinguals are obscured and replaced with a deficit view of their abilities. Further evidence of the deficit positioning of students' linguistic repertoires is the absence of any questions about students' languages on the school application form. This is not to say that this deficit positioning is intentional within the school, but rather that the scant attention paid to language policy in South African schools has this deleterious consequence for children whose home language does not match the dominant language of the school – i.e. the vast majority of South Africans.

The positioning of African language speakers as deficient English monolinguals is extended to the policy on communication with parents:

> *Extract 3.2 Success High language policy – parents*
> The language of communication with parents shall be English, but steps will be taken to ensure that, while the standard of English is not compromised, the level of English usage shall not be such that it denies access to communication and comprehension by those whose *linguistic abilities in English are less developed than those of the average English home language speaker.* (emphasis mine, p. 1)

In the section in italics, we see the shadowy figure of the 'average' language user making an appearance. In the context of South Africa, those who reported having English as a home language in the 2011 census totalled 9.6% (Statistics South Africa, 2012), the majority of these being white South Africans. It becomes difficult to see how the parents of Success High could ever be imagined to be 'average English home language speaker(s)'. Furthermore, scholars have critiqued the notion of 'home language speaker' (Makoni & Pennycook, 2005) or 'native speaker' (Rampton, 1995) especially in a context of African multilingualism. I suggest the term is used here as a cover for positioning the ethnolinguistic repertoire of Whiteness (McKinney *et al.*, 2015) as the norm and as a desirable, but unattainable, standard for Success High parents. The anxiety about compromising the standard of English is particularly jarring in this context as what is at stake here is not students' ability to cope with the curriculum and assessments, but clear communication with parents. In practice, as I will describe in the next section, the principal flouts the English-only parent communication policy and uses interpreters and other strategies resourcefully.

These examples of an ideology which positions students' and parents' language use as a problem, or deficient, is a common one all the way through the schooling system, as highlighted by McKinney (2017). McKinney argues that:

> the intimate relationship between language and power in schools works to position children from dominant backgrounds as legitimate language users while those from non-dominant linguistic, cultural and class backgrounds are frequently positioned as linguistically deficient. (2017: 63)

I have discussed how the 'non-dominant' isiXhosa resources of the students and parents are cast as a problem in the policy and the principal's interview in that they are not English resources. McKinney also draws our attention to an ideology that positions any variety other than the 'standard' (i.e. the variety used by the powerful in society, in this case, white, middle-class South Africans) as deficient and problematic. This 'monoglossic ideology' prevents the non-standard resources of the majority of students being recognised in policy documents, government reports or language tests, where:

> the 'normal' student is imagined as already a competent user of the language variety that schools should in fact be giving him/her access to. (McKinney, 2017: 64)

Overall, the Success High language policy positions the average Success High student and parent as linguistically deficient. Furthermore, the linguistic resources that the students and parents do have are rendered invisible in the policy. It is the coloniality of language (Veronelli, 2015) which enables these racialising processes to occur with the policy as a vehicle.

Linguistic Landscapes

While the language policy is silent on environmental text in the school, a journey through the school to examine the linguistic landscape of the school buildings is illustrative of languages being used for specific purposes and audiences in a patterned way. In this section, I will lead the reader on an imagined physical journey through the school premises

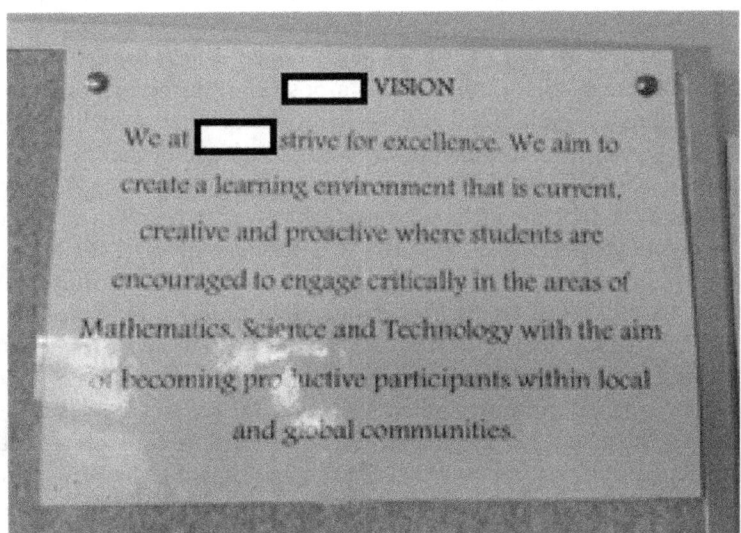

Figure 3.1 School vision displayed in the entrance lobby

pointing out texts that were on display in order to provide an analysis of hierarchies of language use in the domain of environmental text.

As a visitor enters the school, the first environmental text they encounter is the school motto printed large above the door leading from the reception area into the rest of the school buildings: 'No excuses – just success'. By referring to 'excuses', this motto positions the school in opposition to other schools, or students, which may try to make excuses for their lack of success. It also emphasises its singular focus which is academic success. This message is voiced in English and oriented towards the visitor as it is the text appearing closest to the entrance.

The representation of the school in English is echoed by the vision statement which is pinned to a noticeboard in the lobby and aligns with 'success' in the motto by stating in the opening sentence that 'we…strive for excellence'.

Appearing next to the school's vision are newspaper clippings of articles in English extolling the school as a fine example of a township school which is beating the odds and achieving success. As this is an area in which visitors wait, the audience can be assumed to be outsiders.

After leaving the formal printed text environment of the entrance lobby, one enters a space of buildings separated by paved thoroughfares and courtyards. There is a set of noticeboards outside the library with information regarding special student groups and extra-murals, mostly printed with instructions in English. Midway through the cluster of school buildings, there is a brick wall which occasionally was used to tack messages and notices on to which were aimed at the students. This was only visible if you were facing towards the exit of the school. The predominance of English in these texts was noticeable, with Figure 3.2 opposite being a typical example of a printed poster.

This notice with text in English has been word-processed. The use of English is remarkable because this is a poster produced by students for students about a social, not academic, event. A phrase such as 'come through' is not one that students would use with each other face to face when they would likely address one another in isiXhosa. It is possible that the association of printed text with English is very strong for the author/s of this poster and the use of isiXhosa was unimaginable.

One handwritten note from a teacher was heteroglossic in its use of register, employing a convention from mobile phone text-messaging, '2MORO'. This orthography has the advantage of allowing the message to fit easily onto an A4 page and to be written quickly.

Continuing on our return journey through the school, there is a notice written by the groundsman on a piece of used cardboard, and it is found attached to a grill near a flowerbed (Figure 3.4). It employs translanguaging in forming an instruction text aimed at students in a familiar township register. Features associated with English and isiXhosa are drawn together into one heteroglossic text. Its purpose is to influence behaviour, and the

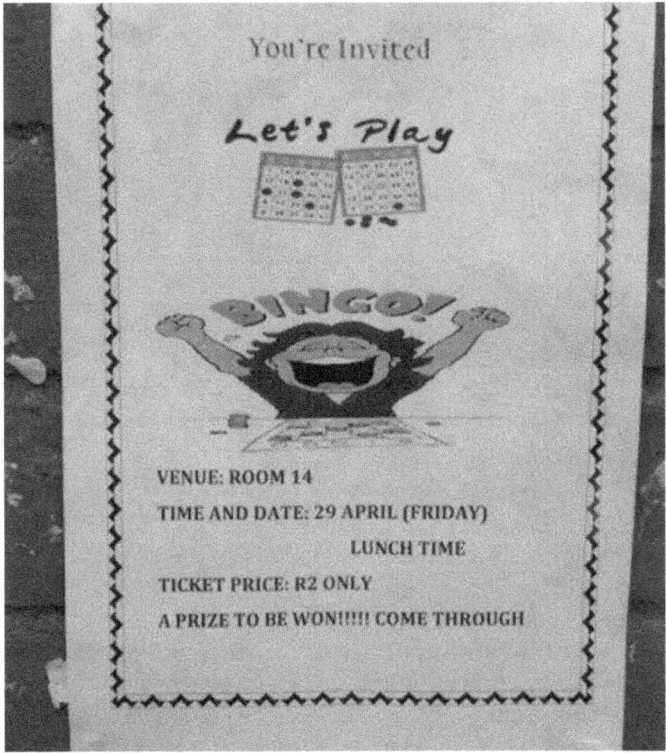

Figure 3.2 Bingo advertisement on the 'student wall'

Figure 3.3 Notice about Saturday school on the 'student wall'

groundsman might have appealed to students in a shared familiar register as a strategy of influence. Equally he may have been freely using the written language resources with which he was most familiar as he operates

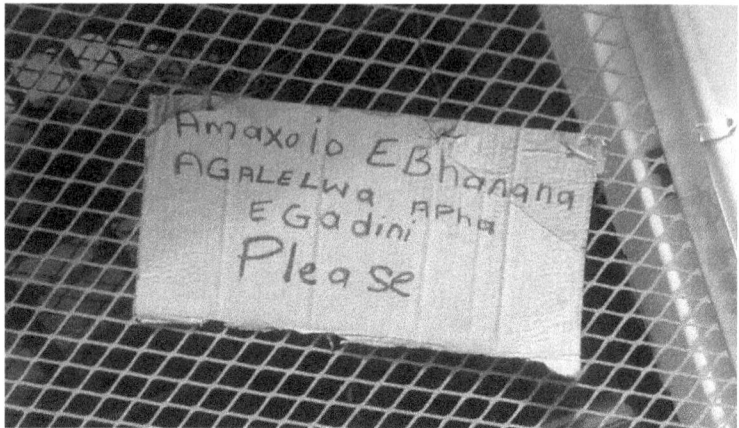

Figure 3.4 Banana peel sign
English gloss: Banana peels must be thrown here in the garden, please.

outside the language policy of the academic spaces of the school, unlike the students who produced the sign in Figure 3.2 who are influenced more by the language policy which exhorts them to display English competence at school. In their linguistic landscape, the study of signs in Khayelitsha, Stroud and Mpendukana (2009) differentiated (following Bourdieu) between sites of luxury and sites of necessity and tracked how signage differed in these sites. The examples of signs at Success High reveal sites of luxury and of necessity operating within the school grounds. Stroud and Mpendukana argue that 'representations found in sites of necessity (are) highly contextualized in the immediacy of task-interaction' (2009: 373) and that they appear using materials that are non-durable, cheaper and usually found in the local environment. Stroud and Mpendukana found that the language use on signs in sites of necessity is usually heteroglossic with features of English and isiXhosa being used, while in sites of luxury, there is more use of English and less mixing of linguistic features. All these features of sites of necessity apply to the sign in Figure 3.4, firmly placing the sign, its author and the activity of composting food waste in a site of necessity. Nevertheless, given the sign's visibility in a public thoroughfare, it functions as a decolonial crack in the edifice of printed text in English.

We have now returned to the entrance lobby of the school – a site of luxury (Stroud & Mpendukana, 2009) positioned as it is near the offices of the school management. Just as we walk out through the entrance doors to the school, there appears in large, printed letters an exhortation: 'Fun'ulwazi – Be curious' (the English following the isiXhosa being a translation). Orientated as it is towards the school and students as they exit the building, and written in both isiXhosa and English, this sign is intended for students as a spur to be curious about the world they are entering as they leave the school premises. It is unique in featuring English and isiXhosa side-by-side with the English functioning as a translation of the isiXhosa. Its position at the exit of the school, only to be viewed on leaving, diminishes its impact as a sign in a site of luxury; however, it is significant in that it contains the only formally printed text containing isiXhosa to be found in the out-of-classroom premises of the school. This sign is typical of signage in sites of luxury in Khayelitsha, as argued by Stroud and Mpendukana (2009), in that it employs highly edited English features as well as isiXhosa features which functions to link the present place (school) to other imagined places (university and the world of work). The environmental text outside the classroom is self-reinforcing in that it expresses the values of the community but also upholds those values through its presence.

Academic learning spaces at Success High included: classrooms, computer laboratories, the library and the hall. I observed teaching and learning in four classrooms. Displayed writing in these classrooms was sparse and included subject-specific posters, motivational quotes and lists of names of students. I found no examples of isiXhosa language and no examples of students' work in classrooms. The library was the place where our study group was held and therefore another key learning space for the research. Apart from the scant availability of isiXhosa books in the library, there was also only one example of isiXhosa text displayed. After my first visit to the library, I made the following entry in my fieldnotes:

Extract 3.3 Library language
Interestingly, no displayed language appears in Xhosa, except the handwritten word 'amasiko' (rituals) on a sticker which has been stuck on a poster which advertises different career paths for different subjects. I ask the assistant librarian what 'amasiko' means and she tells me rituals but seems uncertain and so I point out the sticker and ask her if the word relates to the poster in any way. She says no and hastily removes the sticker. Is she embarrassed by its presence in the library? She says a child stuck it there. I wonder if she thinks I'm criticising its presence. Or perhaps she is just playing policeman to the transgressions of the children.

As I intimate in my fieldnotes, the librarian censures the tacked-on, handwritten text in isiXhosa. It may have offended her for other reasons than its isiXhosa lexeme: it may have been unsightly to her, cluttering up the poster, or the reference to a traditional isiXhosa practice in the context of an English poster giving information about career paths may have seemed illegitimate to her. However, I would argue that her hastiness in removing it without engaging with my interest in it reveals a sense of shame about it which is deeper than its perceived untidiness – revealing Anglonormativity. It was not the only time I experienced a pro-English sheen being applied to the cultural life of the school in my presence.

In sum, English language text in the environment of the school is given prominence, by its appearance on more durable materials and printing resources being allocated to it, while isiXhosa is displayed using makeshift materials and is not as prevalent, with the exception being the printed bilingual text: 'Fun'ulwazi – be curious', although this is placed at the exit to the school which makes it peripheral rather than central to the printed discourse of the school. The language hierarchy in written text on school grounds contributes to the under-valuing of isiXhosa in the school community.

The Principal and Staff

During my interview with the Principal of Success High which took place right at the start of my fieldwork, we discussed the three official languages of the Western Cape and the role they played in her repertoire. For transcription conventions, see Appendix 3. She began haltingly with what she called her 'home language':

Extract 3.4 Principal's home language
Principal: I **am** . Afrikaans as
my home language is Afrikaans
um so
but I can make myself understood in English

Far from merely being able to make herself understood in English, the principal is actually highly proficient in this language, and it is the dominant language she uses at work. This backgrounds her linguistic skill in two languages and constructs her as a monolingual, whose identity is bound up with her 'home language' ('I am Afrikaans'). This treatment of her Afrikaans and English was brief, although when I probed her on her use of Afrikaans at school, more detail emerged. I reminded her that I had overheard her speaking Afrikaans to a member of the grounds staff. She responded by indicating that both men responsible for the grounds were isiXhosa speakers who spoke better Afrikaans than English. These were men with whom I myself had only spoken isiXhosa and so I had a limited knowledge of their repertoires. A further probe I used was stating that there were other home language speakers of Afrikaans on the staff. She responded to this by explaining the limits she places on using Afrikaans at school. She described how if she were speaking Afrikaans to a fellow speaker in the staff room and someone entered who was not Afrikaans-speaking, she would revert to speaking English 'just to include everybody and that they know that it's all above board' (Principal interview). Of the 17 academic staff who were regulars in the staff room that I polled, only three indicated English as one of their home languages. However, the principal assumes that using English in a multilingual environment such as this staffroom automatically constitutes inclusion and legitimate, comprehensible speech. Her assumption is testament to the power of the ideology that English is a neutral lingua franca which includes rather than excludes (Phillipson, 2009).

The story of the principal's isiXhosa part of her repertoire is one of language learned both formally and informally. She reports having studied isiXhosa at university 30 years ago but admitted that when 'you don't practise it it goes away' (Principal Interview). She added that the isiXhosa she learned was 'Oxford isiXhosa' and different to 'what I hear spoken here'. Schools and universities teach and emphasise the standard (or 'Oxford') varieties of languages. This practice is especially strong for African languages (Guzula, 2022) whose guardians in the academy hold to notions of purism as a strategy of language preservation. The principal's metaphor for standard isiXhosa is particularly apt given the 'colonial invention' of standard African languages (Makoni & Pennycook, 2005). Despite her limits in isiXhosa, she reflected that she could 'get the gist looking at body language' and was able to respond in English to students, staff and parents who spoke in isiXhosa. In her interview, despite claiming a monolingual identity, the principal reports on her multilingual life in which she uses adaptive strategies to negotiate a working environment in which the majority of the community members are isiXhosa dominant.

Table 3.1 provides a summary of the 17 staff responses to my questions about language use. The other six members of staff were not available to respond.

In contrast to the students of Grade 9B (see p. 64 for Table 3.2) whose home languages were significantly multilingual, only one staff member professed to have more than one home language. I posit that this is due to the principle of inheritance working more strongly in the adults and the principle of affiliation to new heteroglossic ways of speaking and being working more strongly in the teenagers (Rampton, 1995). Also notable in Table 3.1 is that only 12% of the teachers in my sample reported to be exclusive English home language speakers. This reveals that the staff body reflects the demographics of South Africa more broadly where 9.6% of

Table 3.1 Language information gleaned from 17 of 23 academic staff (74%)

Language	Number of staff	Percentage
isiXhosa home language	8	47%
English home language	2	12%
Afrikaans home language	3	18%
Zulu or Setswana home language	3	18%
Shona and English home language	1	6%
Other languages known	Sotho, German, Dutch, Korean, Venda, Siswati, Ndebele, Sepedi	

people are English home language speakers (Statistics South Africa, 2012). In addition, the fact that the majority of Success High teachers have a home language other than the language of instruction is closely aligned with the situation in the majority of South African schools (Probyn, 2001) where not only do teachers have the challenge of the mismatch between the students' home language and the language of instruction, but their own as well.

Probing staff attitudes, beliefs and practices regarding language in learning took place mainly through the use of a questionnaire and the principal and Science teacher interviews. However, one interaction I had with a long-serving teacher at the school, captured in my field notes, was particularly revealing of underlying ideologies. Early in my fieldwork, this teacher asked me what I was researching. After I answered that my interest lay in bilingual learning, the teacher retorted, 'but we don't have any bilinguals here'. The teacher was displaying assumptions that commonly accompany discussions of bilingualism in South African schooling. As outlined in Chapter 1, 'bilingual education' is still only conceived of as English-Afrikaans bilingualism within a colonial paradigm, and in the absence of an explicit definition of 'bilingual' by the teacher, I assume he meant English-Afrikaans bilingualism. Be that as it may, his contention nevertheless results in positioning of the Success High students as deficient English monolinguals rather than bi/multilinguals. This positioning is evident in teachers' responses to the questionnaire below where the name of the language 'isiXhosa', like in the policy, is not mentioned. Instead, English is referred to predominantly, and the terms 'mother tongue' or 'indigenous' or 'their own language' are present in the place of isiXhosa.

Of the 17 academic staff who responded to my orally administered questionnaire, 5 also completed the more detailed written questionnaires. Two of the questions related directly to language for learning. The written answers given by the five respondents are transcribed below each question. The subjects taught by the teacher are given in brackets after their pseudonym.

1. *Do you have any rules about language use in your classroom? Please describe briefly.*
    T1 (English enrichment): Speaking English is compulsory.
    T2 (English): English as far as possible.
    T3 (Mathematics): We must only use English in the classroom. You cannot learn Mathematics in another language as it will be tested in English.
    T4 (Life Science): If a student wants to express him/herself in the mother tongue, I would allow them to do so – for short spells.
    T5 (Geography and English): I know I'm supposed to enforce that only English is used in class, but I feel that they are helping each other more in their own language.

2. *Do you experience any challenges relating to language in your classroom? Please describe briefly.*
   T1: Students struggle sometimes to express themselves or explain in English.
   T2: Students are prone to revert to their mother tongue when they struggle to express themselves. They converse in their mother tongue with one another even during the English lesson.
   T3: Some students find it difficult to express their views in English.
   T4: It may contribute to relations if teachers have an understanding (basic) of the mother tongue of students at a school. It will also be helpful if teachers use mother tongue words, phrases (indigenous) to help explain complex concepts.
   T5: Sometimes students do not know a word, but they just ask another student and the word always comes.

Although this is a small sample of the academic staff (22%), the answers to these questions reveal influential attitudes and beliefs about language use in the classroom. All five teachers described oral language practices, which reveals that it is the dominant communication channel of the public space of the classroom and is at the front of these teachers' minds when reflecting on language practices, despite only written language being assessed in all content subjects, including Science. Two teachers (T1 and T3) report that they insist on exclusive English use in the classroom. The other three teachers express more nuanced language rules with conditions attached ('for short spells'; 'as far as possible') or awareness of how practice diverts from school language policy ('I know I'm supposed to enforce that only English is used'). These teachers display a more inclusive attitude towards students' most familiar languages and see the benefit of using these languages as resources for peer-to-peer learning and whole-class teaching. The unspecific and concessional language rules governing classroom practice used by these teachers are aligned with the anxieties expressed by the principal regarding classroom language practices which will be discussed below. Even when teachers expressed clear and confident language policies in their classrooms, there may be more complex practices happening in reality. One Science teacher whom I met early in my fieldwork was very confident about her language use in the classroom. I met her in her classroom, and she explained her adjustments to the language use in her classroom while three Grade 11 students worked on homework in a group near us. The following extract is taken from my fieldnotes:

Extract 3.5 Students mixing while learning
She said she used to use a methodology of getting her students to translate explanations to each other in Xhosa, but now doesn't use that anymore, rather she asks them to explain to each other in English. She says this is

better. When she asks some students in the classroom if this is better they give a much more hedged answer. They seem unsure. ... I ask the students in the classroom what language they are using to discuss the science problems they are working on and they say 'we are mixing'.

The gap between the teacher's perception of student practice and their reported practice is stark here. Overall, teachers' comments on the languaging practices they employ in classrooms often reveal more about their own language ideologies than actual classroom practice, especially languaging between students. The principal shared a number of her management practices regarding language learning in her interview.

Following directly from the brief overview of the language policy given by the principal in her interview, she began to broach the topic of the role of 'code-switching' in teaching and learning. She had been informed about my research topic by way of a letter and informal conversations we had previously, and this is probably the spur to her introducing this topic.

Extract 3.6 Principal views on code-switching
Principal: And it's um we we we do um allow and possibly encourage code-switching if it will help the understanding of the students but there are certain teachers that can't code-switch for me for instance I can't I know certain words in English but I think I'm gonna do more damage if I want to use a Xhosa word to explain things (laughing) more harm than good you see, so there are certain people, we have Zimbabwean teachers we have um teachers that cannot speak isiXhosa um so the the code-switching in the sense to help them understand the work better by explaining it in their mother tongue, that doesn't really work for for us who don't speak isiXhosa

The principal's speech here is hesitant and hedging. She hesitates through repeating 'we' in the first line and hedges through the use of 'possibly'. This is a topic about which she feels some awkwardness and possibly irresolution. She also acknowledges those staff (including herself) who cannot 'code-switch' as they are not proficient in isiXhosa, recognising their lack in this regard. She continues to describe her informal directives to staff about code-switching as follows:

Extract 3.7 Principal views on code-switching continued
(T1) **Principal:** I didn't I don't explicitly say um when I but in the staff meeting that code-switching is allowed but when I do speak to individual students I feel that there is a place for code-switching um ... if say a Xhosa-speaking person would speak to students and they have difficulty explaining a concept or they have difficulty not explaining the concept let me just not say it that way, they have difficulty getting the kids to understand a particular concept, but they know that there is a word in Xhosa that will make them just easily understand it they they can say they have

the vocabulary to say it in English but the kids they don't grasp it (Robyn: m) but when they just have the word or the phrase or the idiom in isiXhosa that will make the kids grasp it and see the picture clearer then that is that is quite acceptable for me, so I'll when I speak to individual um people then I'll do that however when I do my rounds and I hear people teach in isiXhosa then I will speak to the teachers about that because you not supposed to teach in isiXhosa

(T2) **Robyn:** ...so what's the difference in your mind between...teaching in isiXhosa and . teaching in English with some code-switching when when understanding is difficult

(T3) **Principal:** you see, what we need to um we we let me let me put it to you this way, when the kids come here they some of them actually have difficulty conversing in English (Robyn: m) but at the end of grade 12 and that is their passport basically for higher education, all the exams are going to be in English and our job is to make sure that they understand the work in such a way that they can express it (Robyn: m-hm) in English correctly

The principal here presents an understanding that there is more than one practice that she classifies as code-switching, some of which she condones, others which she doesn't. In the first turn, she focuses on the need for her students to 'understand', 'grasp' and 'see the picture clearer' in their classes. However, she makes it clear that the use of isiXhosa should be limited to a 'word', 'phrase' or 'idiom'. In other words, the use of isiXhosa is a concession towards students to ameliorate lack of understanding, but it should not become dominant or visible as a resource. Condoning the use of code-switching publicly in a staff meeting is going too far for her. However, when probed (Turn 2) to provide a distinction between 'teaching in isiXhosa' and 'teaching in English with some code-switching', she avoids answering the question and rather moves on to the topic of 'our job'. She understands this to be the responsibility of herself and her staff to the students, to make sure that they 'can express (their work) in English correctly'. The reason she gives for this is the high stakes in higher education placed on English proficiency. The ideal of preparing students for a world of English dominance is a safer topic than dwelling on the messiness of the mechanics and politics of teaching and learning in situ with the multilingual reality of her classrooms. Her discomfort can be described in terms of the double burden that teachers in English-dominant multilingual contexts are under where they have to balance the pressures of providing access to new concepts and to the language of power (Setati & Adler, 2000).

The principal's view on code-switching is pivotal as the leader of the school. Also, her views here are representative of many South African teachers who hold strong opinions, but do not have a nuanced understanding of the practice of the use of different languages in teaching and learning. This has been attributed to the lack of penetration of recent developments in applied linguistics in education research in general and therefore into teacher education programmes (McKinney, 2017; Probyn, 2021).

While the policy states that 'the language of communication with parents shall be English', in practice, the principal flouts the English-only parent communication policy and uses languages resourcefully. In her interview, the principal described a number of techniques she uses to cross language barriers in communicating with parents: she uses staff as interpreters; she prioritises listening in meetings even if her comprehension is limited, and she has had letters to parents translated previously. In all these measures, she flouts the language policy to aid communication and establish trust with parents. The measures are journeys towards communication but are limited by the principal's level of proficiency in isiXhosa and by the dependence on the parents voicing their objection to using English only in the one-on-one meetings, an act requiring high levels of agency from the parents.

In the walkways and quadrangles of the school, teachers and students interacted with each other in familiar registers. A close analysis of this talk was not conducted, but observations I made as I walked through the school yielded a sense of the easy camaraderie of school peers talking inside the school grounds as they would outside the school grounds. During the study group meetings, I pushed the participants to find a term to define this familiar register that they use with each other. This was somewhat disingenuous of me as I would not be able to use one term to describe my most familiar spoken register as of course this is an idiolect and unique to me. However, the students pressed on and used descriptors recorded in Chapter 6. This familiar register was also used between staff members, particularly among support staff, and when teachers speak one on one with students. The teachers who shared this register with the students used it in conversation with students around the school. Even the Principal who purports not to speak isiXhosa is able to understand students when they speak within earshot of her.

Extract 3.8 isiXhosa proficiencies

Principal: when teachers, when the kids converse with teachers outside of the classroom in most cases when it's a Xhosa-speaking teacher they will converse in isiXhosa in most cases, right, when they speak to me they will sometimes because they so used to me, they will also start speaking in isiXhosa and (laughing) then they will check themselves (laughing) you don't understand (laughing) you know and they surprised sometimes when I actually answer (laughing) because I do

Robyn: in Xhosa, or in English //oh you answer in English but you understood//

Principal: // in English I answer in English but I //understood

The principal laughs often in this section of her interview. She clearly enjoys recollecting moments of linguistic facility on her part and the rapport it builds with the students. This mood is in contrast with her earlier serious comments about code-switching in the classroom. The social life of the school and its academic life constitute two very different interactional frames with different rules for language use. Debates about language in academic learning for multilinguals are often rife with anxiety and the playful flexibility with which we use language everyday are sometimes ignored and left out of discussions of appropriate language for learning.

I visited one school assembly where all members of staff and students were invited. As was customary, a senior isiXhosa-speaking teacher led a devotion in isiXhosa, and the principal led the rest of the assembly in English. The use of isiXhosa in this setting was reported by a member of staff to be very much appreciated by the students. The assembly functions as a high-status domain, and the use of isiXhosa in this space is symbolically powerful for the students, although its use was reserved for a teacher. This instance of the use of a formal register of isiXhosa in the assembly and the isiXhosa used in the isiXhosa Home Language subject classroom were the only two ratified uses of the standard variety of isiXhosa for high-status functions that I witnessed.

The discourse employed by the principal and staff in reference to their own and others' language use at school is multi-voiced and dilemma filled. The principal expresses reductive views on her own language use initially, but then tempers these with anecdotes about her broader repertoire which she employs at school. While stopping short of an unequivocal endorsement of code-switching in class, she explains a variety of translingual strategies which she supports. Classroom translanguaging and the use of interpreters during parent–teacher meetings are, however, positioned as concessions, not proactive employment of isiXhosa resources.

The Science Teacher

Twenty-four-year-old Ms B reports her home language as isiXhosa. Her family is originally from the isiXhosa-dominant Eastern Cape, but she grew up in Cape Town and attended primary school in a neighbouring suburb and also in Khayelitsha. English was her language of instruction throughout her schooling, although with varying multilingual practices being employed by her teachers each year. She started high school at another school in Khayelitsha and then moved to Success High in Grade 10 and completed Grade 12 there. She qualified with a BSc in Microbiology and Biochemistry and a Postgraduate Certificate in Education – a qualification to teach high school – in 2014 from the University of Cape Town and completed her teaching practice at Success High. In 2015, she took up a Natural Science position at Success High and one other Cape Town school. At the time of my fieldwork, she was in her second year of teaching at the school. While her interview responses are included as a staff member in Table 3.1, more detail is available on Ms B's language repertoire which is pertinent to the study. My first prompt about her language repertoire opens the following extract.

Extract 3.8 Ms B's language repertoire
(T1) **Robyn:** and then I'm interested in your
your languages that you know and that you speak and you use
(T2) **Ms B:** ok
(T3) **Robyn:** um
can you tell me a little bit about that
(T4) **Ms B:** um well
home language is isiXhosa for starters
and then I teach in English
well I speak English most of the time
I can say and only a couple of times or with a couple of individuals that I speak Xhosa with

Ms B goes on to say that apart from English and isiXhosa, she doesn't speak any other languages, but then further on in the interview added 'Xhosa is so similar to Zulu' and 'the people from Joburg their Tswana I can understand'. Ms B's multilingualism requires some probing to uncover. She claims to be English-dominant 'I speak English most of the time', but I witnessed her speaking isiXhosa to colleagues during breaks. She learnt Setswana from her roommate at university. She also mentioned picking up Afrikaans from the area where she lives in Somerset West, and she studied this language in school. She speaks mostly isiXhosa with her granny and her mother. That Ms B's multilingualism requires probing to uncover points to the unmarked nature of African people's multilingualism (Makalela, 2016). The invisibilising processes of the coloniality of language (Veronelli, 2015) that makes Ms B unused to valuing or highlighting her multilingualism.

I also asked Ms B about her language use on social media:

Extract 3.10 Ms B's social media language
(T1) **Ms B:** (laughs) I think honestly just use English um with most people
(T2) **Robyn:** ja, ok
(T3) **Ms B:** because, especially with typing and whatever its so much easier than Xhosa, I think you'd rather speak Xhosa than write it (ok) it gets really complicated so if I'm texting if I'm well Twitter or whatever I would use English cos it's a shorter and whatever

While in reality Ms B's language use in digital communication may include a mix of languages, she reports to using only English because it is easier and isiXhosa is complicated. This is her preference and perception indicating her developed digital literacies and not an inherent characteristic of either English or isiXhosa as multilinguals frequently translanguage in digital communication. When I ask her where and how she learnt English she laughs and says 'what do you mean' and 'I honestly don't know how to answer that' (Teacher Interview 1). Her discomfort with my question could be due to her learning of English being dispersed in time and space throughout her life, from primary school onwards. She reports that she didn't feel confident in English on leaving primary school, only after high school. The whole of her school career was a steep learning curve for her. This moment of discomfort also occurs against the backdrop of a power differential between me as a white English-speaking interviewer and herself as black interviewee having to account for her proficiency in a language through which she must make her living. Certainly, her experience at high school was difficult given the English immersion environment of the Success High classroom, as she goes on to describe:

Extract 3.11 English at Success High
(T1) Ms B: well I didn't want to at first like I I hated the idea of coming here (Success High) I felt like I was forced to come here
(T2) Robyn: whose idea was it then
(T3) Ms B: remember (the headhunters) yes they went and approached the school so basically everyone at the school the teachers were saying I should go and whatever and whatever (in-draw of breath) so but I didn't want to cos you know your friends are there and everyone (Robyn: yes) so now you thinking it's just gonna be me at this new school and ja but ja I was forced to come (Robyn: m) but I didn't enjoy it for maybe like the first month or so until I started well be comfortable and get used to the environment (Robyn: mhm) and then after that it was it was fine it was ja (in-draw of breath)
(T4) Robyn: And do you remember feeling a bit at sea with, with all the English, do you remember it feeling like a much more English than you've ever been exposed to and now you learning through English and it's difficult or or what was it like?
(T5) Ms B: Ja, I think it, that's how I felt throughout the high school (laughs) yeah, yeah I think that's how I felt, like there was something to learn each year and mmm sometimes it was a bit too much

In this extract, Ms B describes her recruitment to Success High and her accommodation to the new environment. As outlined earlier, Success High is a selective school which recruits top-achieving students from local schools to study Mathematics and Science subjects. The environment that Ms B describes getting used to is also significantly better resourced that other schools in the area with more comfortable facilities and IT equipment. Ms B's bodily expressions of discomfort (in-drawing breath, Turn 3) as well as the strong expression 'forced to come' (Turn 3) reveal that her integration into English-dominant education was difficult. This experience affects her ideological position on language for learning to be discussed later.

Ms B's language use is discussed much more informally during the final study group meeting. I asked the students about different people's language use in class, and this extract opens with my direct question about Ms B's language use.

Extract 3.12 Student observations on Ms B's language

Turn	Actor/Action	Speech	Gloss
1	Robyn	UMiss B uyakhumsha nje?	Miss B speaks English only
2	Thandile	Yhu Ewe	Wow Yes
3	Yonela	But simphendula ngesiXhosa xa sifunayo nje	But we answer her in isiXhosa when we want to
4	Thandile	Ewe, ngamany'amaxesha athethe ngesiXhosa	Yes, she speaks in Xhosa sometimes
5	Robyn	Ok ok, so uMiss B uyakhumsha nje	Ok ok, so Miss B just speaks English
6	Thandile	//At first I thought she's was like white//	
7	Robyn	//You're not aware of that//	
8	Thandile	Nooo and even like my mom asked	
9	Robyn	Did you have your eyes closed at that time?	
10	Thandile	(laughs) No Miss	
11	Students	(laughter)	
12	Thandile	I thought like she was mixed or something cos even my mother came home the other day from meeting and I was like Miss B Miss B like speaks English or something	
13	Student	She's really speaking English	
14	Thandile	She's fluent	
15	Mbulelo	Fluent in which?	
16	Robyn	You are you're also all fluent but uh I so so say more about her English?	
17	Thandile	Yoh she like yoh she like it's like	
18	Robyn	What do you say?	
19	Thandile	She's smooth in English like like it's her mother tongue	
20	Robyn	Ja, no it's hard to find a word of Xhosa that she says (Thandile: and and) and you didn't mention it when I asked you who speaks what in the class	
21	Thandile	And it's funny to hear Miss B speak Xhosa in class cos the other time like during break like 'Thandile ndicela undiboleke i-pen'	'Thandile please lend me your pen'
22	Yonela	'Hey Yonela Yonela yintoni le uyenzayo'	'Hey Yonela Yonela what is this that you're doing'
23	Thandile	E-e! But it's very funny	Yes! But it's very funny
24	Robyn	Very strange, ja, Ok	

I want to draw two points out of this multi-voiced discussion. The first is the interest the students show in their teacher's language use. Despite the school language policy requiring teaching and learning to happen in English, the students find their teacher's near-total use of 'smooth' English remarkable due to her racialised identity. Within the first few seconds of my asking the question, Thandile and Yonela have provided three distinct opinions or observations on Ms B's language. They go on to provide elaborations and quote their teacher directly to give examples of her language use. Thandile displays high interest through affect-laden interjections which demonstrate the intensity of his opinion ('yhu' Turn 2; 'yho' Turn 17). The second point is the complex way language and race are intertwined for Thandile. His concept of race in Turn 6 is more nuanced than the one I express to tease him in Turn 9. He uses the adjective 'white' to reference a potential racial explanation for Ms B's language use. He implies that perhaps she has white ancestors. He later changes his racial term to 'mixed' (Turn 12), still citing that her proficiency in English as the reason for his categorisation of her in these racial terms. Ms B's accent when speaking English aligns more closely to what has been described as White South African English (WSAE) (McKinney *et al.*, 2015; Mesthrie, 2010) than her students'. For me, this was the most marked difference between their 'English' and hers. However, these students do not refer to accent, rather they use the following qualifiers and adjectives: 'she's really speaking English' (Turn 13), 'she's fluent' (Turn 14) and 'she's smooth in English like it's her mother tongue' (Turn 19). This favouring of Ms B's linguistic features reveals a prevalent monoglossic ideology which favours phonological features associated with white speakers. The use of 'smooth' in relation to features of WSAE has been reported in other South African school discourse data (McKinney, 2007). The students' reaction to Ms B's language use is indicative of the coloniality of language which racialises black speakers of English and positions the kind of English more typical of white speakers as superior, by comparison positioning black Englishes as inferior and deficient (Flores & Rosa, 2015). To be a black teacher in this school is to be required by policy and management to use English to teach, but a certain variety of English is recognised by students as being out of place. Ms B's variety of English would be recognised as unproblematic in a historically whites-only school in the suburbs of Cape Town by contrast.

In reflecting on her journey of acquiring English, Ms B identifies being 'forced to talk to speak in English' at school as pivotal in her acquisition of English.

Extract 3.13 Ms B's views on English at school
Ms B: I think I would say obviously in primary you had to like try and whatever but um I wasn't comfortable with it [speaking English] I think

until I came to Success High so around Grade 10 whatever so yes I used to speak it before that but it wasn't as comfortable… and actually um some of the teachers, not some, most of the teachers were teaching in Xhosa and which is why I didn't like that because um the only time students get to be exposed to English is in class and now if in class you still are not going to like teach them in English, I remember even our English teacher was teaching us in Xhosa, Biology, Xhosa, you understand, so it never gets to a point where you feel ok I am comfortable with the language until you actually are forced to talk to speak in English and whatever, so.um. I think maybe that forces students to to learn it at a (indistinct) late stage if I can say cos Grade 10 if maybe you are only gonna get comfortable with English in Grade 10 that's a bit late

These comments by Ms B contrast with her views in Extract 3.11. In Extract 3.11, Ms B describes her own experience of an 'English' high school environment as 'too much' and agrees that she felt 'at sea' and that it was 'difficult'. In Extract 3.13, she demonstrates a preference for teaching in 'English' rather than 'Xhosa' for the purposes of language learning. She supports this by noting that students only get exposed to English in classrooms. While this is somewhat overstating the situation, certainly the Science classroom is an important place of language learning. Ms B's view here should be understood keeping in mind the success that she has enjoyed at university and in becoming a professional. This may make her defend the status quo as it worked for her. However, the research reviewed in Chapter 2 shows that most South African classrooms are characterised by translanguaging or code-switching; therefore, Ms B's success may have been in part due to pedagogical translanguaging employed by her teachers.

Ms B's views on language in learning are further unpacked in the discussion of the students' language use.

Extract 3.14 Students' language use

(T1) **Robyn:** and do you see, do you notice in your students a similar experience of suddenly coming across a lot of English when they come (Ms B: ja) into Grade 8

(T2) **Ms B:** eish, ja it's actually the problem with Grade 8 I think also they had a similar experience with not being taught in English and whatever cos with some of them I would see that they do not have a problem with the work, but they have a problem with the language and even in class if I ask questions no one wants to answer and whatever until I ask cos I usually ask is the problem with my question or is it the language then they will always say it's the language and then they will say can we please answer in Xhosa, you understand

(T3) **Robyn:** and then what do you say

(T4) **Ms B:** uh sometimes I say yes sometimes I say no (Robyn: ok) but uh what what I'm trying to do is is to get them comfortable um I like I give them talks and whatever it's fine if you make mistakes its fine um that's what you here for so I'm just hoping like the Grade 9s um by we can even say 10 too it's not like a big of a thing by 10 too they should at least um be able to uh well not feel the need to speak in Xhosa every time like try and try to express themselves in English cos that really the only way they gonna learn (Robyn: m)

Ms B's language strategies in working with her bilingual students include: sometimes allowing isiXhosa to be used, sometimes insisting on English, giving her students motivational talks to encourage them to use English. Her overall goal is for them to speak as much English as possible as she believes this is 'the only way they gonna learn' (Turn 4).

She diagnoses the students' difficulties as follows: 'they do not have a problem with the work, but they have a problem with the language' (Turn 2). She explains how they often have correct answers written in their books but will be reticent to give the answers orally. This separation of 'work' (i.e. content) and 'language' is revealing of Ms B's pedagogy which holds that English is something the students need to work on orally and by their own volition and that by doing this, they will improve in their ability to express Science concepts in writing. This contrasts with the view of language and learning which holds that language is learnt in context, which in this case is the Natural Science topic under study, and that this language can and should be taught through metalinguistic teaching – i.e. explicit reference to aspects of grammar and lexicon associated with Science. When pressed about students' ability to write in Natural Science, Ms B allows that it is mostly 'definitions' that she marks and not any 'creative writing' or 'using their own words' (Teacher interview 1). The only exception to this kind of writing she finds is in the mandated activity, Investigations, where students have to use extended writing to express, for example, the conclusions they have drawn. The kind of writing that Ms B describes as being appropriate for Natural Science is what Lemke (1990: 91) calls 'fixed words'. He warns against this as the only kind of language production being offered to students and prefers 'flexible words' or in Ms B's terms 'using their own words' in which more meaning is made.

Drawing on her own experience of learning through a new language at school, Ms B identifies the difficulties that her students face with English. However, she stops short of articulating a clear method for employing both isiXhosa and English in teaching and learning, although she concedes that both play a role in her classroom. This is not surprising given the lack of teacher education on the topic of multilingual pedagogies and the injunction against code-switching by education departments (Hattingh *et al.*, 2021). The lack of clarity results in an *ad hoc* and often guilt-ridden use of students' home language in teaching and learning (Probyn, 2009). Furthermore, due to raciolinguistic ideologies, translingual practice is marked as deficient in racialised individuals (Flores & Rosa, 2015). Therefore, Ms B may adhere more strongly to standard language ideologies and avoid translingual practice in order to prove her competence. The tension between official language policy and practice is equally strong for students. The following section highlights some of this tension.

The Students of 9B

I collected data on students' language knowledge and use from the 36 members of Grade 9B through a questionnaire. Key results are summarised in Table 3.2.

As the table indicates, the questions about language were formulated as open format questions with space for students to include as many languages as they liked. Some of the questions probed reasons for their answers such as Questions 1 and 2 below:

1. What is your home language/s?
2. How did you decide on your answer to 1? (e.g. It is the language I use the most/They are the languages spoken in my home.)

The table summary reveals that students' linguistic repertoires overlap, with all 36 identifying isiXhosa as one of their home languages. They also have highly heteroglossic repertoires with a third of the class (12) reporting having more than one home language and a plethora of languages listed as 'known', 'spoken' or 'loved' by the students. The student who identified 'Japanese' as the language he loves the most is a karate buff. This highlights the affiliative aspect of language use which is well discussed by Rampton (1995). This multilingual self-identification by the students stands in stark contrast to the school's language policy.

Table 3.2 Grade 9B language data from questionnaire

Linguistic category: open format questions	Number of students out of 36	Percentage
Students identifying isiXhosa as a home language	36	100%
Students identifying as 'knowing' more than one language	36	100%
Students identifying isiXhosa as their only home language	24	67%
Students identifying isiXhosa as one of multiple home languages	12	33%
Students identifying isiXhosa and English as their two home languages	6	17%
Languages 'spoken', 'known' or 'loved' by students	isiXhosa, English, isiZulu, Sesotho, Siswati, Afrikaans, Sepedi, Japanese, Tshivenda, Setswana, Portuguese	

The language for learning part of the students' questionnaire focused on language preferences and self-evaluation of language proficiencies. Because, as shall be described in Chapter 4, the students operate in a system which is highly constrained in terms of meaning-making, I wanted to shift the focus onto their own learning processes and to provide for some nuance in the language choices on the questionnaire. Heugh (2002) discusses how the Department of Education and Training language policy survey of 1992 and the Pan South African Language Board survey of 1999 found that when African language-speaking parents were given a choice which included both English and the home language used as languages of instruction, the majority opted for this. Taking direction from these surveys, I created a student questionnaire that was as nuanced as possible.

As the questionnaire was a minor data gathering tool within my data set, I limited the number of questions I used and only used open questions five times. The third variable in Table 3.3 included an open question for students to give reasons, which will be reported on in the next section. 'In Natural Science lessons, do you prefer working in (tick) English, isiXhosa or both English and isiXhosa? Why?' In offering these choices on my questionnaire, I describe a situation that the school's language policy does not imagine, and therefore a transgressive, but also hopeful possibility.

Using the data in the table, I will discuss first, the differences in students' self-identified proficiencies in reading and writing languages and second, that there is a majority preference for both English and isiXhosa for learning Natural Science. First, the number of students who chose isiXhosa as the language in which they write best (13) was nearly double those who chose isiXhosa as the language in which they read best (7). The majority selected English as the language in which they read best. These differences, while not probed in the questionnaire, align with frequency of language use in productive and receptive modes in these students' schooling. Students have many more opportunities to read English than to write it. Equally, reading material in isiXhosa is scant. On my first visit to the school library which is well stocked, I could find only 42 fiction texts in isiXhosa and no non-fiction texts. This is in contrast to the shelves and shelves of English texts. In an informal chat on meeting the librarian,

Table 3.3 Language proficiencies and preferences in the 36 students of Grade 9B

	English	isiXhosa	Both English and isiXhosa
1. Language in which you read best (open choice)	25	7	4
2. Language in which you write best (open choice)	19	13	4
3. In Natural Science lessons, I prefer working in: (restricted choice)	9	2	25

she gave some reasons for the dearth of isiXhosa books. This is encapsulated in my fieldnotes on that day from which I quote:

Extract 3.15 isiXhosa books in the library

I teased her about there being so few Xhosa books and she said, yes, she realised the dearth after Mrs George left (she also ran the library). She said she struggled to find good Xhosa books. Some she found (Fundza series), and the teen romances went 'flying out' of the library. The problem was that they didn't come back! (Isn't this a good reason for buying more?!)

The lack of isiXhosa reading material, notably the absence in non-fiction genres, is not surprising given the lack of academic literacy development in African languages beyond Grade 3 in South Africa. The second point that Table 3.3 highlights is that a majority of students (69%) would like to use both English and isiXhosa to work in Natural Science class, with only 25% preferring to work in English exclusively, despite the school's exclusive English-medium policy. The reasons that the students gave in part 2 of this question have been summarised in Table 3.4.

Here, we see the majority of responses (66%) invoke understanding of the content of Science as the main reason for the preference of language of learning, whether this is English, isiXhosa or both, although the majority of these opted for both English and isiXhosa. If we assume that those who wrote that they 'like' using both, or that it is 'easy' to use both, were referring to understanding as well, then this majority is even greater. This aligns with the discourse data from the class lessons which showed that isiXhosa was being used primarily in class to work on understanding orally when the students discussed their written exercises with each other. Important here too is that an equal number of students who opted for English only for use in Natural Science work, did so for understanding as those who did so for external factors such as access to tertiary education and because the assessments are in English.

Further evidence of these language preferences and proficiencies of the students was present in the interactional data. During the first lesson

Table 3.4 Students' reasons for language choice for working in Natural Science

Language preference for working in Natural Science	For language reception ('understanding')	For language production	It is a universal language	It is the language of assessment and the academy	Easy/preferable	No reason given
Both English and isiXhosa	17	2			5	1
English	4	1	2	2		
isiXhosa	2					

which I observed, students would frequently call out 'speak English' (fieldnotes, 270116) to each other if someone spoke using isiXhosa in the public space of the classroom. This public policing of each other's language use only occurred during that first lesson I observed and fell away after that, indicating an observer effect.

Conclusion

The coloniality of language is present in all manifestations of language at Success High. I have surveyed a wide range of data in this chapter, including: language policy, written language in the school environment, fieldnotes, interactional data and interview transcripts. This variety of data sources reveals how the complex language environment of Success High is constructed explicitly through metalinguistic talk and writing, in material ways through objects in the environment and discursively through the language used by members of the community. In this way, the coloniality of language is reproduced daily and language diversity remains rather latent. Anglonormativity (McKinney, 2017) is present in policy, environmental text and participant language attitudes and practices. The school language policy emphasises the use of English for all school functions, without offering much guidance to teachers about how to use language for learning in their multilingual classrooms. This results in a diversity of responses by staff and sets up practices in classrooms where the language use of teachers and students often diverges quite dramatically from the policy, as is typical in many South African classrooms (Probyn, 2009; Probyn *et al.*, 2002). The discomfort and ambivalence about bilingual practices and a very hazy understanding of good bilingual practice are mutually reinforcing. Therefore, language ideologies obscure real engagement with productive solutions to the problems of language and learning in post-colonial classrooms (McKinney, 2017: 71). Added to this, standardised assessments and university aspirations cast a long shadow on attitudes and beliefs about language use at school. A virtual tour of the linguistic landscape of the school both inside and outside the classroom revealed a hierarchy of languages found in displayed text in favour of English, with a fair amount of heteroglossic (Bakhtin, 1981) language use displayed in less-visible, less-durable texts.

The goal of English language proficiency for the students becomes the unassailable good (Alexander, 2000) in considerations of language use at Success High, and this crowds out most isiXhosa use or consideration in formal academic spaces creating a strong colonial edifice. However, decolonial cracks are also evident in the doubts that some staff express about a strict English-only policy in their classrooms; in the preferences that the students have about their own language use in learning and in the isiXhosa and heteroglossic texts on display in sites of necessity. In the next chapter, I will outline the constraints imposed on Ms B and her students by the curriculum, assessment and classroom discourse styles. I will argue that these constraints endure due to the coloniality of language in this context.

4 Constraint in Curriculum, Assessment and Classroom Discourse

Introduction

In this chapter, we enter Ms B's classroom during the study of chemical reactions. In preparing for these lessons, Ms B was bound by the nationally prescribed curriculum, state-sponsored textbook and school-generated worksheets and summative assessment in the form of a written test. All these resources are available in English only. The test that was designed by another teacher at the school is patterned on questions on the high stakes school-exit examination which all students take at the end of Grade 12. These expectations in the form of curriculum and assessment shaped Ms B's pedagogy, even though as reported in the previous chapter, she had her reservations about how the Science was presented in the materials. Her teaching was also shaped by her close adherence to the official English-only language policy of the school. In that, she is a recently qualified teacher still growing in confidence, particularly committed to monolingual English teaching and by her self-description English dominant, this is not surprising. Because only English was officially allowed, this constrained the kinds of learning activities that took place due to the still-emerging English language proficiency of the bilingual students. Constrained learning activities in turn led to a constraint placed on the depth to which the concepts of the topic could be explored by Ms B. Although in the under-life of the classroom where students worked together with the concepts, translanguaging was the norm. This is described in more detail in Chapter 5. Coupled with Ms B's strict adherence to monolingual English use was a reliance on more authoritative discourse patterns for teaching and learning, such as lengthy revision of written exercises which kept learning within the whole class plenary domain and under the teacher's control. Given that the assessment of the topic under study consisted entirely of a pen-and-paper test to be written in standard English and no practical work, the teacher's language and pedagogical choices are understandable. Equally, given that she is unlikely to have been exposed to translanguaging pedagogy as part of her pre-service teacher education (Hattingh et al., 2021), nor has isiXhosa been used as a language of learning and teaching in her own Science education, this is expected. However, the consequences of these features of classroom practice for the development of conceptual depth and bilingual students' appropriation of scientific registers will be outlined in the chapter. These features are born out of, and reinforce, the coloniality of language and the coloniality of the curriculum, standardised assessments and schooling more broadly.

I will begin by outlining the scope of the topic of Science which was under study and how it manifest in activity types (Lemke, 1990) of the classroom. Then, in order to get a sense of how the coloniality of language is manifest in the discursive practices of the classroom, discourse data will be presented from the full reach of the topic studied, from the first lesson to the final test.

The Curriculum Topic and Activity Types

The Natural Science curriculum is nationally prescribed. All students are required to enrol in this subject in Grade 9. As was described in Chapter 1, all curriculum documents and state-funded learning materials are provided in English and Afrikaans only from Grade 4. Science topics are drawn from the canon of Western Science, with an exhortation for teachers to include 'indigenous knowledge' while marking it as supplementary (Soudien, 2015; Taylor & Cameron, 2016). The Natural Science topic 'chemical reactions' was studied by Grade 9B at Success High over four weeks during which the interactional and textual data was collected. In this section, I will sketch the extent of this topic as it was realised during 10 hour-long lessons. The data that I draw upon here is the entextualisation of the topic in planning documents, namely, Ms B's term plan for Grade 9; the Grade 9 Natural Science curriculum; the textbook unit headings; and the test. The topic's theoretical foundation is the particle model of matter. It forms part of a term-long chemistry unit called 'Matter and materials' and is the first of four topics in this unit. The three subsequent topics all include practical work on testing for acids and bases and on different kinds of chemical reactions involving metals and non-metals. This first topic therefore forms the theoretical basis for the practical work which comes later. While other topics in Natural Science focused on processes with more links to students' lifeworld experiences (Gee, 2004), the chemical processes of this topic were approached in an abstract conceptual way. This first topic was concluded by the summative test (included in Appendix 2). As is typical for all Grade 9 assessments in South Africa, this test was designed internally by the Science department at the school in previous years and administered and graded by Ms B. The students are

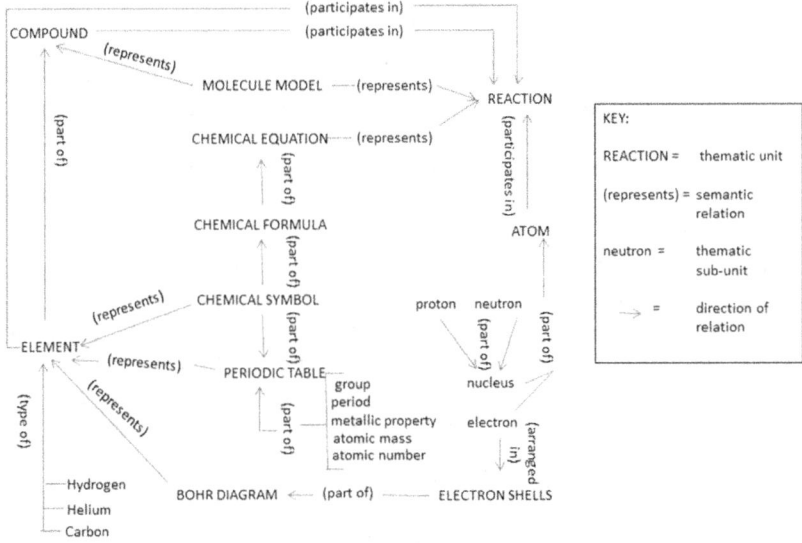

Figure 4.1 Informal thematic diagram of the semantic relations between thematic units of the topic 'Chemical Reactions'

also assessed on their practical work in Science, but by far the dominant form of assessment is pen-and-paper tests.

Figure 4.1 constitutes an informal thematic diagram of the Science topic. It offers an overview of what Lemke (1990) calls the semantic relations (named in brackets and linked by arrows) between thematic units which comprise the topic. Key thematic units (here realised as one- or two-word terms) are linked in a web of meaning comprising the topic and extending beyond it. The thematic units and sub-units were selected based upon my study of the topic at Grade 9 level.

While the thematic units and the semantic relations between them are entextualised in the diagram using verbal English language, their expression in the classroom discourse, textbook, test and boardwork occurred in a variety of modes. I do not claim to present a comprehensive list of semiotic modes but suggest the following as an open-ended list in my analysis of the meaning-making practices of the classroom and study group: colour (in the Periodic Table and molecule models); mathematical symbols (in chemical equations and chemical formulae); gestures; drawings (Bohr diagrams, molecule models); and verbal language (spoken and written). Manipulation of objects was suggested in a textbook activity (Bester et al., 2013: 83) where students were required to use playdough to make 3D models of compounds. This activity was undertaken in the study group but not in the classes. I will present the organisation of the semantic relations within the topic of chemical reactions in the class as a series of activities arranged into types.

In Science classrooms, as in any classroom, there are a multitude of distinct discursive activities that teachers and students engage in. Lemke's (1990) proposal of activity types of the Science classroom builds on Goffman's (1981) interaction order. Activity types enable an analysis of multilingual and multimodal meaning-making without analytical categories which are logocentric or named language-specific. Lemke has proposed a taxonomy of activity types found in Science classrooms (Lemke, 1990: 215). The 30 activity types that he identified over hundreds of hours of classroom discourse analysis structure the teaching and learning of Science topics in different ways. In my analysis, I used Lemke's taxonomy as a reference point, changing or merging these in response to the data and limiting my analysis to only those activity types that comprised chemical reactions topics and not social activities. The final descriptions of topic-specific activity types based on Lemke's taxonomy and used in this book are:

- individual seatwork (students work independently on written exercises);
- true dialogue (discussion between students and the teacher with unknown-answer questions);
- group seatwork (students working together on written exercises);
- siding (speaking or gesturing between students concurrently with the teacher's discourse);
- cross-discussion (discussion between students as part of the plenary discourse);
- student-questioning dialogue (students asking the teacher questions), go over (reviewing seatwork where Initiation-Response-Evaluation (IRE) discourse dominated);
- teacher exposition/review (new or reviewed work explanations by the teacher where IRE discourse dominated);
- and testing (strictly independent seatwork).

I noted also the start and end time of each activity type, using a contextualisation cue by the teacher, such as 'okay', indicating a shift in the discourse as a transition between activity types. This helped me to critique and refine Lemke's notion of activity types in terms of their boundedness. I began to see that they could occur concurrently and were sometimes nested inside each other. Activity types had a strong influence on the kind of meaning-making, including register and mode variations, that occurred at that time. A student, for example, may draw upon different elements of her semiotic repertoire during a 'student-questioning dialogue', 'seatwork' (a writing-dominant individual activity) and 'cross-discussion' (a collaborative, oral-dominant student-to-student activity) in dynamic ways. Lemke's activity types will be used to organise the practices reported on in this chapter and in Chapters 5 and 6.

In the oral-dominated activities such as 'teacher exposition/review' and 'go over' (Lemke, 1990: 217), monologue and IRE discourse (Sinclair

& Coulthard, 1975) are prevalent. In the writing-dominated activities such as 'seatwork' (Sinclair & Coulthard, 1975) involving working through textbook exercises, students respond in brief to written instructions in prose given by the authority represented by the textbook writers. The main activity types that occurred in the dominant communication channel of the classroom are presented in Figure 4.2 along with the amount of topic-specific time each comprised.

Figure 4.2 reveals that the dominant activity type was 'go over' (41%) – an activity in which the teacher leads the class through the answers to a written activity usually employing the three-part structure of IRE, with the initiation comprising the written questions that were read aloud. This activity enabled Ms B to model correct answers in preparation for the test. The second most frequent activity was 'seatwork' (28%) where students completed written exercises in their notebooks, usually accompanied by talk with their neighbour. 'Teacher exposition or review' (21%) involves the exposition of new or previously taught content, usually employing IRE discourse. 'Testing' (10%) is similar to seatwork, but it is completed individually and assessed formally by the teacher.

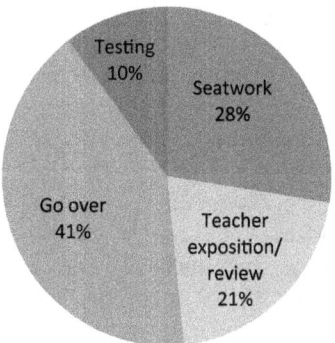

Figure 4.2 Main activity types in the dominant communication channel of the class lessons group as a percentage of total topic-specific time

Restricted Triadic Dialogue

Learning environments in which there are multiple participants, such as classrooms, can form more than one communication channel. Goffman (1981) recognises a dominant communication channel and subordinate communication channels in these settings. In classrooms, one of the common ground rules for discourse is that the teacher sets the dominant communication channel. Subordinate channels are those that are opened between students or in private conversation between a student and the teacher. So, as I discuss dominant classroom discourse practices here, I note that subordinate channels of communication can be operating concurrently with the dominant, constrained channels. Some of these channels that are productive sites for decolonial cracks to emerge are explored in Chapter 6. The teacher does not as a matter of course shut down these subordinate channels of communication. In so doing, she enables productive meaning-making between students even though she is not privy to it.

Teacher exposition/review and go over are ubiquitous activities in Science classrooms (Lemke, 1990). The Success High classroom was no exception (see Figure 4.2). In these activity types, the teacher may present new information, or review previously presented information in different ways, sometimes through reviewing seatwork. The teacher selects material to be presented and leads their students through it either in monologue form or, more commonly, in an IRE discourse pattern (Lin, 2007; Sinclair & Coulthard, 1975). The IRE pattern, or triadic dialogue, allows the teacher to retain control over the pace and topic of content coverage while maintaining a level of student involvement during their 'response' turn. While the quality of this dialogue pattern for learning depends upon the content of the teacher's 'initiation' turn, the length of the 'response' and the content of the 'evaluation', the dominant type of triadic dialogue in Ms B's classroom was restricted to closed-question initiations which required very short student response turns. In these oral-dominated activities in the 9B classroom, Ms B usually responded only to the oral mode of meaning-making. Students were seated at tables facing the teacher and sometimes contributed by means of action modes, for example, gesture, but this went unremarked. Ms B stood at the front of the classroom and moved around, gesturing while she talked. The oral discourse took the forms of a monologue or triadic discourse.

In the class lessons and study group sessions, there were few moments of exposition through monologue, and they were short-lived. The dominant structure for exposition and review was triadic, or IRE, discourse. In this discourse structure, students have clearly cued response slots to fill, which the teacher then explicitly or implicitly evaluates. The cues for a required response are well understood by all participants: the teacher poses a question, or perhaps requests a filler response through rising intonation. Triadic discourse supports learning to different degrees depending largely on the moves that a teacher makes during the evaluation (or feedback) stage. An example of triadic discourse (Extract 4.1) is drawn from the first lesson in the topic where Ms B is reviewing the prior knowledge of the Periodic Table with the students.

Extract 4.1 Teacher triadic review

Turn	Actor/Action	Speech
1 Initiation	Ms B stands at board where Periodic Table is displayed and points to Periodic Table while gaze is towards class:	what do we call the elements in this group in the last group Group 18

2 Response	Mthobeli raises hand Ms B points to Mthobeli with ruler Mthobeli:	Noble gases.
3 Evaluation Initiation	Ms B smiling: Ms B gaze to Mbulelo	The noble gases, yes what does that mean Mbulelo what are noble gases
4 Response	Mbulelo:	Eh, misi eh, <SLOW>they are called noble gases because <SLOW>. they are not very reactive.
5 Evaluation	Ms B nods:	Yes, they are not very reactive.

This is an example of the most restricted variety of IRE discourse in the data set. Although Mbulelo answers hesitantly, Ms B accepts his answer without probing the meaning of 'noble' or 'reactive' any further to check his understanding, much less to check other students' understanding. The three moves of the IRE discourse are very clear, and turns are taken predictably by the teacher and the students. This is aided by ground rules for classroom talk (Mercer, 1995) such as students raising their hands if they are offering a response; rising intonation from the teacher acting as a cue to students to offer a response; and the teacher selecting students by name for response turns. The register used in these responses was typical for students' responses to the teacher's initiations and constitute register ground rules: Turns 2 and 4 are uttered using a formal scientific English register. Students' turns tend to be few and short, guaranteed by the use of closed questions, and they are rarely engaged in exploratory talk (Barnes, 1992) through the teacher's initiations, which would lead to a more openended IRE discourse. This can be an effective way of ensuring student participation especially where students are emergent bilinguals, still learning the named language of which scientific English is a variety. However, the disadvantage of this tight IRE structure is that students are more likely to adhere to 'fixed words' (Lemke, 1990: 91) as these can be memorised (McKinney *et al.*, 2015). As students' responses are expected to be presentational in nature, there is a risk that conceptual depth may be sacrificed, and misunderstanding masked as in 'safetalk' (Chick, 1996). The example of the adjective 'reactive' (Turn 4) in this extract is a case in point. Later on in the lesson series (Extract 4.2 below), Thandile reveals in discussion in his group that he is confusing 'reactive' with 'radioactive', an indication that the meaning of 'reactive' here has not been sufficiently determined.

Extract 4.2 Thandile confuses 'radioactive' and 'reactive'

Turn	Actor/Action	Speech
1	Mtho:	It is radioactive.
2	Thandile	Redi^{active} re^{active}

The example in Extract 4.3 shows a triadic structure in which there is a smooth movement between the three parts: initiation, response and evaluation. This occurs when students are relatively sure that their responses are correct and the teacher accepts the response without contesting it. I will now present an extract where the student's response is hesitant and eventually incorrect. The students' meaning trajectory in these instances depends very much on how the teacher scaffolds, probes and follows up during the evaluation move.

Extract 4.3 Incorrect student response

Turn	Actor/Action	Speech
1 Initiation	Ms B: Both hands open with fingers splayed at chest height Ms B: shifts gaze from Mthobeli to other side of class briefly. Eyes widen, head tilts down, gaze to Mthobeli Ms B:	Where What do we find in the nucleus ^{All} of it
2 Response	Ls:	No, Miss
3 Initiation	Ms B: Both hands hold the ruler (Ms B stands still for duration of Mthobeli's next Turn)	What do we find
4 Response Evaluation Response	Mthobeli: Fingers of right hand come together at tips. Fingers separate and hand makes a swift movement to the right Ms B: nods head Mthobeli:	Em. We. we find protons and electrons (Ls: indistinct) <FAST>Protons<FAST> are moving outside the
5 Initiation (probe)	Ms B:	Outside ^{the}
6 Response	Mthobeli:	(Indistinct) negative and the electrons are moving inside the (indistinct)

Mthobeli's response in Turn 6 is incorrect in that, although he may not have provided the term 'nucleus', he has intimated that electrons are found inside this atomic structure. In considering how Mthobeli's meaning-making is constrained here, I will focus on the actional modes employed both by Ms B and Mthobeli. During IRE discussion such as this, the teacher has more physical room to employ actional modes as her body is unconstrained by furniture in contrast to the students who are seated at desks. In this instance, Ms B employed gesture, facial expression and gaze to select Mthobeli as respondent (Turn 1), affirm his speaking rights (Turn 3) and evaluate his response (Turn 4). Although constrained by furniture, Mthobeli was free to use his hands, and he employed them in making meaning even while his speech faltered. While he doesn't utter the word 'nucleus', he symbolises a circle and his hand movement that mimics the movement of electrons around the nucleus. His gestures in Turn 4 preceded his speech and captured the meaning of his words that followed, as described by Roth (2004). He had a critical audience and adjusted his responses according to their back-channelling. Also, he did not associate the sub-atomic particles correctly with their place in the atom; however, he distinguished, through gesture and speech, between the nucleus and particles moving outside the nucleus. Ms B did not draw attention to his gestures and did not extend the meaning trajectory from these gestures to the oral scientific register. She could have said, 'you are showing us the nucleus and the protons; but are the protons inside or outside the nucleus?' As it stands the exploratory meaning-making of the student was not valorised, and he was not required to link these exploratory gestures to the high status and demanding scientific register in English.

One of the activity types used by the teacher to provide exposition of content is what Lemke (1990: 217) calls 'going over seatwork' or 'go over'. After a seatwork activity (usually done in writing) has been brought to a close, the teacher initiates an activity where the written answers of the students are reviewed through a whole class discussion – a traditional teacher-led practice as detailed by Lin (2007). Figure 4.2 reveals that this activity type dominated the class lessons in terms of time, taking 41% of topic-specific teaching and learning time. By going over work, the teacher can develop ideal answers in relation to the topic, and these can be queried or developed by either the teacher or students in preparation for the written test at the end of the topic. Also, the written questions offer a predetermined script which would provide some security for an inexperienced teacher such as Ms B. This activity type often takes the structure of IRE in which the teacher or a student reads out the written instruction from the worksheet, test or textbook, a nominated student responds with her version of the answer, and the teacher evaluates and gives feedback on this response. If the response is deemed incorrect by the teacher, they may call upon another student to give an alternate answer.

Going over seatwork was an activity that was often disrupted by student challenges to the ratified answers. This would then be followed by another period of exposition of a particular concept by the teacher. Indeed, much of the exposition of the concepts happened in this way as part of the 'going over seatwork'. The teacher often employed the use of trans-semiotising (Lin, 2015), or shifting between modes, during 'going over seatwork' to achieve thematic development. If the seatwork answer required was a chemical equation, she would re-package the answer through drawing a Bohr diagram on the board. Students thus had an alternative expression of the same meaning, often one that allowed more detail to be added – fulfilling a 'why?' question from students. The meaning being transformed from the written symbolic mode into the diagrammatic visual mode enabled understanding and functioned as 'message abundancy' (Gibbons, 2006: 55) which is a powerful strategy in bilingual classrooms.

Restricted triadic dialogue presents the possibility of opting out as well as resistance. Like in all classrooms, some students at times opted out of making meaning within the Science topic through siding (in speech, gesture, writing or reading) about other things (Lemke, 1990: 75). At times, 9B students also resisted the strictures of restricted triadic dialogue spontaneously. These occasions are described in Chapter 6.

Standardised Seatwork

During the study of chemical reactions, the dominant text used in class was the monolingual English textbook – although this was mostly used for seatwork exercises, not reading of explanatory definitions – supplemented by a few monolingual English worksheets. On the shelves of the classroom sat 30 copies of a multilingual Mathematics and Science glossary (Young *et al.*, 2005). Ms B reported never having used these glossaries which were written by language and Science experts at a university and donated to the school. Their donation predated Ms B's employment at the school, and she had not received any introduction to these materials. She used the set textbook and some existing monolingual worksheets made by other teachers at the school. The lack of use of the language supportive materials is not surprising in a context of Anglonormativity where it is assumed that all Science texts will appear in English. It underscores the need for specific interventions using these materials and accompanied by teacher professional development. Indeed, there are no studies in South African schools describing teachers using these materials. The seatwork activities that dominated 9B Science lessons were activities that constrained students' responses and seatwork that constituted formal, individual testing. Written questions in seatwork activities such as this were usually closed questions – those with one correct answer – and the implied required register for meaning-making was written scientific English or a written symbolic register (see Figure 4.3). These kinds of activities dominated the textbook. In an analysis of the 13 activities in the chapter dealing with this topic in the textbook, all constituted this kind of constrained seatwork activity.

Ms B drew all her seatwork activities from the textbook, and it was the dominant learning material in the class lessons. However, in an interview with me, Ms B expressed a dim view of the textbook: 'I don't really like it' and 'it's too simplified' (Teacher Interview 1). She expressed feeling compelled by higher authorities to use the textbook: 'that is what we have to use' (Teacher Interview 1). One of the senior teachers in the Science department confirmed that the students' textbook is supplied by Western Cape Education Department (WCED) and not chosen by the school. This teacher also told me that she encourages teachers to use a variety of textbooks for their own reference, but teachers have to apply to the principal for funding for these books. The students used only the textbook, one worksheet and two tests as written resources during the class lessons on the topic.

Ms B's criticism of the textbook was expressed in more detail during the first interview as follows:

Extract 4.4 The textbook

Ms B: it is so: simplified
and then it skips
um sections of the work that
uh
for example they can't understand
um reactions without understanding bonding and whatever
(Robyn: right)
but the textbook does that
and CAPS does that

This comment was borne out by the content of the textbook. 'Bonding' is only referred to in the textbook topic as 'joining', such as in the statement: 'Compounds are made of elements that are joined together'(Bester *et al.*, 2013: 79). The colloquial phrase 'joined together' is used instead of the scientific term 'bonded'; therefore, this important part of the conceptual framework of the topic remains in the everyday register and is not given the further scientific meaning that 'bonding' implies.

Figure 4.3 consists of two photographs: the first is of the first three questions in Activity 2 from my copy of the textbook (Bester *et al.*, 2013: 77); the second is of a student's exercise book with her written answers to these questions.

As Figure 4.3 demonstrates, the kind of seatwork activities present in the textbook and worksheets produces a narrow set of responses, either a single word or only one correct answer. This narrow set of responses is easy to assess and correct but does not reveal much about the students'

Activity 2 Use the Periodic Table to understand elements

Study the Periodic Table at the back of this book.
1. How many groups are there in the Periodic Table? 18
2. How many periods are there? 7
3. What elements are in the same group as hydrogen? Li Na K Rb Cs Fr

Name
Zinc
Co...
Gold

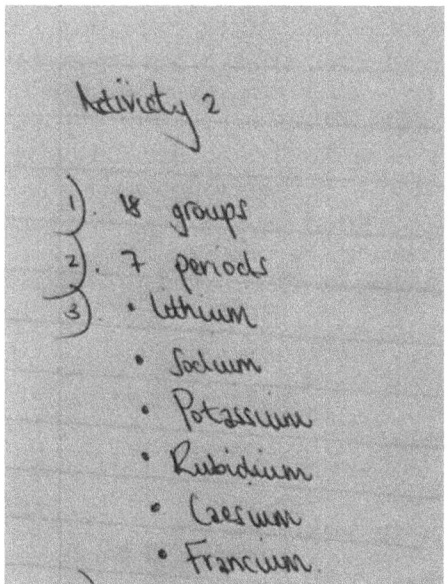

Figure 4.3 Textbook activity and Nomsa's answers

thinking process as they use the Periodic Table as a reference and decode it to answer the questions. Some of this 'hidden thinking' is, however, available in the spoken and bodily discourse of the students as they discuss their answers while working with seatmates. This discourse was allowed but not encouraged by the teacher. On occasion, concomitant with this speech was spontaneous and exploratory writing in the form of notes and doodles aiding meaning-making towards the final answer. This spontaneous speech, action and writing is discussed in Chapter 5 when data is presented in which the teacher circulates in the classroom and talks with students about their answers and when students discuss their answers with each other.

Test writing was unique in the discourse of both the classroom and the study group in that it is the only activity type where students have no interaction with anyone else. Tests were undertaken in both class and study group settings, although in class the stakes were far higher: the class test was the only form of formal assessment in the topic. The test results of the students were generally poor with the average being just above 50%. While completing a test, students interact solely with the text of the test. Written presentational discourse adhering to a narrow definition of academic English for Science is demanded of students in both receptive and productive forms of meaning-making (i.e. reading and writing) when answering test questions. Other modes, such as the drawing of diagrams, are occasionally included in Science tests, but when written language is required to be read or written, it must conform to the register of reported science – one of many registers in which science gets done (Yager, 2004). Unless teachers write a memorandum for a test or create their own worksheet, they may never themselves have to produce the written scientific register that is required by students in a testing situation (Shohamy, 2004). They may therefore be out of touch with the cognitive work required in framing an answer in the written scientific register. In her interview when we discussed the low test marks, Ms B indicated that 'I wouldn't say that the writing is a problem'. However, in contrast to the single-word responses required in class seatwork (Figure 4.3), the literacy demands of the test were greater and therefore could be experienced as problematic by the students. An example from the test follows where the scientific register in English which is used to phrase the question contains a nominalisation ('arrangement') and is lexically dense:

Question 2
Helium is an unreactive gas used to fill up balloons and power air ships.
2.1.3 Neon is also an unreactive gas. How is the arrangement of electrons in Neon:
(a) similar to the arrangement in Helium? and (1)
(b) different from the arrangement in Helium? (1)

The 10 students whose test answers I collected performed poorly on this question. Only one scored full marks, and only three others scored half marks. All received full marks on the question in which they had to draw a Bohr diagram which also dealt with the concept of the arrangement of electrons. The students were able to understand a question and/or express themselves in the graphic mode but could not understand/express themselves successfully in scientific English. Although I would not argue for a straightforward correlation between the poor performance and classroom discourse, it is important to note that there was no metalinguistic discourse used in the class lessons to unpack nominalisations. Furthermore, there was no use of the nominalisation 'arrangement' to refer to electrons in an atom in the textbook, the worksheets or Ms B's oral discourse. Neither was there a class activity in which students could practice writing the kind of scientific register that was required to answer this question. Setati *et al.* (2002) have described the lack of scaffolded practice in the English academic register as an 'incomplete journey' from oral forms of discourse in more familiar registers to written forms in English in South African classrooms. In contrast, a study of bilingual Science students in the US, teaching using metalanguage, including nominalisations, can improve students' ability to construct and deconstruct scientific texts (Gebhard *et al.*, 2014). The scientific register in English is challenging for monolingual English speakers and much more so for emergent bilinguals such as these Grade 9 students. I argue that the kind of safe-talk (Chick, 1996) that took up so much class time for Ms B and her students militated against grappling with the science register in English using exploratory talk (Barnes, 1992). Approaches employing metalanguage or translanguaging might have helped the Grade 9 students become familiar with the new register. The lack of attention to the demands of the new register by Ms B is also a consequence of the normalised English immersion education that these students have received since Grade 4. If the English immersion reality were recognised as a programme with a label such as English Medium Instruction (EMI) (Probyn, 2021), more attention may be given to supportive measures such as a focus on teaching the language of Science. As it stands the lack of guidance for Ms B and her students on learning the register of Science in English is part of what Ngũgĩ Wa'Thiongo calls 'normalising the abnormal' inherent in the coloniality of language for learning in this context (Ngũgĩ, 2018).

Conclusion

There are several layers of constraint operating in the class lessons. The tightly specified curriculum topic culminating in a standardised monolingual English pen-and-paper test had a washback effect on the kinds of activities that Ms B initiated in the class. In addition, Ms B's close adherence to the school language policy of English-only in her classroom constrained the kinds of meaning-making in which the students engaged. All text was available in English only, despite multilingual glossaries being available, and all teacher-talk in the dominant communication channel happened in English. Exploratory talk was not possible in English only, and this may be why it was avoided in favour of a restricted form of IRE dialogue. The use of isiXhosa language resources or action modes was not encouraged and at times even discouraged (as reported in Chapter 3 when students censured each other with the call to 'speak English!'). In this way, both the familiar register resources of the students and their bodies as meaning-making resources were invisibilised and excluded. Equally constraining was discourse structure of 'safe-talk' which dominated: turn-taking in the oral IRE discourse in the whole-class setting was circumscribed and shorter student texts predominated with only one 'voice' or 'view' being heard (Mortimer & Scott, 2003: 33). There were few opportunities for students to practise the written scientific English register required by assessments and/or the scientific community.

The pedagogical choices and linguistic choices made by, and imposed upon, Ms B were both constraining factors for learning. These factors are interdependent and cannot easily be teased apart. When only English may be used, certain teacher-led activities become more dominant. Likewise, if more student-centred and exploratory activities are used, bilingual language use becomes advantageous.

In the next chapter, some spontaneous learning practices of the students of Grade 9B in the class lessons and the study group are described and proposed as decolonial cracks.

5 Decolonial Cracks Introduced by Students

Introduction

Leaving behind the dominant teacher-led classroom practices of Chapter 4, this chapter focuses on the spontaneous learning practices that the Success High students engaged in. Despite many teachers' concerns that students will use any unratified channel of communication in a classroom to pursue non-academic topics, when left to their own devices, students do engage in a variety of on-topic learning activities. The activities during which Success High students engaged in spontaneous learning practices were, following Lemke's activity types: student-questioning dialogue; group seatwork; siding (communication between participants in a subordinate communication channel); individual seatwork; and the very rare, cross-discussion (topic-related engagement between students in the plenary). Data from the two learning sites, the class lessons and the study group, relating to each of these activity types will be presented in this chapter as decolonial cracks initiated by the students.

There are two salient features of these grassroots decolonial practices. First, they are spontaneous and student driven. In contexts where the coloniality of language endures through monolingual language policy, these practices by non-dominant multilinguals occur in an adaptive translanguaging space (García & Li, 2014) where no official space or validation is given to translanguaging or trans-semiotising. The practices themselves engender a decolonial borderland: official language policy and semiotic hierarchies which privilege linguistic over other semiotic resources rub up against a different order introduced by the students. In analyses of only the trans-linguistic aspects of these practices, they have been described as 'natural translanguaging' (García & Li, 2014) or 'spontaneous translanguaging' (Cenoz & Gorter, 2017). In this way, they are distinct from pedagogical translanguaging which encompasses some of the planned and facilitator-driven activities which are described in Chapter 6. The Science content that is focused on in these activities has been shaped by the students' interests in an active way (Kress *et al.*, 2014; Rosebery *et al.*, 1992). The centrality of the students' interests often lends these practices a playful quality.

The second salient feature of this category of practices is that they employ a broad set of semiotic resources, often simultaneously. Whereas the resources in play in the activities in Chapter 4 were constrained, in grassroots practices, the set of resources expands. A decolonial lens on these practices allows the body as meaning-making tool to come to the fore (Menezes de Souza, 2021). Rather than being merely accompaniments to the linguistic mode, bodily modes such as gesture, facial expression and posture contribute discrete meanings to learning activities which reveal complex identity processes, such as identity meshing (Tyler, 2022). These bodily meanings are immediately available to others with whom students may want to collaborate. Lin's terms 'trans-semiotizing' (Lin, 2015) and 'whole-body sense-making' (Lin, 2019) account for the flexible practices of these multilinguals as they draw upon different elements of their semiotic repertoire including language, gesture, facial expression and body movement. In addition, the linguistic resources expand with features of different registers of isiXhosa and English as well as other languages being drawn upon by students to make meaning.

The episodes that have been selected in this chapter and the next have gone through different transcription iterations. The comic strip presentations used here (Figures 5.2 and 5.4) and in Chapter 6 have been co-created with artists to foreground the trans-semiotic nature of the grassroots decolonial meaning-making of the students (Tyler, 2021). By disrupting the conventions of classroom discourse research writing in this way, I am signalling a dissatisfaction with the traditional genres and inviting us to look at new ways of thinking about discourse in Science classrooms, particularly in classrooms where students recruit the resources of languages other than the sanctioned English to make meaning. In these contexts, it is often the named languages which are the foci of analysis, identified in transcripts through translation, separated from each other by being presented in different font styles or in separate columns. This is often because the imagined audience is English monolingual, or the focus of the research is on the functions of different languages. The comic strip genre introduces a narrative element to the meaning-making and represents movement in space and time. It avoids the hierarchy of modes created by a transcript in a table where whatever is on the left is given priority due to European norms of literacy (Ochs, 1979). In a comic strip, the modes of gesture, facial expression and verbal expression are represented simultaneously and laminated on top of each other. An element of drama is attained through the use of different cinematographic 'shots' (medium close-up, long shot) to tell the story of the episode. In representations of classroom discourse, this helps the researcher to recreate the drama of a learning moment. The cartoons also centre isiXhosa-based languaging in an academic text. The presentation assumes a bilingual isiXhosa/English reader-viewer by leaving the oral mode uncluttered by translation and requiring the non-isiXhosa-speaking reader to do the work to get to understanding by searching for the translation in an endnote. Another perspective which a non-isiXhosa-speaking reader might take is articulated by bell hooks as a 'space to learn':

> Think of the moment of not understanding what someone says as a space to learn. Such a space provides not only the opportunity to listen without 'mastery', without owning or possessing speech through interpretation, but also the experience of hearing non-English words. (hooks, 1994: 172)

By curating a particular experience for the English-speaking reader, the comic strip is intentionally subjective and partial, which Ochs argues cannot be avoided in a transcript, but should be made explicit (Ochs, 1979).

I now proceed to examining the decolonial cracks present in the different activity types.

Student-Questioning Dialogue

In Chapter 4, I presented the distribution of the topic-specific activity types (Figure 4.2) of the classroom. The activities, which were conducted as whole-class, English-dominant discussions ('go over' and 'teacher exposition/review') with the teacher standing and able to move around and the students seated, comprised the majority of classroom activity time (62%). The content of these discussions was controlled by the teacher, and the only ratified way of spontaneously engaging with the teacher was to bid for a turn and ask a question. Lemke (1990) holds that this 'student-questioning dialogue' is a rare classroom activity. This was certainly the case in my study. A student question was a rare thing and sometimes served as a catalyst for further questions from other students, producing a phenomenon of clustering of questions, as described in Lemke's study (1990: 52). As space opens up for conceptual challenge and lack of understanding or student interest to be aired, students embrace it and questions abound. On occasion in the Success High classroom, this extended into engagement with peers through cross-discussion, an activity type that is represented further on in this chapter.

Students' interest came to the fore to a greater or lesser degree depending on the kind of questions they asked. Chin (2001, in Alvermann, 2004) distinguishes between *basic information* and *wonderment* questions asked by students. Teachers find wonderment questions challenging as they require them first to understand the thought processes that initiated the question. In the following interview extract, Ms B reflects on the kinds of questions that different students ask.

Extract 5.1 Student questions
Ms B: Yonela I never have a problem with the questions she

she's usually clear (Robyn: clear)
ja what she needs to know
but um Asanda not so much
I think she .
ja I I usually struggle to understand what she's asking
and Bongeka is worse
I can never understand what Bongeka is saying

An analysis of the classroom discourse data reveals that Yonela, whose questions are 'clear' to Ms B, usually asks basic information questions and Asanda and Bongeka usually ask wonderment questions which are those Ms B 'struggle(s) to understand'. Ms B begins to place the locus of misunderstanding with Asanda ('I think she') but backtracks on this and places it on herself ('I usually struggle to understand'). Perhaps this is so that she does not appear condescending or critical of one of her students to me as researcher. Ms B's discomfort with Asanda's wonderment questions is evident in the extract from a class lesson below. It follows an episode of triadic discourse on the sub-topic 'naming compounds'.

Extract 5.2 Asanda's wonderment question

Turn	Actor/action	Speech	Gloss
1	Asanda: (action?)	miss can I ask you something	
2	T:	Yes	
3	Asanda: (action?) T approaches Asanda and stands about 3m from her facing her.	If if . if it happens that um . the the the compound formula doesn't have i- a a a a ele an element that's that's that's not a metal kwenzeka ntoni	If if. if it happens that um. the the the compound formula doesn't have a- a a a a ele an element that's that's that's not a metal what happens then
4	T: Turns away from Asanda towards the whiteboard	\<FAST\> usually_does \<FAST\> remember I told you the other day	
5	Asanda: (action?)	//but//	
6	T:	//that um//	
7	Asanda: (action?)	but but i-hydrogen and oxygen…	

Unfortunately, the camera's view did not extend to where Asanda was seated during this lesson, so there is no action data for her question. However, I observed that exploratory talk of this nature is usually complemented by meaning-making in action modes. Asanda's question is uttered in a meshed register (Gibbons, 2006) to make meaning. She draws on features of 'isiXhosa' ('kwenzeka ntoni') and 'English' ('can I ask you something') and technical terms from the topic ('compound'). Her exploratory utterance is halting and hesitant (she pauses and restarts) as she orders her thoughts. Ultimately, she poses an exception to the rule of naming compounds which Ms B has been positing. The wonderment question is challenging due to its exploratory nature and in that it confronts the rule which Ms B has been teaching about how to name compounds.

Ms B's response to Asanda's question is conflicted. She initially demonstrates an interest in Asanda's question by approaching her physically (Turn 3). She then attempts to avoid the question in Turn 4 by using 'usually', speaking quickly and physically moving back towards the physical anchor of the academic content, the whiteboard. Her own words spoken in the past 'remember I told you', as well as to a standard 'English' which is associated with the authority of the test and textbook also serve as a bulwark against the discomfort of the Asanda's question. However, she then allows Asanda to interrupt with an elaboration on the question (Turn 5 and 7). Asanda re-asserts her interest through objecting ('but') to Ms B's diversion by providing a correct example of a compound consisting of hydrogen and oxygen, neither of which is a metal. She also re-introduces the meshed register, including the Xhosalised 'i-hydrogen' which is more familiar to her. Xhosalisation is a version of borrowing in which an existing English word, typically one for which there is no obvious isiXhosa equivalent, is attributed an affix with isiXhosa features (Paxton & Tyam, 2010). In this way, Asanda resists the constraining presentation of the teacher and asserts her voice in the meshed register. As Asanda engages in exploratory talk to tackle a complex problem, she needs to recruit her most familiar linguistic resources to ease the task. In a less powerful position as student, she is also posing a challenge to the simple answers of the curriculum. It is perhaps easier to take up a challenging stance from a linguistic place of confidence and comfort.

Group Seatwork

During class lessons, when students were given a written activity to complete at their desks, they were usually allowed to do this in collaboration with the other students seated in their group. This seatwork constituted 28% of classroom time spent on the topic. The kind of interaction captured in Figure 5.2 was typical of groups working together in this way. Groups were facilitated by the placing of tables together into a hexagonal shape. The extract below features a group of four boys sitting at such a table with an audio recorder positioned in the middle. They are working on an activity in the English textbook in which they are required to 'read'

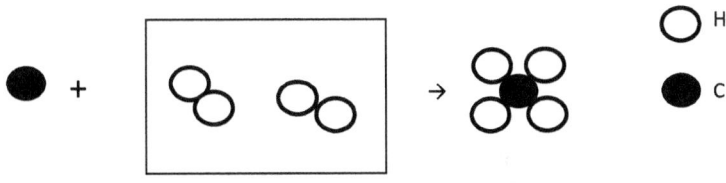

Solution: C + 2H$_2$ → CH$_4$

Figure 5.1 Worksheet chemical equation problem and solution

a series of coloured circles as atoms belonging to different elements in a reaction and translate this into an equation representing the reaction using chemical symbols. Mthobeli begins to talk through the procedure of representing the diagram of two Hydrogen atoms in symbolic form. Then, Mbulelo experiences a breakthrough in his understanding of diatomic elements and shares this with the group. He has been problem-solving by reading an explanation of diatomic elements in the textbook on the opposite page to the activity they are working on. It gives him insight into how they should represent the four white circles (enclosed in a box here for ease of reference) in chemical symbols. The question and solution are reproduced in Figure 5.1 followed by the interaction in comic strip form (see Figure 5.2).

Mbulelo as the central figure in this group seatwork episode engages in a rich whole-body sense-making performance. Mbulelo is clearly excited that he has discovered how to continue with the activity and pursues this interest by drawing the others into dialogue with him. He is insistent that Mthobeli 'look' and listen to him. He then embarks on a multimodal explanation using both his and Mthobeli's textbook, his body and his most familiar meshed register to argue that they should not represent the four hydrogen atoms together as four. In Frame 5, Mbulelo draws two texts together through the use of gesture indicating that one has bearing on the other. This flurry of gestural activity is in contrast to the static nature of all the boys' bodies up to now. Goldin-Meadow (1999, in Roth, 2004) has shown physical gestures 'used in conjunction with spoken utterances represent the leading edge of cognitive development' (Roth, 2004: 48), i.e. that gestures express understandings which cannot be expressed yet in spoken words. In the case of Mbulelo, his gestures and gaze connect the current activity with the notion of a diatomic element before he begins to express this in words to Mthobeli. His meaning-making originates in the body. This is congruent with previous findings in a bilingual Mathematics setting where gestures prefigured the use of a mathematical word (Tyler, 2016). With his hands, Mbulelo points emphatically to text in the two textbooks, establishing the authority of what he is about to explain by beginning with drawing attention to the written statements in the textbook. Like Asanda, Mbulelo makes his conceptual points using a meshed register. This is patterned: technical

Mthobeli: You first write here then you say four Hydrogen what what
Mandla: There oh I didn't see it
Mbulelo: (singing)

Figure 5.2 Zibayi-two: Trans-semiotising in group seatwork

features relating to the science content are usually Xhosalised versions of 'English' words ('two', 'molecule' and 'hydrogen') some having come to English from Latin or Greek; some conjunctions are also English; most features are recognisable as 'isiXhosa'. I should pause here to note the awkwardness of using named language descriptors for the features of

Mthobeli: (indistinct)

Mbulelo: Oh no!

Figure 5.2 *Continued.*

Mbulelo's speech as expressed through the use of scare quotes. It is my attempt to navigate around the feature identification paradox (Seargeant & Tagg, 2011 in Bhatt & Bolonyai, 2019) of using the names of the very categories I am trying to debunk. However, the assignment of features to one language or another is not so easy. Can 'hydrogen' be said to belong more to English than isiXhosa, given its common use in many world languages? Is 'ihydrogen' an English, Greek or an isiXhosa word, or none of these? The assignment of a feature of discourse to one or other named language may be necessary during analysis in order to demonstrate meshing of features which in a different context would be said to belong to different languages, but more important for the point being made here is that Mbulelo and his peers are engaged in enregisterment (Agha, 2006). The signs that he uses are recognised by all participants as belonging to

92 Translanguaging, Coloniality and Decolonial Cracks

Mbulelo: Look! Look!
Mthobeli: Mh?
Mbulelo: But look you see then the Hydrogen is a molecule that exists, they are two when they exist, so you don't count them as four

Mbulelo: here they are two, they count as two

Figure 5.2 *Continued.*

Mbulelo: because Hydrogen when there is one and you add Oxygen

Mthobeli: Hydrogen can never be one

Figure 5.2 *Continued.*

a register for doing Science learning in a peer group and the meaning-making flow (Lin *et al.*, 2020) continues. The meshed register allows Mbulelo to engage in exploratory talk in order for all three boys to work towards conceptual understanding.

94 Translanguaging, Coloniality and Decolonial Cracks

Mbulelo: Yes so you write two here so you're not gonna write four

Mthobeli: Why didn't you say so?

Figure 5.2 *Continued.*

The interaction ends with Mthobeli and Mbulelo jostling for position as the most helpful or knowledgeable peer in the group, a playful one-upmanship pattern which played out in every lesson within this group. This is an example of what Ballenger describes as a learning situation

Mbulelo: Why didn't you say so?

Figure 5.2 *Continued.*

where 'social intentions remain enmeshed in the arguing and theorising' (Ballenger, 1997: 10) enabling multiple identity positions to be enacted simultaneously. I describe this as identity meshing (Tyler, 2022). In this whole-body sense-making performance, Mbulelo has argued convincingly for the relevance of the theory of diatomic elements to the current activity. In this way, he enacts a successful academic identity. At the same time, he joins his friend in a teasing dialogue to shore up his social identity. While the boys find Mbulelo's academic knowledge helpful, they are all careful to incorporate this within a frame of social competitiveness.

Siding

Communicating with someone other than the ratified speaker in a speech event has been described as byplay (Goffman, 1981), or in a classroom setting, as siding, or side-talk (Lemke, 1990). This activity forms part of the underlife of a classroom (Gutierrez *et al.*, 1995) in that it is not ratified by the teacher. Lemke identifies three important social functions of side-talk: it provides a channel for students to sustain their personal relationships; it fulfils a need for students to talk to someone other than the teacher about the current learning activity; it provides an option for students to disengage from the classroom activity altogether (Lemke, 1990). In a South African university setting, Antia (2017) found that translanguaged siding by students in lecture halls supported academic learning through recontextualising the content as well as through linguistic brokerage. The second function articulated by Lemke, relating to the learning of the academic topic, is exemplified by the example below. Lemke describes a process very similar to what unfolds in Extract 5.3:

> Side-talk serves students' needs to talk with someone other than the teacher about what is going on at the moment in the class... Students first share their question, or confusion, or idea with another student, and only then do they go public with it and ask the teacher. Students...get very little practice speaking the language of science. Just to phrase a question they need to get a running start, and dialogue is the practice ground... (Lemke, 1990: 75)

Mbulelo and Thandile are talking about the word 'radioactive' and together they set up the question that Thandile asks the teacher.

Extract 5.3 Radioactive

Turn	Actor/Action	Speech	Gloss
1	Mbulelo: gesturing from Mthobeli to Ms B	Buza miss. It's important.	Ask miss. It's important.
2	Mthobeli:	Ndithi what does it	I'll say what does it
3	Mbulelo: leans towards Mthobeli, whispering	What does the word radioactive mean	
4	Mbulelo: Points to Mthobeli	Miss, uMthobeli uyabuza.	Miss, Mthobeli is asking
5	Mthobeli: smiling	Xa i-element i-radioactive ithetha 'ba ithini	When the element is radioactive what does it mean
6	Student	ithini?	what?
7	Mthobeli:	It is radioactive	
8	Thandile	Rediactive Reactive	
9	Ms B: Raises hand with fingers splayed and palm facing towards Mthobeli	Ok	
10	Mbulelo:	Radioactive.	
11	Thandile:	Rediactive	
12	Khethiwe:	Like a radio.	
13	Students and Ms B:	(laughter and clapping)	

The function of siding as a rehearsal of Science language is particularly evident in this example. For at least a minute before this extract,

Mbulelo, Mthobeli and Thandile have been discussing the word 'radioactive' in a side channel concurrently with the dominant communication channel of the student-questioning dialogue. Mbulelo then prods Mthobeli to seek clarity from Ms B (Turn 1). Then, Mthobeli begins to rehearse the question (Turn 2) followed by Mbulelo's rephrasing (Turn 3). Then, Mbulelo, who is interested in the question of radioactivity, gets the teacher's attention orally as well as using a gesture and sets Mthobeli up as the questioner (Turn 4) and someone who runs the risk of losing face if the question is deemed to show him in a bad light in any way. This face-saving technique is typical of Mbulelo's identity work in general where he often moves to put himself in a superior academic position in relation to his peers (see also Figure 5.2). Mthobeli's smile may indicate that he realises he's been set up, but he goes ahead with the question anyway. Natural translanguaging plays an important role in providing three versions of the question with which Mthobeli eventually 'goes public'. He begins by phrasing the question haltingly in a familiar register. Mbulelo then builds on this expression and produces a version of the question in 'scientific English'. Mthobeli then publically expresses a well-formed question in a meshed register of isiXhosa and English. By delivering his message in this meshed register, Mthobeli flouts the explicit classroom rule that students should speak in English when addressing the plenary. This example demonstrates that this rule is not strictly upheld. Mthobeli's translanguaging allows the question to be 'chewed over' and tested as different versions as Mthobeli gets comfortable with the meaning of the question. This movement between registers in dealing with the same content resonates with Setati *et al.* (2002) in showing that there are different pathways between registers to gaining conceptual understanding. The unexpected direction of the discussion in Turns 11 and 12 also provide a light-hearted moment of verbal play contributing to positive class affect. This use of familiar register in this episode converges with the students' interest, or sense-making purposes (Ballenger, 1997), which the questions pursue. The converse is also possible: if students are denied the opportunity to use their most familiar registers, their wonderment questions may also be suppressed.

Siding sustains student interest in the topic, which is apparent in the next example, Extract 5.4, involving Thandile. Ms B is aware of side-talk continuing between Thandile and his neighbour during a class discussion of metals and their states at different temperatures. As an admonishment for breaking the rule against side talk or 'talking' (Lemke, 1990), she asks him to account for the content of his talk. Thandile shapes a response which expresses some of the meaning he has already been making in his side-talk. Mbulelo and Mthobeli, seated at the other end of the classroom from Thandile, then begin to side about Thandile's response.

Extract 5.4 Terminator

Turn	Actor/Action	Speech	Gloss
1	Thandile: Gaze to neighbour softly	Like uTerminator	Like The Terminator
2	Ms B Gaze to Thandile	Ja it has properties of a metal that's why it reacts like a metal even though it's a it has that exception of being a liquid <FAST>Ok. Thandile. </FAST> what you talking about cos you not talking about Mercury	
3	Thandile	(indistinct) Mercury	
4	Ms B: to Thandile	Ok please tell all of us cos we'd like to know	
5	Thandile: aloud	Ndithi Misi like ndibona iTerminator mna imetal (indistinct) ajika ayiliquid but same time i-metal (indistinct) ajikayo	I am saying Miss like I watched Terminator, it's a metal (indistinct) which changes into a liquid but at the same time is a metal (indistinct) it changes
6	Mbulelo, to Mthobeli	Yhe?	Hey?
7	Mthobeli, to Mbulelo	e-e le ma̱khi leya le ikhala kanje La nxi nxi nxi	Yes the my friend the one that sounds like this That nxi nxi nxi
8	Mthobeli, to Mbulelo Mthobeli's arms are bent and his side and he moves them back and forwards	Le ijik' ithi	The one that turns and does this
9	Ms B gaze to Thandile	Ok we believe you let's move on to non-metals	

Thandile must first assert the relevance of his side-talk to the plenary discussion before he can win the right to speak in the plenary. His contribution, made in his most familiar register, seeks to show how a fictional character made of metal which is at different times liquid or solid has relevance to the discussion of Mercury, a metal that is a liquid at room temperature. His example comes from the popular action film series 'Terminator' which features a robot which is made of a liquid metal alloy. On the other side of the classroom in this moment, Mthobeli picks up the semiotic flow (Lin *et al.*, 2020) and is able to display his knowledge of popular culture to Mbulelo by mimicking the sound and movement of the robot. Both Thandile and Mthobeli are performing their scientific and social identities simultaneously in this moment of side-talk (Ballenger, 1997) through engaging in repartee and the Science topic at hand (Lemke, 1990). While they are both students of Science in a classroom, they also position themselves as teenage boys who watch science-fiction movies.

Thandile's contribution also reveals a misconception which he shares with at least Khethiwe (as came to light in one of the study group sessions) but probably more students. He fails to distinguish between the taxonomy of metals/non-metals and the taxonomy of states of matter. Unfortunately, this contribution, centring on a student's interest but also his misconception, is not taken up by the teacher. Rather, she takes control of the pacing of the lesson by indicating that we are all going to 'move on' (Turn 9) to the next topic. Lemke (1990: 65) suggests that this is a strategy for teachers to keep to their own agenda or interests:

> Teacher control of pacing can be used strategically to create a sense of the 'pressure of time' which can make it easier for a teacher to forestall student initiatives and keep to his or her own agenda for the lesson.

The opportunity for engaging the students' interest as well as working through a misconception was missed by the novice teacher.

Cross-Discussion

The next example of grassroots decolonial practice is taken from the study group data. Cross-discussion is an activity type where students take control of the topic-specific discourse and engage each other about it without deferring to the teacher/facilitator. It requires extraordinary agency to be taken up by students and is extremely rare in secondary school contexts. This instance of cross-discussion straddled a formal and informal learning space, as I will describe, and this perhaps created the necessary conditions for cross-discussion to flourish.

Khethiwe, the central actor in the episode to be presented, is the top-scoring Science student in her class. She was also the only member of the Grade 9 Natural Science class to respond to my invitation for further comments at the end of the language questionnaire that I circulated (Figure 5.3).

Khethiwe's response on the questionnaire echoes and illuminates her performance in the study group. She employs different modes and voices

100 Translanguaging, Coloniality and Decolonial Cracks

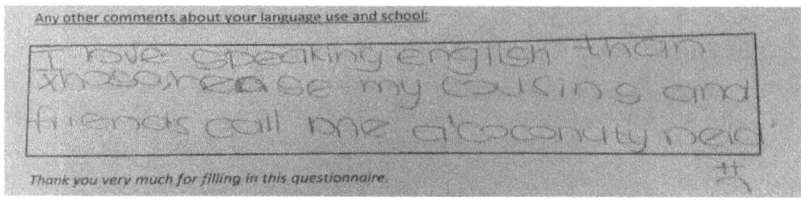

Figure 5.3 Khethiwe's questionnaire response
Transcription: I love speaking English than xhosa, hense my cousins and friends call me a 'coconuty nerd' ☹.

to make her point: academic formulations of English ('hense') and quotation marks, but also a playful emoji to illustrate her response to the name-calling – 'coconut' being a derogatory metaphor to describe someone who has brown skin on the outside, but displays aspects of white culture and is therefore 'white on the inside'. She creates a meshed register here in which her feelings of love and sadness around her use of English are juxtaposed. It is this meshed register that expresses the conflict in her life in the borderlands where her academic and social identity positions meet.

The comic strip in Figure 5.4 represents a moment in the study group, just before we closed the meeting one Thursday afternoon, when Siphosethu became interested in a box of coloured pencils lying on the shared table. Having read the text on the back of the box ('wood-free coloured pencils'), Siphosethu was puzzled about the raw materials used to make the pencils. I challenged the group to find out more about what the pencils were made of by 'writing down the question'. The challenge was given impetus by my offering them all 'a prize if you give me a good answer'. It was soon after this challenge was made that the action in Frame 1 ensued. Phumeza sought help from her peers in interpreting my instruction by asking whether she was correct in assuming that the task at hand was to answer the question about the composition of the pencils. Khethiwe then identifies her error in Frame 2 and poses an alternative task in Frame 3 – finding the aim of the investigation – which the group take up in Frame 4.

Figure 5.4 represents a moment of interaction in which multiple semiotic modes come together to create meaning. Frame by frame, the interaction shifts from the uncertainty of which activity the participants are involved in (Frame 1) through a period in which a new activity is suggested by Khethiwe (Frames 2 and 3) to a place of settling upon an activity (Frame 4). It is through this process that Khethiwe appropriates Science discourse.

At least eight modes are discernible in the whole-body sense-making moment captured by Frame 3, relying on the audio and video recordings and my memory of it: facial movement (eyebrows raised, eyes wide, smiling), gesture (fingers forming 'o'), body positioning (leaning forward), gaze (at the friend who asked the question), a meshed linguistic register (isiXhosa and English), voice volume (increased), vowel length (extended) and intonation (rising tone). These modes combine in a powerful meshed

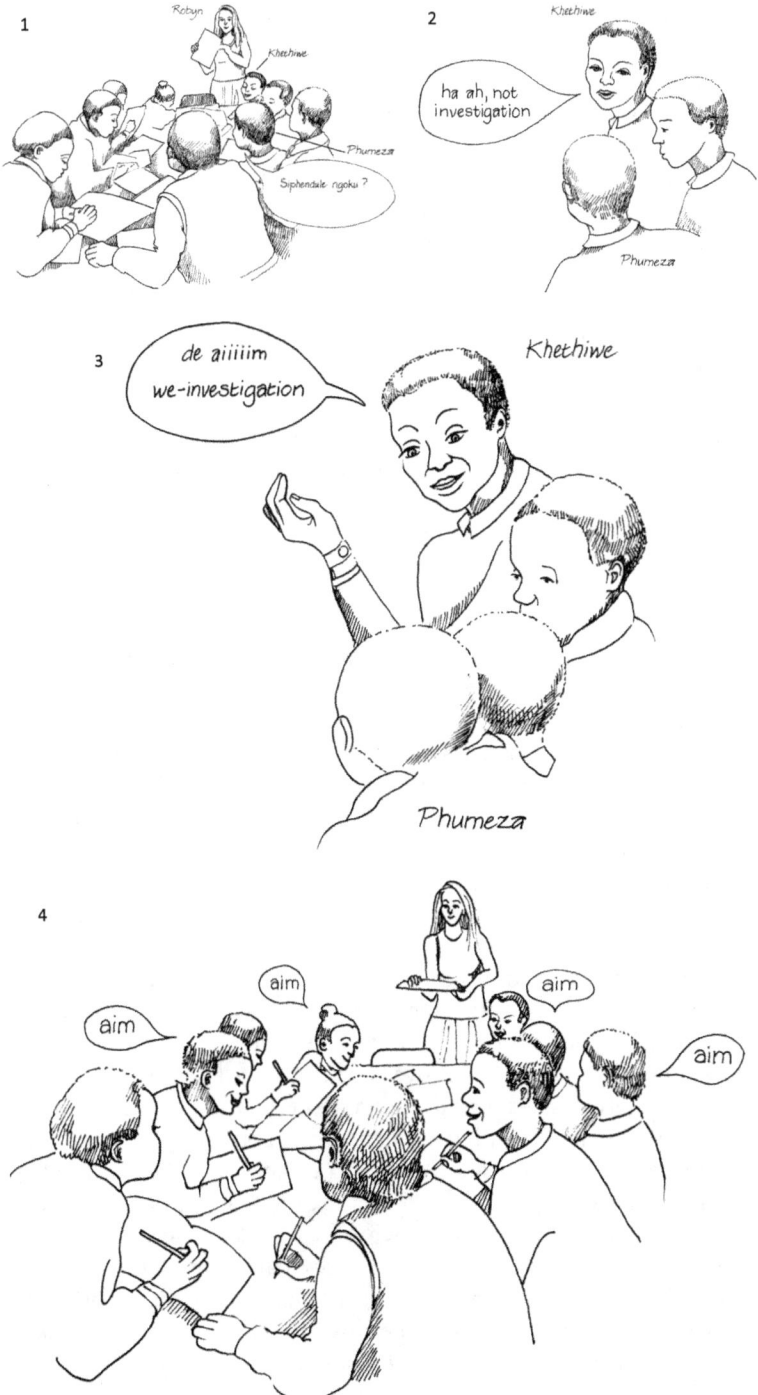

Figure 5.4 Comic strip representing Khethiwe's language and identity meshing (Siphendule ngoku? *Must we answer now?*)

identity performance to realise a complex and nuanced meaning. Through the simultaneous use of these multiple modes, or trans-semiotising, Khethiwe brings different identities into play which could be seen as incompatible by virtue of, for example, the school language policy which holds that Science should be taught and learned in English.

In Frame 3, Khethiwe continues to situate the current task within the investigation genre which she introduced in Frame 2 by pointing to a specific investigation activity: finding the *aim* of the investigation and articulating it. However, the lexical features she uses do not conform to the notions of scientific English espoused by the textbook or curriculum documents. It is a meshed register that she utters, employing features of the familiar register in use among the youth of Khayelitsha: 'de' and 'we-', and features of scientific English: 'aim' and 'investigation'. She layers her lexical meaning-making with other modes in order to: (a) draw attention to her skill at applying a Science genre to a task which the teacher/facilitator has not framed as such, (b) distance herself from an academic identity position to which she does not want to appear attached in order to maintain good social standing among her peers and (c) and create a moment of playfulness.

Her raised volume and extended vowel sound as she utters the word 'aim' are enough to draw attention to her skill at recruiting this academic discourse into the informal task of finding out about pencils for a prize. Adding stress to the word 'aim' in Frame 3, where 'investigation' in Frame 2 received no stress, is listed by Lemke as a common 'thematic development strategy' (Lemke, 1990: 226) that teachers employ to build up a network of meaning relationships across a topic of Science. Like a skilled teacher, Khethiwe has used vocal stress to highlight a significant scientific unit of meaning which facilitates her peers' understanding here. The action modes, such as gesture, facial movement and change in body position, go further. Because they are so exaggerated when compared to the other actions in the group immediately prior to Frame 3, I argue that Khethiwe is seeking distance from the performance of an academic/scientist/teacher identity position in this moment.

Owing to the censure Khethiwe has received for her use of English and her academic prowess – being a 'coconuty nerd' – she utters scientific discourse in an informal learning moment at her peril. Within what began as a social interaction, she risks identifying too closely with the predispositions and value systems of Science that Science words carry. Khethiwe's identity work here is in contrast to what we have seen Mbulelo doing, who sought to align himself with an academic identity by putting his friends down during academic activities. Apart from the difference between the activities in which Mbulelo and Khethiwe engage as academically knowledgeable – an academic activity versus a social activity which shifts to an academic one – their responses are also affected by their gender. Whereas a boy displaying academic prowess may be well received by his peers, a girl's academic prowess may be negatively received (Carlone *et al.*, 2015).

Drawing on Bakhtin, McKinney and Norton recognise that:

> the appropriation of the words of others is a complex and conflictual process in which words are not neutral but express particular predispositions and value systems. (McKinney & Norton, 2008: 193)

Kapp (2004) found similar risk management in her study of English in a high school in Cape Town where she concluded that 'to be seen to be investing in English... is to risk humiliation and derision' (2004: 258). Even when the named language of the students and the Science discourse is the same, the appropriation of the register of Science can pose identity risks for students. In his study of African American Vernacular English-speaking youth in Science classes in the US, Brown (2006: 96) found that the black students struggled to appropriate the discursive practices of Science and had to 'balance the tension between their academic and personal identit(ies)'. The students in Brown's study actively resisted using 'slang' or features from their familiar registers in talking about Science as they argued, 'It isn't no slang that can be said about this stuff' (2006: 96).

In order to mitigate the conflict of appropriation, Khethiwe folds the Science discourse into her social discourse through trans-semiotising. The message that I argue Khethiwe intends through her performance in Frame 3 is, to repurpose the words of Goffman (1975) as: 'whatever I am, I am not just someone who can only speak scientific English'.[1] Goffman's phrase 'whatever I am' poignantly captures the borderland of identity flux and experimentation in which a 15-year-old such as Khethiwe finds herself. This performance constitutes identity meshing in that rather than switching between two identity positions, Khethiwe meshes them in order to create a new position for successful science learning.

Khethiwe's performance is supported by her peers in Frame 3, particularly Siphosethu (out of frame) and Phumeza, who respond through uninterrupted gaze directed at Khethiwe, smiling and positioning their bodies to face her. The responses of Khethiwe's peers in Frame 4 – smiles and the validating action of taking up her discourse in echoes and beginning to write – are also indicative of this support. In this way, Khethiwe sets in motion a flow of meaning-making (Lin, 2019) in which many of the members of the study group participate, so that the translanguaging which is achieved is a communal endeavour. In Frame 4, we see participants picking up the scientific term 'aim', and it echoes around the group. The flow of meaning-making results at the end of the episode with one of the students, Thandile, co-uttering the question, 'What do wood-free coloured pencils made of?' as he inscribes the words into his exercise book. The result of the joint trans-semiotising is the phrasing of a question for scientific investigation.

Another motivator of Khethiwe's utterance is her human interest in joy and humour, or what Huizinga (2014, in Blommaert, 2017: 3) describes as, 'the playful character of many social, cultural and political practices'. This motivator is in evidence in her catching her friend's eye as she looks on in Frame 3. Having not asked the participants about their laughter during this episode, I can only speculate that it is due to their delight in their own cunning at having linked a seemingly social activity of working towards a potential prize to an academic genre used in class lessons and the fun they are having in simultaneously playing and ridiculing 'the academic'. Support for the concept of identity-meshing and the affect it engenders comes from Wu and Lin (2019) who argue:

> Naming these phenomena in a simple and encompassing way in terms of switching between traditionally named languages and registers would rob away the rich and delicate feeling-meanings engendered from the symbiosis of all the available communicative semiotic features entangled simultaneously. (Wu & Lin, 2019: 265)

Individual Seatwork

The practices discussed so far have predominantly enlisted body and oral-linguistic meaning-making resources. In this last section, I present examples of grassroots practices which centre on the written (including graphic) mode. Although not exhorted to do so, some students made notes during teacher exposition or go-over activities. Figure 5.5 is a photograph of Khethiwe's notebook including some of her spontaneous notes taken during Class 3.

This page from Khethiwe's exercise book depicts two kinds of writing. The first is notes that she has copied verbatim from the board as the teacher wrote them up. This activity was referred to by Ms B as optional as she explained that the notes appeared in the textbook as well. The second kind of writing was not referred to by the teacher but was produced spontaneously by Khethiwe. This demanded active listening on her part as she followed the teacher's talk and determined what was important enough to write a note about, hence revealing her interest.

Figure 5.6 is a copy of the text that Khethiwe produced during just over four minutes of individual seatwork on the problem: 'What is the chemical

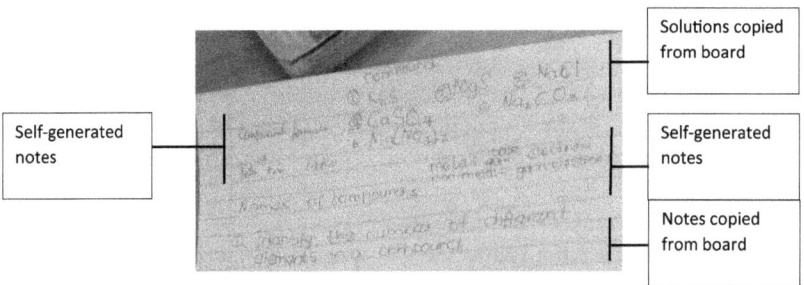

Figure 5.5 Khethiwe's exercise book

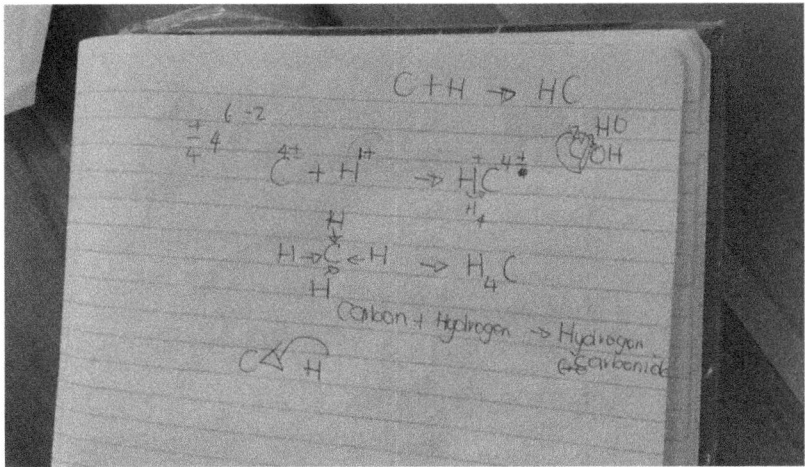

Figure 5.6 Side drawing while working on understanding

equation for this word equation: carbon + hydrogen → hydrogen carbide?' It is typical of what populates students' notebooks the world over, and indeed much of what scientists scribble about on the 'back of envelopes' (Lemke, 2004: 33). Khethiwe was the only student to produce this volume of notes. It is exploratory rather than presentational (indeed, she does not reach a solution) and therefore cannot be said to follow conventions of text-image presentation or a grammar of visual design very strongly. Space has been used on the page for convenience rather than in an ordered way. On the video recording, Khethiwe is shown skipping from one part of the page to another without linear progression over time. Its purpose rather is to contribute to Khethiwe's meaning-making as she tries out different expressions of the problem. Some parts of her text-image are representational – such as the arrows of different shapes representing processes, the chemical symbols and the chemical names – and should be considered as part of the text which she can review. Others are mere traces of her meaning-making in the actional mode, such as circling 1+ (top-middle of Figure 5.6), which serve to help her focus on that part of the problem in the moment and are not reviewed.

Khethiwe's two notes were produced during activities which were set up by a teacher or facilitator. As an indication of the range of what students draw upon from their semiotic repertoires when making meaning outside of the ratified class activity of taking notes from the board, I present a text-image (Figure 5.7) copied from the inside cover of a reader for the school subject isiXhosa Ulwimi Lwasekhaya Ibanga 9 (isiXhosa Home Language Grade 9) which I happened upon in the staff room as part of the 'rubbish collecting' (Blommaert & Dong, 2010) of ethnography.

This text-image is a mind map or concept map of the characters in a short story called 'Kuthiwani xa kunje?' which is an isiXhosa Home Language prescribed literature text for Grade 9. The student has used the names of the characters and in brackets, a short description of each as an

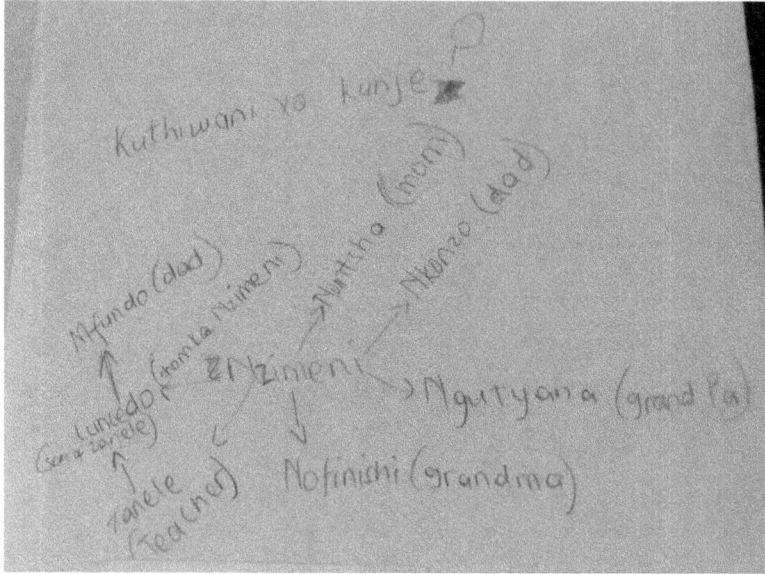

Figure 5.7 Spontaneous mind map

aide memoire. Through the use of arrows, they have indicated their relationship to each other. The short descriptions employ different features from their repertoire which would be considered transgressive in formal writing for isiXhosa Home Language. 'Chomka' (friend of) reflects isiXhosa and township youth features, while 'son of' and 'grandma' and 'teacher' are English features which can occur in township youth registers as well. The inclusion of the English features is particularly interesting given that the isiXhosa Lwasekhaya subject, like other language subjects at this and most Western Cape schools, ascribes to a monoglossic ideology which insists on 'pure' use of the target language and so this kind of languaging would be frowned upon in written work in the classroom. This is evidence of the register-meshing which occurs naturally when students are completely unfettered by language policy and have as their goal simply conceptual understanding.

The three examples of private writing/drawing given here echo the rich multi-semiotic nature of the oral/actional meaning-making presented earlier in the chapter.

Conclusion

In this chapter, the grassroots decolonial practices of Khethiwe, Thandile, Mbulelo, Asanda, Mthobeli and others have been described using the concepts translanguaging, trans-semiotising, whole-body sense-making, register meshing and identity meshing. The students created decolonial cracks (Mignolo & Walsh, 2018) in five different classroom activities and inserted their interests and sense-making resources. The features of grassroots decolonial learning practices which have emerged are:

- They are a form of resisting the coloniality of the English-only classroom space.
- They sustain student interest in the academic topic and their sense-making purposes (Rosebery *et al.*, 1992) often through playfulness.
- They are often collaborative and involve semiotic flow between students (Lin *et al.*, 2020).
- They usually involve multiple modes and registers, often meshed together, such as in whole-body sense-making (Lin, 2019).
- They can be challenging to teaching interests which are constrained by curriculum coverage.
- They provide opportunities for performing different identity positions simultaneously (Ballenger, 1997) and hence provide a decolonial borderland of Science discourse appropriation.

The bilingual, spontaneous learning practices reported on in this chapter are easily comparable to those which would appear in a 'monolingual' classroom. In such a classroom – as has been described by Lemke (1990) – students learn 'bilingually' through employing different registers, moving back and forth between everyday language and scientific language as well as embodied modes. Otheguy *et al.* (2015) articulate the difference thus:

> The difference between monolinguals and bilinguals is that monolinguals are allowed to deploy all or most of their lexical and structural repertoire mostly freely, whereas bilinguals can only do so in the safety of environments that are sheltered from the prescriptive power of named languages. (2015: 295)

The bilinguals in this study are racialised students learning in a language in education context of coloniality, and therefore their translingual and trans-semiotic practices here are described as grassroots *decolonial* practices. The activity types of the classroom in which they can enact the grassroots decolonial practices are the sheltered environments referred to by Otheguy *et al.* (2015): student-questioning dialogue, siding, cross-discussion and talk accompanying group seatwork and individual seatwork. In the following chapter, I describe the interventions made in the study group to enlist a wider range of learning resources and learning activities in the study of chemical reactions as processes of decolonial design and pedagogies.

Note

(1) Writing about a five-year-old's irreverent actions while riding a merry-go-round horse, Goffman reflects: 'To be a merry-go-round horse rider is now apparently not enough, and this fact must be demonstrated out of dutiful regard for one's own character… The child says by his actions: "Whatever I am, I am not just someone who can barely manage to stay on a wooden horse"' (Goffman, 1975: 124).

6 Decolonial Cracks in Pedagogy: Freedom and Resistance

Introduction

The focus of this chapter shifts to the study group setting: an intervention that I as researcher was free to design in any way I liked. I intentionally created an established translanguaging space in which bilingual language use was encouraged and pedagogical translanguaging (Cenoz & Gorter, 2021, 2017; Probyn, 2015) was a structuring strategy. Furthermore, the study group allowed an opportunity to engage with the curriculum (and extend it) using more student-centred pedagogies as it was free from the time pressures and large numbers of students in the classroom setting. When an established translanguaging space is brought into being through naming the resources that can be drawn upon, then participants begin to mobilise these resources. The translanguaging stance (García *et al.*, 2017) which I as a facilitator adopted included encouraging 'flexible wordings' (Lemke, 1990) in order to appropriate the Science content in greater depth. Equally, by designing tasks that require the use of invisibilised resources, the space becomes more open to translanguaging/trans-semiotising practices. These designed translingual learning tasks such as translation, writing in more than one language and discussing multilingual resources have been described as 'official translanguaging' (García & Li, 2014) and 'pedagogical translanguaging' (Cenoz & Gorter, 2021; Probyn, 2015). In the language of Catherine Walsh, this is the planned work of 'open(ing) cracks' of decoloniality (Mignolo & Walsh, 2018: 83). But, as I will show, the coloniality of language was also present as the cracks were being opened. It was visible in the resistance students showed to new ways of learning and new languages being legitimised for learning. These practices were often transgressive as they flouted the English-only language policy of the school, drawing on linguistic resources from isiXhosa as well, with the authority of having been designed by an adult facilitator within a sanctioned learning space. In Chapter 5, activity types were presented which were initiated by the students: siding, cross-discussion and student-questioning dialogue. In this chapter, other activity types were initiated by me as the facilitator of the study group and constituted some form of seatwork accompanied by student-led meaning-making. One other activity type forming part of the pedagogical approach was true dialogue.

Critical True Dialogue

The data from study group discussions presented below comprises examples of true dialogue (Lemke, 1990). True dialogue occurs when a teacher asks her students questions and does not know ahead of time what the answer would/should be. This differs from the typical triadic dialogue found in classrooms and described in Chapter 4 where teachers ask known-answer questions. Lemke laments the scarcity of this type of dialogue in Science classrooms as it enables productive discussions of issues of judgement and opinion (Lemke, 1990). In these examples, I have described the dialogue as *critical* true dialogue in that it challenges language ideologies and Anglonormativity in discussions of potential and actual language use for Science.

My limited capacity to use isiXhosa to learn Science certainly contributed to the English dominance of the discourse in the group. However, being a learner of the language also had its advantages in positioning me as a student, in effect turning the power binaries in this context of teacher–student and white South African–black South African on their heads. It also evoked metadiscourse about isiXhosa which drew students' attention to their own language use. I was also something of an anomaly as a white person who could speak some isiXhosa. Certainly, I never heard another white (or coloured) person speaking isiXhosa at Success High during my time there. Hence, I was immediately an object of some interest and an oddity. At the first study group meeting, I felt nervously determined to use isiXhosa myself to model bilingualism and so establish a translanguaging space. Figure 6.1 follows my first greeting of the students and the ensuing moments. I had previously met them in class to introduce my research study and the study group.

This interaction – or rather false start – in the first few moments of the inaugural study group captures some of the vulnerability and awkwardness of my role at Success High. The people pictured around the table in the library are in uncharted territory. My initial question is out of place within the logic of the coloniality of language on three levels. First, I am a white South African greeting black South Africans in their home language, which is an act against the grain of the stratification of social power which was set up by Apartheid, namely that the language of white South Africans predominates in interactions between white and black people (Botha, 2012). Second, in a semi-formal teaching and learning space, I am a teacher opening the interaction in an African language. The third level exists as a compound of the first two levels, bringing a unique strangeness to the interaction. I am a white English home language South African teacher greeting black isiXhosa home language students in their

Figure 6.1 Weird language in the study group ('ninjani?' = 'how are all of you?')

home language in a content subject teaching and learning space which is never imagined as anything other than English dominant. My out-of-place initiation highlights the Anglonormativity of the learning environment.

I am prepared for my 'out-of-place'ness in that I have had time to prepare for my fieldwork and observe student speech patterns. Students are unprepared for me, especially my ability to speak isiXhosa, and Khethiwe's response in Frame 1 is refreshing and out-of-place in equal measure. It is out-of-place in that students do not habitually respond to teachers' discourse evaluatively, yet it is a disarmingly honest emotional response to the Anglonormativity being challenged. It is also an opportunity for Khethiwe to perform important social identity work as a peer of the other students, as indicated in Chapter 5. By enacting youth slang ('weird', Frame 1) and upstaging the teacher through diverting the attention from my utterance to hers, she presents herself as a socially powerful member of the peer group. My reading of her desire for the recognition of this identity is strengthened by her gaze cast towards her friend with the concomitant smile of success (Frame 3).

I allow her response to 'hang in the air' by repeating it (Frame 2) which allows space for other students to respond, which they do tentatively by laughing softly. Then, I put on naivete, playing the sincere language teacher, while at the same time revealing my disguise by leaning forward and joining in the laughter (Frame 3). Through this joke, I am trying to win rapport and therefore trust. The discussion continues as I risk an explicit discussion of race.

Extract 6.1 Language and race

Turn	Actor/Action	Speech	Gloss
1	Robyn	Ja ndithetha…Ndifuna ukuthetha kanjani ne?	Yes, I speak Xhosa. I want to speak isiXhosa how, hey?
2	Nandipha nods		
3	Khethiwe	Freaky	
4	Robyn	Why is it so weird? You've never seen a white person speaking Xhosa?	
5	Khethiwe	No, I've never imagined you speaking Xhosa // that's why//.	
6	Robyn	//But I already//spoke Xhosa in your ^{class}.	
7	Ls	Yes	
8	Thandile	But in class	
9	Robyn	Kancinci nje nhe?	Just a little bit
10	Students	Ja.	

My opening the conversation in Extract 6.1 in isiXhosa (Turn 1) does little to unsettle the school norm that students speak English with white adults. This instance of racialised language use which structures social interaction has two possible causes. First, it is so unusual for a white person to use isiXhosa in communicating with a black person in the Western Cape that Khethiwe remains in the convention of English for white interlocutors. Second, Khethiwe herself is unusually invested in speaking English and as she is the first respondent to my question, she sets the language of further engagement. Then, in Turn 4, I introduce the question of race and language use. This is avoided by Khethiwe. Perhaps this involves too much risk for her: negotiating the ground rules of this subject in discussion with a newly acquainted white adult is too complicated. She quickly brings the subject round to me as an individual and Thandile introduces the setting change. Perhaps using isiXhosa during the podium event (Goffman, 1981) of addressing the whole class is more understandable than in a small group where the possibility for conversation between individuals opens up. Just as my use of isiXhosa is limited by my proficiency and the students' willingness to converse with me in that language, so my struggle to talk about the elephant in the room is limited by taboos around talking about language and race in certain public spaces in South Africa. Kell (2010) argues that this is not an unusual predicament for South African linguistic ethnographers:

> South Africa is a country that is still very divided. Ethnography offers a way into understanding such divides. In South Africa it is not an easy way. At the same time as it 'entails trust and confidence' (Hymes 1996, p.14), it also involves grappling with issues of identity and risk. (Kell, 2010: 231)

The informal discussions we had in the study group provided further opportunity to probe language attitudes. In the first study group meeting, there were nine students present. Shortly after the meeting started, the students and I embarked on a discussion about which languages are useful for speaking about Science. This conversation reveals much about the students' different notions of what it means to speak or even 'do' Science.

Extract 6.2 Language for Science

Turn	Actor/Action	Speech	Gloss
1	Robyn:	Masithethe kancinci. Uyakwazi ukuthetha iSayensi ngesi … ngesiXhosa?	Let's talk for a little bit. Do you know how to speak Science in… in isiXhosa?
2	Students, shaking heads	Hmh.	
3	Robyn:	Huh?	

4	Nandipha	(Indistinct)	
5	Robyn:	Nithetha isiNgesi nje?	You speak English only?
6	Nandipha nods		
7	Phumeza	Ndingazama.	I can try
8	Robyn:	Hey? You've never spoken Science in Xhosa?	
9	Students, shaking heads		
10	Khethiwe	I try. Always fail.	
11	Robyn:	Where do you try?	
12	Khethiwe	At home (indistinct) day to day.	
13	Robyn:	Then why do you fail?	
14	Khethiwe	Because I don't know most of isiXhosa, most of the words.	

In an effort to win rapport with the group on this our first meeting, I posed my first 'focus group question' in Extract 6.2 in the register most familiar to the students. By turning the conversation to a discussion of Science learning, I was modelling how this register could be used to speak about Science topics. The students surprised me by refuting that they could do this, despite exhibiting this exact skill during Science lessons that I had already observed. Phumeza is generous in offering to try this new way of communicating Science, but I unfortunately did not hear her suggestion. However, the reason they did not attribute this Science talk in lessons to 'isiXhosa' was because of their definition of speaking Science in isiXhosa. The students' understanding of language for speaking Science has been circumscribed by the coloniality of language in which their Science education has been steeped. The only way they can define appropriate Science language is according to European language theory which emphasises bounded, 'pure' language codes. The assumption is that if a language is to be used for Science learning, it needs a fully developed, home-grown set of terminology. This assumption belies the hybrid nature of the 'English' Science register which has a history of borrowing and meshing terms from other languages such as Latin and Greek. For Khethiwe, at least, this assumption indexed knowing all the English scientific word equivalents in isiXhosa. As the data has already revealed, the students already use isiXhosa for meaning-making in Science and coin heteroglossic words as they go. Many of these are still in development, or contested, by experts. Things became more complex when I shifted the focus from 'isiXhosa' to 'mixing', which was much more readily accepted as a viable register for 'talking Science'.

Extract 6.3 Speaking Science with a mix

Turn	Actor/Action	Speech	Gloss
1	Robyn:	Can you mix Science in… Can you speak Science with a mix? isiXhosa ngesingesi?	Can you mix Science in… Can you speak Science with a mix? isiXhosa and English?
2	Thandile	Mhm. Only explanations.	
3	Khethiwe	Ja.	
4	Thandile	I'm speaking isiXhosa.	
5	Robyn:	Only with the explanations?	
6	Thandile nods		
7	Robyn:	What's an explanation?	
8	Khethiwe	Like when you're explaining something.	
9	Robyn:	So what's not an explanation in Science? Give me an example of when you're not explaining something in Science?	
10	Thandile	It's a statement, like saying something, saying something then you are confident, sure. But when I'm trying to explain to the whole class, like it gets difficult to explain it in English. So…	
11	Robyn	Then you change. I would have thought you have to really know the Science to explain it. So if you're explaining something, you really know what you're saying. So the words that you use have to be right.	

In Extract 6.3, Thandile holds that you can only speak Science with a mix for 'explanations'. In order to explain what he meant, he drew a distinction between an explanation which is 'trying to explain to the whole class' (i.e. exploratory talk) versus a 'statement' which is when you're confident and sure (presentational language). His use of 'only' as a preface for using a mix demonstrates its low status as a science activity – a widely held view where exploratory talk is under-valued as a learning device. Using Barnes' (1992) distinction, we can say that Thandile has been exposed exclusively to 'presentational' language use in English while learning Science at school. However, as reported in Chapter 5, I frequently observed Thandile and his peers using isiXhosa/English bilingual language practices in order to solve Science problems and to complete tasks collaboratively in their classroom. However, Thandile clearly asserts that one can only 'mix' isiNgesi nesiXhosa while providing *explanations* in Science lessons and that a marker of successful Science is providing 'statements' about which 'you are confident'. In my last utterance, I push Thandile to see that providing explanations is an essential indicator of successful languaging for learning in Science. However, given Thandile's experience of the Anglonormativity of school Science where all learning support materials and all assessments have been available monolingually in English, and the dominance of summative assessments, his perspective is not surprising. The circumscription of isiXhosa to its use in less visible and predominantly oral academic functions is a manifestation of the coloniality of language for learning.

Later on in the study group sessions, I set the students a translation task that is described below. Here, Thandile's views on appropriate language for Science were challenged in that he was required to read a Science definition in isiXhosa. The translation activity as a whole offered students the opportunity to talk explicitly about language for Science in a way that potentially developed their critical faculties and enlarged their awareness of the role of language in learning. I set up the activity of translating the dictionary definition within a critical frame ('I want to know how did they [authors of the dictionary] do in terms of translating' and 'you're the experts'), encouraging critique of both the source text and the task. The redesign (Janks, 2010) of the task was in fact a response to the students' criticism of the definition in a scientific isiXhosa register that I provided. Despite the fact that they had not completed a task like this before, nor in fact produced any written definitions of their own in their lessons, students were very comfortable in taking up the position of knower and talked about the language use in the source text critically as the following three examples show:

> Miss do you realise this is like…deep…deep Zulu. (Thandile)
>
> Asithi like 'ba formal Xhosa thina (We don't speak like like formal Xhosa) (Yonela)
>
> 'Funeka sizibhale kaloku but kengoku sisiXhosa esidibene ne-English (We must write them but it's Xhosa that is combined with English). (Thandile)

Thandile complains about having to provide a translation into English when, according to him, some of the words in the source text are already in English (e.g. hydrogen). This criticism highlights the hybrid nature of Science language in that the words which Thandile is criticising in the source text are

Xhosalised (Paxton & Tyam, 2010) versions of English words originally borrowed from Latin ('imoletyhuli') and Greek ('iathom', 'hayidrojini'). The engagement with the borrowing which infuses all scientific registers is a process of disinventing named languages for Science. While his comments were not pursued in the study group, Thandile is speaking into a debate around appropriate ground rules for the intellectualisation of African languages – whether new terms have to be coined, old words re-purposed for academic disciplines, or borrowing with or without Xhosalisation.

For these bilingual students, the written scientific definitions in isiXhosa were very unfamiliar. Not only was the secondary discourse of Science unfamiliar, but it was presented to them in isiXhosa. Since the start of their Science education (formally in Grade 4), they have only been exposed to written science in English – due to the policy, curricula and publishing constraints described in Chapter 1. The students feel more empowered to be critical of the isiXhosa Science register due to its unfamiliarity brought about by the coloniality of language which marginalises colonised people's language resources. isiXhosa is not positioned as a language of power and knowledge production. Hence, more rigorous standards of intelligibility are applied by these students than those which they might apply to their school textbooks in English, for example. The task opened up conversations among the students and myself about the registers being used to talk and write about Science. Three themes emerged from that discussion: some kinds of language we claim as our own ('claimed by the students'), some kinds of language we disclaim ('disclaimed by the students') and some kinds of language are 'used in/useful for this exercise'. The names for registers which the students used in the discussion have been listed in Table 6.1 below, categorised according to the theme they constituted.

The variety of register descriptors used by the students during the discussion implies the keen insight which they have into their own language use. They describe, creatively and clearly, different registers in relation to how much they identify with them. The discussion also contained a fair amount of negotiation and conflict around the descriptions of the registers revealing the emotional investment students had in accurately describing their language use. They distanced themselves from a particular kind of isiXhosa which they dubbed 'deep Xhosa' or 'formal

Table 6.1 Registers referenced in the translation exercise

Register	Examples in the discourse
Claimed by the students	'kasi Xhosa', 'isitsotsi', 'isigingqi', 'isiXhosa', 'siya-mixa', 'Capetonian Xhosa', 'si-incorporata ubutsotsi' (we incorporate gangster-language)
Disclaimed by the students	'deep Xhosa', 'deep isiZulu', 'formal Xhosa',
Used in/useful for this exercise	'tsotsi taal', 'isiXhosa esidibene ne-English' (isiXhosa that is mixed with English), 'isiXhosa esivakalayo' (proper isiXhosa)

Xhosa' and displayed an affiliation with urban vernaculars (Makoni *et al.*, 2010) such as 'Capetonian Xhosa' and 'isitsotsi' (language of gangsters), although not as languages for academic discourse. The students observed that the isiXhosa used in the glossary book included both formal isiXhosa ('isiXhosa esivakalayo') and mixed language ('isiXhosa esidibene ne-English') which they criticised, displaying a keen metalinguistic awareness. Important too for this identity work is that all the references to the registers used by the students were made using plural pronouns such as 'we', referencing a strong group identity constructed around language use.

In the examples of true dialogue described above, the coloniality of language played a significant role. It governed the ways in which race and language use are constructed and the ways in which a language, in this case a black African language, is linked (or not) to high-status activities such as presenting Science information. While these critical true dialogues were short, they present examples of the kind of dialogue that is important in accompanying translingual work in contexts of language inequality. While the coloniality of language was strongly asserted, the dialogues can be seen as decolonial cracks which can be exploited in a variety of ways over a longer period of time between a teacher and her students.

Whole-Body Sense-Making in Posing Problems

Posing problems as a way into new content learning has a long history as a productive, transformative and decolonial pedagogy. Since Freire's proposal of problem-posing versus banking education (Freire, 1996), inquiry-based approaches to teaching Science have gained in popularity (Yager, 2004). Yager holds that:

> Often, the best context for learning occurs when issues (questions, problems, or concerns) are used to define and exemplify science content. Whenever possible, these issues should arise from student experiences, concerns, or both. (2004: 102)

In this section, I describe a problem-posing activity which was used in the study group. This is an unusual seatwork activity in that it only lightly guides the content under study, as opposed to very rigid closed-question activities in the textbook. This activity spanned the length of the study group's existence with references to these questions in the final sessions. Below I describe the three phases of the activity.

I was fortunate to have started the study group meetings before the topic began in class and so could do some work with our prior knowledge. Determined as I was to make the study group a context for real learning, and free as I was from the constraints of the curriculum, I asked the students to formulate their own questions related to the topic of chemical reactions in the first study group. These questions, including my own, were formulated during the first study group meeting. I then wrote these up on two large sheets of newsprint and displayed them against the library shelves at most study group meetings. I proposed the activity as follows:

Extract 6.4 Setting up the activity
Robyn: Um but let's just do a quick activity, and that is write down three questions that you have about chemistry or chemical reactions. Anything. Try and write on something you've really been wanting to know. Or if you think about chemistry, what would you want to know. Even if it's what is the point of studying, how can this help me in my career. Even if it's something like that. Any three questions that you have about...about chemistry, chemical reactions.

By framing the questions as those 'you've really been wanting to know', I focused on eliciting the students' interest. They took up the challenge and wrote down their questions. I did not specify which linguistic resources they should use, but they all unsurprisingly used only English resources given their schooling acculturation. After they had each selected one of their questions, I wrote their 'wonderment questions' (Chin, 2001, in Alvermann, 2004) up onto newsprint. Chin found that students did not generate wonderment questions on their own and:

> this suggested to her that leaving such questioning to chance was tantamount to letting students' puzzlements go undetected – in effect, stifling further inquiry. (Alvermann, 2004: 232)

Chin therefore makes a strong case for designing learning activities which require students to ask wonderment questions. Some questions were transcribed verbatim, and others were changed slightly by members of the study group to aid coherence. As scribe, I tried to remain as true to the author's intentions as possible, without ironing out any conceptual inaccuracies I noticed as I imagined these would be good fodder for discussion later on. One example of the joint construction of a student's question follows:

Extract 6.5 Joint construction of a wonderment questions

Turn	Actor/Action	Speech
1	Palesa:	(Indistinct)When gas particles diffuse, are the particles com-
	Looks up from page, shakes hand by twisting wrist	pletely disappearing or they just float til an en' where they (indistinct)

2	Robyn:	Ok. Say the first part again?
3	Palesa: Holds book with both hands and reads	When the gas particles diffuse are the particles disappear completely or they
	Lets book go, looks up at Robyn and others, smiles Describes circles with extended hand and moving fingers looks at neighbour who is smiling with raised eyebrows Robyn writes	float around
4	Ls laugh	(indistinct)
5	Thandile: smiling	They don't float.
6	Robyn:	Ok. So what do we write down for the end? Do they disappear completely or just float? Or do you want me to write something else?
7	Robyn Writes: 'When the gas particles diffuse do they disappear completely or just invisible/float?'	
8	Khethiwe:	Or just like invisible.
9	Palesa:	E-e. (yes)
10	Robyn:	I'll put float and invisible. We're gonna have to we'll have to decide what to

Palesa and her peers engage in a variety of meaning-making practices during the presentation of her question for inscription. Instead of merely reading the question verbatim, Palesa prefers to elaborate and extend her meaning through the use of gesture and exploratory talk. The question is an intriguing one with many concepts or semantic relations (Lemke, 1990) caught up within it. There is so much to define before the question can be answered. When her written words begin to fail to capture her meaning, she looks up from the page and employs gesture to try to communicate her intentions better. This demonstrates her interest in being understood and in the question. She could have just followed my instruction to read her written question aloud, but she prefers to 'work on understanding' in a more public space before committing to it.

The full list of questions as they appeared on my newsprint after that first study group meeting are as follows:

Extract 6.6 Students' elicited questions

1. Fezeka: When you have mixed atoms and they've made a chemical reaction, can you separate them?
2. Thandile: Is everything around me made of atoms?
3. Lindelwa: Why are electrons and protons always equal?
4. Siphosethu: Why do chemical reactions happen?
5. Khethiwe: Why does oxygen and hydrogen make a liquid (water) when both are gases?
6. Nandipha: Why is an element made out of atoms?
7. Phumeza: What effect do chemical reactions have on our lives?
8. Lelethu: What jobs are closely linked to Chemistry?
9. Palesa: When gas particles diffuse do they disappear completely or just become invisible?
10. Yonela: Are there any jobs in the field of chemical reactions?
11. Mthobeli: What are the things that you will see or notice if the reaction has taken place?

Apart from Questions 7, 8 and 10, which relate the topic to the life worlds of the students, all the questions can be classified as wonderment questions about Chemistry in that answering them requires higher level processing and a complex and lengthy answer. The aim of the question-writing exercise was not to create scientifically accurate questions, but rather to begin to explore ideas about the topic. The questions do contain inaccuracies. In Khethiwe's question, for example, she states that oxygen and hydrogen are both gases. This is not always the case, as both of these elements can change state and become liquid or solid at different temperatures. However, as stated above, this inaccuracy was left unrevealed until the fifth study group when we reviewed the students' questions to see whether they had gleaned any answers from their study of chemical reactions.

The second phase of the activity was to track the progress of the students' thinking in relation to their question as the topic progressed. Extract 6.7 is of the discussion of Khethiwe's question:

Extract 6.7 Khethiwe's question

Turn	Actor/Action	Speech
1	Robyn Robyn looks from question on the newsprint to Khethiwe	and Khethiwe, how are you doing with your question
2	Khethiwe	mm

3	Robyn	What would you what would your answer be to your question at the moment and let's see if it changes from now until the end of the term just read it out
4	Khethiwe, reading: Robyn's gaze is on Khethiwe Khethiwe looks at Robyn Khethiwe:	Why does oxygen and hydrogen make a liquid which is water when both are gases? Miss I have no idea (indistinct)
5	Robyn: Eyebrows raise and gaze moves to Anelisa	How much can how much can you answer like give something towards an answer cos it happens ^{right}. so
6	Khethiwe: Hand holding pen goes to mouth, Anelisa looks down at her pencil case Khethiwe:	mm … <FAST> I think because hydrogen has um metal properties </FAST>right
7	Robyn: Khethiwe: strokes paper with pen, gaze to Robyn Robyn:	It's on the left hand side ja Ja With the metals ja
8	Khethiwe traces a circle with her pen on the paper while gaze is still to Robyn Gaze is to page Taps pen on paper and gaze to Robyn	And it reacts with uh oxygen I think um the oxygen you know kind o- loses that gas form I think they come to a compromise
9	Robyn, smiling, spoken very quietly	They come to a compromise
10	Khethiwe Looks from her book to Robyn and back. Draws circles on her page	Metal liquid liquid's like in the like a semi-metal cos water is a semi-metal so those are metal here those are non-metal here and they come to a compromise to uh (indistinct) that's what I'm thinking

I will begin with an examination of the epistemological assertions about Science which are expressed in the guiding moves made in Extract 6.7. First, I emphasise to the students the *process* that is involved in conceptual development in Science. 'What would your answer be to your question at the moment' (T3) and 'give something towards an answer' (T5) leaves open the possibility that that answer may change and that an incomplete answer is also useful for learning. This also draws attention to the students' thinking – or introduces metacognition which Khethiwe picks up in Turn 10: 'that's what I'm thinking'. Second, I draw attention to the empirical nature of Science, reminding the students that this is not just a theory but that 'it happens ^{right}' (T5).

Khethiwe is on the receiving end of my probing as I withhold my own ideas and push her to express hers. Khethiwe expresses her thoughts on how liquid water is formed from two elements which are, in her current understanding, always gases. The concept around which Khethiwe's question pivots is that matter can be described in different ways: two of which are states and the metallic properties of elements. The pauses in her speech indicate her hesitance and discomfort with these ideas. She also hedges by using the phrase 'kind o'' and 'you know' (Turn 8). She arranges information into different patterns in Turn 8. These features of her speech indicate that she is engaged in exploratory talk (Barnes, 1992). Mental effort is often also expressed physically and Khethiwe's effort is revealed through her actions: she draws circles on the page; her gaze is on the page and not on her interlocutors. Then, she engages sophisticated concepts from her life world to provide an analogy using personification for what happens in a chemical reaction ('they come to a compromise'), thereby engaging in the thematic development strategy of rhetorical connection (Lemke, 1990). I am able to support her in this strategy by repeating what she says and smiling which allows her the space and confidence to talk further into the concept. Lastly, she reveals her conceptual error in conflating state of matter with the metallic properties of elements through her exploratory talk 'water is a semi-metal' which I pick up in the following few turns.

Differently to her peers when they engage in exploratory talk, Khethiwe uses English. As her main interlocutor, I am English-dominant and so she accommodates my language repertoire through this. But Khethiwe is also particularly proficient in English in comparison with her peers due to her bilingual home. Other students might not be able to engage in such conceptual depth in English and would need interlocutors with a wider repertoire than I have to engage successfully in exploratory talk of this nature.

Part way through the study group series, I added another piece to this problem-posing activity in an effort to make the questions part of scientific inquiry more broadly. I sent the 11 student questions to three adults I knew who are, or have been, involved in scientific inquiry post-school. I was careful to select a racially diverse group to act as positive role models for the students. One is a professor of Biology at a university, one holds a doctorate in Microbiology and one is an Economist. I asked them to select a question that they would be interested in answering and record a video of themselves answering it. They were asked to address the student whose question they were answering and to keep their response to 1–2 minutes. They were free to answer in any way they liked. I then asked them to send the video to me via WhatsApp so that I could show my students. The purpose of these videos was threefold:

- to expose the students to another authority on the topic of chemical reactions and to demonstrate the relevance of the topic beyond the classroom walls;
- to provide a development of the topic using Lemke's strategy of 'repetition with variation' (Lemke, 1990);
- to give the students the message that an adult who is part of an aspirational world of work cares enough about them to take the time to make a video which might help them in their learning.

Unfortunately, the time I had to show the videos to the students was very limited due to the school's busy programme and so feedback from them was minimal. However, they watched the videos with rapt attention and reported that they enjoyed them very much. The problem-posing exercise provoked decolonial cracks in centring the students' sense-making purposes (Rosebery *et al.*, 1992). In articulating their exploratory thinking in relation to their questions, Palesa and Khethiwe employed whole-body sense-making drawing on linguistic features associated with Science registers and everyday registers as well as drawing on gesture. They did not draw on features from isiXhosa overtly, but I argue that their full multilingual repertoire is activated as they struggle to make meaning here. Additionally, grappling with the articulation of their questions caused Palesa and Khethiwe to dwell in a borderland (Anzaldúa, 1987) of uncertainty which held the potential of conceptual growth.

Trans-Semiotising in Written Work

As the study group sessions commenced before the start of the topic 'chemical reactions' in class, I began with a review of what the students knew about the topic from previous study in Grade 8 or elsewhere. I asked the students to draw a diagram of a chemical reaction. I explained that it could be a general representation of a reaction or could denote a specific reaction. Once the diagram was completed, I asked students to explain what they had drawn in written isiXhosa. This requirement was met with shock and dismay. This was the first time these bilingual students had been asked to write anything at school, outside of the isiXhosa subject classroom, in their home language. The requirement directly flouted the school's language policy, although this paled in comparison with the huge task of a totally novel register as their only means of expressing themselves. All the students who undertook this activity found it difficult. Below are some of their reflections after completing the activity:

Extract 6.8 Yonela's reflections
'Yoh, very hard…like there were other terms that you couldn't where you couldn't like explain in Xhosa like chemical reaction' (Yonela)

Extract 6.9 Khanyiswa's reflections
'it was quite difficult, it was like a new language' (Khanyiswa)

Terms that they had no problem incorporating into their spoken registers in the classroom such as 'i-reaction' suddenly posed a problem for them in writing. In defining what counts as a register for writing, the coloniality of language caused the students to resist the task of Science writing in isiXhosa. The standardising force of writing bore down heavily on them until they relaxed into flouting the written, standard isiXhosa that they are used to using in isiXhosa Home Language class. The accompanying talk with one another was crucial in achieving this.

Despite the difficulties the students' faced, they all produced a paragraph of text in a short space of time. Figure 6.2 is a reproduction of Khethiwe's complete text+image followed by explanation.

The purpose of this activity was for students to explore their prior knowledge of chemical reactions using an expanded repertoire (Lin, 2015) of semiotic resources. I did not give any instructions about the conventions of the genre of scientific diagrams or explanations as this was not the focus. Nevertheless, students employed generic conventions spontaneously. In Khethiwe's example, we see the use of labels, connecting lines between words to show a process and the use of brackets to show alternative expressions of the same substance to aid clarity: 'isoghum beer (umqombothi) utywala'. This shows a good awareness of what the conventions of these genres are.

While drawing and writing are the two broad mode categories employed in Khethiwe's text, within them there are other modes used to express nuances of meaning. The designed trans-semiotising in the activity has produced a highly multimodal text. The drawing part of the text contains two discrete texts: a realistic drawing and a reaction diagram. In the drawing mode, colour and labels are used to convey meaning. In the meshed register (Gibbons, 2006) of the writing, there are features present from different registers: scientific English ('rea(c)tion', 'alcohol'), formal isiXhosa ('iswekile', 'utywala') and Esenginqi, the students' most familiar language ('isoghum beer', 'iyeast'). Each of the different modes contributes something to the overall meaning of the text: the drawing foregrounds apparatus; the writing foregrounds the human actor and the physical process; the reaction diagram foregrounds the chemical process and the scientific register. Khethiwe's use of brackets is more akin to the bilingual

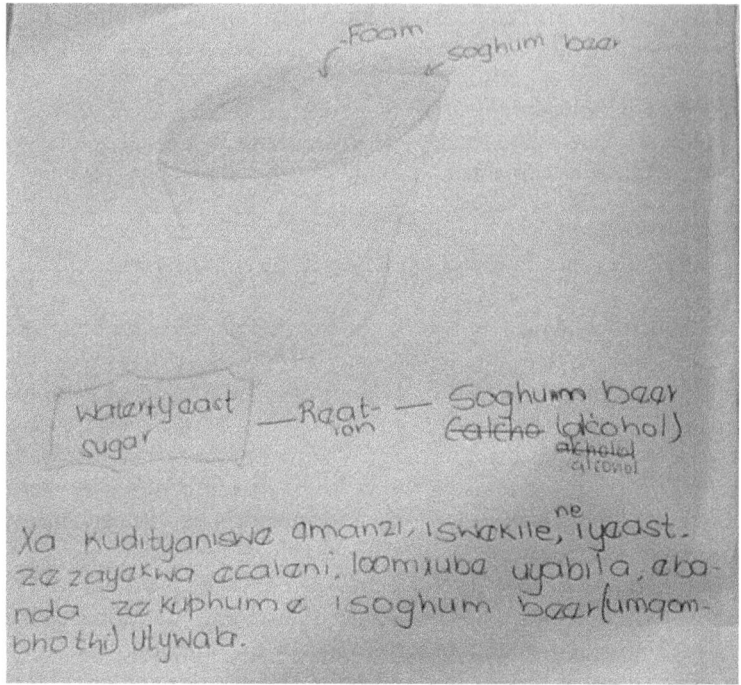

Gloss of linguistic text:

If you mix water, sugar and yeast together, then put it aside, that mixture boils. When it has cooled, it will become sorghum beer (umqombhothi) alcohol.

Figure 6.2 Khethiwe's prior knowledge text

practice of translation as orthographically it keeps the two codes separate through the punctuation marks. If then, Khethiwe were to be restricted to only one mode and register, for example, scientific English for explanatory definition, she could draw on the meaning she has made in other modes to create a more comprehensive text. It could be argued too that the most comprehensive text expressing Khethiwe's understanding of chemical reactions at this point would necessarily be multimodal. The activity of explaining what they had drawn gave an authentic context for meaning-making. Working with authentic texts is highly recommended in literacy studies in multilingual environments (cf. Makalela, 2015). The explanations of the diagrams also made 'fixed words' (Lemke, 1990) an impossibility.

For some students (for example, Yonela), the writing below their diagram was the longest piece of extended writing they completed during the course of studying chemical reactions. Mayaba *et al.* (2013) found that South African children are exposed to very little writing in the Science classroom. The text-type of reflective explanation proved to be a non-threatening opportunity to track their understanding of a topic at a particular point in time. This text could potentially be reflected upon later as understanding developed.

This activity was novel on two accounts. First, it was a transgressive activity in the incorporation of isiXhosa resources into writing about Science. By taking a trans-semiotic approach, I was able to minimise the threat of writing Science for the first time in isiXhosa by using the diagram as a scaffold. Second, it centred a new genre of writing for Science for these students: the reflective explanation.

Translation

The literacy activity of translation might seem out of place in a content learning environment such as Science; however, there is a strong tradition in Science education research of emphasising the literacy demands of Science (Gee, 2004; Halliday & Martin, 1993; Lemke, 2004). Translation itself has been proposed as an appropriate method of deepening Science understanding (Lemke, 1990). From the monolingual English language Science learning context, Lemke proposes translation between colloquial and scientific language as a way of developing the 'flexible wordings' required for understanding and using Science content (1990: 173). Gibbons (2006) argues for the importance of 'meshed registers' in learning Science, where students use parts of colloquial registers and parts of the scientific register in talking about Science. In collaborative translating, such as in the case reported on here, oral meshed registers are available for analysis. For multilingual students who have a wide semiotic repertoire, translation becomes an even richer activity. Baynham and Lee (2019) argue that translation is an activity forming part of the translanguaging competency of a multilingual speaker. In his 1990 book, Lemke describes a Science class activity which I have not yet come across described in empirical research literature:

> Students should regularly have oral, and occasionally written, practice in class in restating scientific expressions in their own colloquial words, and also in translating colloquial arguments into formal scientific language. (Lemke, 1990: 173)

It is the *written* translation activity which has not been reported in school Science literature. Lemke argues that translation exercises can have benefits for increasing 'students' fluency and flexibility in using the foreign register of science' (Lemke, 1990: 173) and helping students to understand which register – or purpose-built assemblage of linguistic features – is which. Translation as a linguistic endeavour has traditionally had no place in Science class. This has been assumed to be an activity suited to language classes only. However, the flexibility of expression of the thematic pattern (Lemke, 1990) which translation enables makes it a rich meaning-making activity for Science. Lemke described translations between colloquial English and scientific English. In my study, I had the opportunity to experiment with a translation between scientific isiXhosa, scientific English and colloquial isiXhosa (Esenginqi) – an activity that was transgressive in the light of the English-only language policy of the school. These translation activities are a typical example of pedagogical translanguaging due to their planned nature: 'pedagogical translanguaging is concerned with the planning, application and extension of multilingual pedagogical strategies and practices based on the student's whole linguistic repertoire' (Cenoz & Gorter, 2021: 19). Translation in academic learning comes close to the activities initiated in a Welsh classroom where the term 'translanguaging' was coined by Cen Williams (Williams, 1996). In this classroom, input was given in Welsh and students created output in English.

The current activity took place during the final study group meeting which was designed as part focus group, part study group. The first half of the session was dedicated to the interview in which we reflected on the chemical reactions unit as studied in the study group and the classroom. Then, during the second half, I set up a translation exercise in which the students worked in pairs. Using a multilingual dictionary of Science and Mathematics terms as a resource (Young *et al.*, 2005), I designed a worksheet with key concepts from the topic described in paragraph form. This dictionary exists in multiple copies in the 9B classroom, but as discussed in Chapter 3, Ms B has never used them. In the dictionary, a concept is defined in English first, then Afrikaans, isiXhosa and lastly isiZulu, with occasional accompanying graphics or diagrams. The order in which the definitions occur is significant in that it indexes a language hierarchy which values English preferentially and then the other three languages in the order in which they appear. On my worksheet, only the isiXhosa definition of each concept was reproduced, and a space was left for the students to fill in an English translation. The translation of one concept from isiXhosa into English comprised the first seatwork activity.

I set up the activity with a critical framing, encouraging the students to critique both the authors of the sources text ('I want to know how did they do in terms of translating') and the task ('you're the experts'). The students embarked on the task in a manner which displayed high engagement and interest[1] and early on began making critical comments about the arcane language in which the isiXhosa definitions had been written. Thandile retorted, 'miss, do you realise this is like…deep…deep Zulu'. They also distanced themselves from this register. Yonela explained to me, 'asithi like ba formal Xhosa thina' (we don't speak like formal Xhosa).

Yonela and Thandile worked together on the English translation of the definition of 'Imoletyhuli' and produced very similar, but not identical, texts, reproduced below. (The first definition, which appears in the dictionary, was not used by the students, but here it is used for comparison with the students' English translations.)

Extract 6.10 Original English, Young et al. (2005) (not made available to students)
A molecule is the smallest unit of an element or compound that can exist alone; it is made up of the same or different types of atoms, e.g. one molecule of water is H_2O; one molecule of hydrogen is H_2 (H_2 is a diatomic molecule – it always exists as two atoms in nature).

Extract 6.11 Original isiXhosa, Young et al. (2005)
Imoletyhuli lelona suntswana lincinci lembumba elinakho ukuzimela; lenziwe ngee-athom zohlobo olunye okanye ezahlukeneyo, umz. Imoletyhuli enye yamanzi ngu-H_2O; eyehayidrojini ngu-H_2 kwaye ihlala izezohayidrojini zimbini endalweni.

Extract 6.12 Yonela's first version
A molecule is the smallest part of matter of the compound that can stand or split on its own, as it is made up of one/different kinds of atoms, for example one molecule of water is H_2O, for hydrogen is H_2 and there are always two hydrogens in nature.

Extract 6.13 Thandile's first version
A molecule is the smallest part of the compound that can stand or split on its own, as it is made up of one/different kinds of atoms, for example one molecule of H_2O/water has 2 hydrogens and that will stay the same in nature.

The production of these texts demanded rigorous intellectual work and collaboration. Neither Thandile nor Yonela was certain of the meaning of 'isuntswana' (part/particle) and discussed this with the other students present. Through this, they began to develop a receptive register for Science in isiXhosa. The collaboration between Yonela and Thandile was filled with contestation which then produced more finely tuned conceptual understanding. Following Kress *et al.* (2014), I argue that the differences in the final texts they produced also revealed their diverging *interests* in creating the texts:

> Students' texts can be read as transformative of the original resources, as their shaping of meaning in what is for them the most apt and plausible way given the resources available to them in a specific context. (Kress *et al.*, 2014: 29)

The first difference in Yonela and Thandile's translations is found in the first line where Yonela includes in her translation of 'isuntswana' the scientific concept of matter (Extract 6.12). In so doing, she produces a register in her translation which is more scientifically technical than Thandile's which omits this term. This references her developed knowledge of the formal isiXhosa word 'isuntswana' as a technical and not an everyday term in this context. The second difference is in the expression of the concept of a water molecule. Yonela renders the section: 'Imoletyhuli enye yamanzi ngu-H_2O; eyehayidrojini ngu-H_2' as 'one molecule of water is H₂O, for hydrogen is H₂ ' and Thandile as 'one molecule of H₂O/water has 2 hydrogens'. Both students have not accounted for the meaning of the semi-colon between the two phrases and the prefix 'eye' in 'eyehayidrojini'. However, they have also both made scientifically accurate meaning in their translations which focus on the part of the definition which they see as salient for their interest. This centrality of their own interest indicates that discourse appropriation is occurring (Bakhtin, 1981). Yonela focuses on the diatomic nature of hydrogen in its natural state, while Thandile focuses on the equivalence of the common name and the symbol in reference to the element in question.

Towards the end of the first translation, I began to respond to students' critiques of the language of the isiXhosa definition by asking them to perform a second translation. This translation was to employ a different register again. Here are my instructions for the pair working on 'atom':

Extract 6.14 Instructions
Robyn: If this is your friend who has never heard English or who never studied science in English you need to write this explanation of an atom, for that person in kasi-Xhosa (township isiXhosa) …So uya-mixa okanya (so you mix or) … but just write the way you'd tell your friend about it

The students shared ideas and debated vigorously how best to go about making this translation. At one point, Thandile rebelled against the set task and redesigned (Janks, 2010) his own activity:

Extract 6.15 Thandile redesigns the task
Thandile: You know what's gonna happen now
I'm not gonna translate this
I'm gonna write it in my own understanding
that's what's gonna happen

Thandile's redesigned activity helped to achieve the goal of appropriation of the Science content which was inherent in the activity. Yonela and Thandile's second versions appear below followed by an English gloss.

Extract 6.16 Yonela's second version

[Handwritten text: Mamela chmy i-molecule yeyona part incinci kuyo uonke into esinggonatleyo enoKwazi uzimala yodwa and neeyu one or more ntlobo ze athomi. Lyk one molecule ya metsi is H₂O kwaye. Kuzosolo ko kukho ihydrogen ezimbini in nature]

English gloss of Yonela's second version:

Listen my friend, a molecule is the smallest part of all the things which surround us, that is able to stand on its own and it is made up of one or more types of atoms. Like one molecule of water is H_2O and there will always be two 'hydrogens' in nature.

Extract 6.17 Thandile's second version

> Kau 1 molecule yeyona well incinci ye compound enozimela ngokwayo. Lo wey yenziwe ngeyi nye ye different atoms. Umzekelo: 1 molecule yamanzi ina 2 hydrogen and lo wey oyihlala injalo unaphakade.

English gloss of Thandile's second version

My friend, a molecule is the smallest 'thing' of a compound that is able to stand on its own. This 'thing' is made up of one of the different atoms. For example: a water molecule has 2 hydrogen and that's how it's going to stay forever.

Yonela and Thandile draw on their semiotic repertoires freely and creatively to develop a register for writing Science for the audience of a peer. Both versions are in a highly meshed register in which features of scientific discourse ('atoms', 'compound', 'imolecule') are found alongside social nomenclature ('kau', 'chmy'). Extended written language ('yonke into esingqongileyo') is found with text messaging abbreviations ('chmy', 'lyk'). Sometimes the students choose features from isiXhosa ('kwaye', 'umzekelo') and sometimes from English ('lyk', 'and') and Yonela includes a feature of Sesotho ('yametsi'). This freedom in drawing on a variety of semiotic features typifies Otheguy *et al.*'s (2015) definition of translanguaging:

> We... define translanguaging as the deployment of a speaker's full linguistic repertoire without regard for watchful adherence to the socially and politically defined boundaries of named (and usually national and state) languages. (2015: 283)

Once again, the choices that the students make reveal their meaning-making interest. For example, Yonela chooses the phrase 'yonke into esingqongileyo' (everything which surrounds us) aligning with a lifeworld register, whereas Thandile chooses 'compound' aligning with a scientific register.

The students have now contributed to a total of six written versions of a definition of 'molecule'. These versions offer opportunity for further critical evaluation of the affordances of each for meaning as well as the development of new versions which extend the meaning of these. The nuances of meaning expressed by students during this exercise as well as their flexible languaging (García & Li, 2014) will not be visible to Ms B or to the Science teachers who set the monolingual English Success High Grade 9 test. These teachers are merely following the assessment guidelines laid down by state education advisers and patterned on the monolingual and monomodal high-stakes school-leaving examinations which dictate what counts as knowledge (Shohamy, 2004). The students' texts also pose a challenge to arguments made about classroom discourse usually, even optimally, moving from oral home language to written English in content subjects (cf. Setati *et al.*, 2002). Rather in line with previous findings (Tyler, 2016), students have moved through different registers in a multidirectional manner ending with multiple versions of the Science content.

The translation activity centred on separate named languages and required students to move between them. This in itself was a productive activity for conceptual development. However, during the activity, a meshed form of languaging emerged through which the students negotiated meaning with each other. Both a meshed form of languaging and the temporary stabilising of registers, or enregisterment (Agha, 2006), were important in completing the activity.

Towards Translingual Seatwork Tasks

In Chapter 4, I discussed the complexities for emergent bilinguals of making meaning in the class test using a nominalisation in English: 'arrangement'. Translations of many of my transcripts were completed by Babalwayashe Molate. She also translated the class test into isiXhosa (see Appendix 2). She translated '*How is the arrangement of electrons in Neon…*' as '*Zibekwe njani ii-elektroni kwi-Neon*' (how are the electrons placed in Neon). By translating 'arrangement' as 'zibekwe njani' (or 'how are they placed'), the essential meaning is retained, but the nominalisation is lost. 'Arrangement' is a noun, but 'zibekwe' is a verb. Thus, the grammatical feature of nominalisation is absent from the isiXhosa version. While the test translation was not used in my fieldwork, it served as a finding that while translations may be able to aid understanding, they may not necessarily model the features of presentational registers such as nominalisations. Potential alternatives to 'zibekwe njani' which include a nominalisation are:

'amalungiselelo' (arrangement – Nabe *et al.*, 1976)

'ukubekwa' (placement – Gononda, 2013)

'i-arrangement' (arrangement –formulated with a language and literacy colleague, Lara Krause, 11 September 2017)

By working with these multiple versions, the uses and benefits of each becomes apparent. Xhosalisations (Paxton & Tyam, 2010) such as 'i-arrangement' might be seen as sloppy language use by purists, but this term retains the nominalisation in a way which the isiXhosa phrase 'zibekwe njani' does not. 'Amalungiselelo' is also a nominalisation but would be less familiar to students, so I argue less ideal than 'i-arrangement'. However, the benefit of introducing students to 'amalungiselelo' is that they can then compare the grammar of making nominalisations in English and in isiXhosa. 'Zibekwe njani' offers an everyday register expression of the semantic relation which is helpful in unpacking the nominalisation. Pointing out these different affordances to students and exposing them to these versions – in other words, the use of metadiscourse – enables the flexible expression of scientific meanings and language awareness (Lemke, 1990).

It is possible also to present questions and tasks aimed to elicit Science content knowledge in different languages, registers and modes in one written task sheet. In Appendix 2, 'A translingual Science worksheet' serves as an example of this. Instructions are written in monolingual English, monolingual isiXhosa and meshed registers. Furthermore, some tasks are more flexible than those usually associated with Science assessment at school. Question 4 allows an open-ended response 'write about how the elements are arranged', rather than restricting students to focusing on one aspect. Also, the instruction at the start of the test to 'Khethani iilwimi zenu freely xa niyaphendula. Ninga-mixa!' (gloss: Choose your languages freely when you answer. You may mix!) encourages translanguaging in written responses from the students. This kind of translingual worksheet models new forms of bilingual language use alongside more standardised versions of language and traditional monolingual forms, validating heteroglossic language use as well as monoglossic use. This is especially important in the early years of discipline-specific language use by students, echoing Lemke's assertions about the importance of learning Science bilingually.

Conclusion

In this chapter, I have presented examples of decolonial cracks that come about through pedagogical design within an established translanguaging space. At the same time, I have shown how these cracks have been resisted by students and the coloniality of language has been reasserted. A variety of seatwork activities were reported on which required students to draw on previously unacknowledged and delegitimised semiotic resources for learning Science. These included exploratory drawing and writing in isiXhosa and an informal, urban variety of isiXhosa used for expressing a scientific definition and gesture. Not all activities were intentionally bilingual, but all positioned the students as agents of their learning, foregrounding their interest and encouraging flexible wordings and wrestling with meaning. These activities were at first very uncomfortable for students and required them to take up identity positions as resourceful bilinguals which they had not been allowed to take up in Science learning until now. At times they resisted this, which highlights how in a colonial system such as South African schooling, children are entrained into a monolingual mindset and shifting from that is difficult discursive and identity work. Woven into the activities was critical true dialogue about language use for Science which shaped the established translanguaging space and supported the designed bilingual and trans-semiotic activities. These also enabled further critical true dialogue in a way which was mutually reinforcing.

The final chapter draws together insights from the data presented up to this point revealing the coloniality of language and decolonial cracks. Recommendations will be made for widening these cracks. I will also connect the ideas I have proposed with other transformative projects in education.

Note

(1) On the video, students are seen leaning in towards their tables and each other and gesticulating during the completion of the task.

7 Conclusion: Widening the Cracks

Introduction

In Chapter 1, I posed the following questions:

(1) *How is the coloniality of language present in a Southern bilingual Science learning context?*
(2) *What decolonial cracks in language and identity for learning are observed?*
(3) *How can these decolonial cracks be widened?*

I have aimed to show two features of a Southern bilingual Science learning context: the coloniality of language and decolonial cracks in language and identity for learning. My argument, following Quijano (2017), is that coloniality is always present within decoloniality. My approach has been to present microanalyses of a wide variety of data to demonstrate processes of de/coloniality unfolding at the level of languaging for learning Science at school. Through the presentation of a case study of two learning sites in a high school in Cape Town, South Africa, I have argued that de/coloniality is an apt proposition for understanding language and identity in learning Science bilingually in the South. The coloniality of language constrains which semiotic resources can be used and how they are employed. But there are decolonial cracks to be found in the edifice of coloniality/Anglonormativity in learning. This concluding chapter offers a summary of how the coloniality of language was present in the research sites and what forms the decolonial cracks took. I will also explore how these cracks might be exploited, widened and connected with other transformative education projects. I begin with a summary of the ground covered in the previous chapters.

In Chapter 1, the conceptual framework of the coloniality of language and decolonial cracks in relation to South African education was outlined. The coloniality of language was shown to pervade the South African schooling system, and its effect on the black student speakers of non-dominant languages was described. The centring of English (and to a lesser extent Afrikaans) and the marginalisation of African languages was shown to be systemic: curriculum, teacher education, learning materials and classroom practices all display Anglonormativity (McKinney, 2017). Here also, the over-arching framework of decoloniality was reviewed with a focus on African thinkers. Two strands of decolonial theory were teased out which have particular relevance for the decolonial cracks highlighted in content learning in this study. The first is border thinking – the epistemological location of borders as fruitful sites for knowledge-making. The second is a recognition and centring of the body as a meaning-making resource. Chapter 2 outlined key concepts in language, the body and identity in learning which are applied in the study. The study was positioned as part of a trajectory of research into language use in content classrooms (especially Science) in South Africa which has adopted different conceptual lenses to account for multilingual and multimodal meaning-making. These are: code-switching, home language use in the classroom, translanguaging, trans-semiotising, trans-registering, whole-body sense-making, and register- and identity-meshing. Chapter 3 presented an analysis of the language environment of Success High demonstrating the coloniality of language present in ideologies, landscape and policy. Both official and tacit language policies were largely uninterrogated by staff and students and functioned at a remove from practice. Long-term patterns of practice in classrooms in the school also reproduced and reinforced the coloniality of language. This chapter also outlined the participants, their language profiles and attitudes, revealing some stark differences between the teacher and her students' views, but also revealing heterogeneity among the students both in language profiles and attitudes to language in learning. Decolonial cracks within the edifice of Anglonormativity were also revealed: the halting, but open ways in which the principal spoke about code-switching and her own language repertoire, the teachers' ambivalent attitudes to isiXhosa use in class, the cobbled-together groundsman's sign with its heteroglossic richness all pointed to cracks already present.

Chapters 4 to 6 presented a view of the Science learning in the two sites: Ms B's Grade 9 class and the after-school study group which I facilitated. In Chapter 4, the constraints of the curriculum and standardised monolingual English assessment placed on Ms B and her students when studying the topic (chemical reactions) were outlined. I argued that the coloniality of language expressed through the official school language policy and Ms B's close adherence to this restricted the activity types (Lemke, 1990) of the classroom. 'Go over' activities where seatwork was reviewed by the teacher in restricted Initiation-Response-Evaluation (IRE) discourse dominated class lesson time. Restricted IRE discourse enabled the teacher to maintain control of the discussion and to steer students towards ideal answers. However, it also comprised a version of safe-talk which did not probe understanding deeply. While English-only, linguistic-only resources were valorised, the features of the written Science register in English were not well practiced or appropriated in class, and this had effects on test performance. Chapter 5 offered the proposal that the spontaneous grassroots learning practices which the students employed in class and in the study group constituted decolonial cracks. The students drew together features of their semiotic repertoires in spontaneous and creative ways in order to forge new and meshed identity positions for learning Science. Siding and gesture as well as groupwork were often found to be about the Chemistry topic under study. The analysis of this 'hidden' meaning-making provided evidence of students' misconceptions; wrestling with concepts towards understanding; and connecting the science with their lifeworld knowledge. Chapter 6 described activities from the pedagogical intervention of the study group which explicitly required students to draw from an expanded semiotic repertoire, i.e. pedagogical translanguaging. These activities, such as versioning of Science definitions, pursuing questions on topics of their own choosing and exploratory drawing, formed decolonial cracks which enabled deeper conceptual understanding and identity development through identity-meshing. However, the activities were also resisted by the students who were unaccustomed to having previously marginalised parts of their repertoires positioned as learning resources. In this way, the coloniality of language was reasserted.

De/coloniality

The coloniality of language and decolonial cracks exist alongside and within each other as expressed by Quijano's (2017) rendering of 'de/coloniality' using the backslash. The findings from Success High provide examples of this. The coloniality of language is present in the systemic invisibilising through policy and learning materials of African language resources at school; in the disavowal by the students of their most familiar language resources as vehicles of scientific communication; in their resistance to employing isiXhosa language resources to write about Science topics; and in the teachers' resistance to using isiXhosa beyond occasional guilt-laden oral code-switching.

Following Veronelli (2015), to escape the logic of the coloniality of language, we need a different paradigm to understand colonised/indigenous peoples as having language in the full sense and being fully capable of expressing knowledge. Languaging (Maturana, 1990) provides one such paradigm. As shown in Chapter 2, languaging has been refined through the empirical study of non-dominant/indigenous/colonised people's meaning-making. In the process, terms used in this study – translanguaging, trans-semiotising, whole-body sense-making and identity-meshing – have been coined by scholars. At Success High, it was these meaning-making processes that opened decolonial cracks providing alternatives to the perpetuation of the coloniality of language in school Science learning.

The decolonial cracks presented in the study were made visible through a research orientation of border thinking (Mignolo, 2000) and a centring of the body in meaning-making (Menezes de Souza, 2021). Border thinking enabled an analysis of register and identity meshing and an appraisal of the meaning-making performance as an integrated whole, with its tensions and conflicts between semiotic modes and registers brought about through their organisation into hierarchies in the colonial system. A centring of the body allowed its affordances as a Science meaning-making tool to come to the fore.

The evidence of decolonial cracks presented throughout the preceding chapters leads me to celebrate these as very good signs, along with McKinney (2017):

> We face significant challenges of unjust standardized assessments, restrictive education policies and general resistance to a heteroglossic understanding of language as social practice. But the good news is that we know it is possible to implement transformative approaches to language and literacy inside and outside of formal schooling because…this is already being done! (McKinney, 2017: 10)

However, it is sobering to have to note, along with Walsh (2014), that the decolonial cracks are easily covered over because the practices are not supported by institutions and are sometimes vilified. They are certainly not yet supported by material resources. Therefore, decolonial cracks require maintenance and widening.

Widening the Cracks in Language for Learning and Research

Walsh's proposal of decolonial cracks is a practical and hopeful metaphor for the possibilities of taking action towards a more socially and epistemically just schooling system. The coloniality of language is pervasive and hegemonic in education; however, the findings from the Success High study join a body of evidence which shows that teachers and students are already designing, resisting and practising within decolonial cracks, however hesitantly, unevenly and ambivalently. Weber and Dyasi (1985: 569) aptly remind us that institutional power – be it at school or state level – affects how wide the 'cracks in the wall of constraint' can be that teachers and students create. Identifying, initiating and widening decolonial cracks enables teachers and students to be positioned as knowers and agents of change. Researchers and practitioners can build upon the innovative practices which teachers and students already participate in. Additionally, this approach facilitates the building of language policy from below while being entangled within a colonial matrix of power (Quijano, 2017). The announcement by South Africa's Department of Basic Education in March 2022 that it will introduce African languages as media of instruction beyond Grade 3 is certainly heartening from a decolonial perspective in that the knowledges and ways of knowing of colonised people will have an opportunity to gain prominence. However, the success of the programme will depend upon meeting the challenges of a complex situation such as language in education in South Africa. Proceeding from the proposal made in this book that it is productive to begin with the decolonial cracks which already exist in the system, the next task is to address Walsh's question:

> How do we, and can we, move within the cracks, open cracks, and extend the fissures? (Mignolo & Walsh, 2018: 83)

First, policymakers, educators and learning materials producers should acknowledge the *grassroots spontaneous practices* of our youth where the decolonial option emerges. Currently, South African schools are functioning as adaptive translanguaging spaces, but they need to transition to become established translanguaging spaces. Both language and curriculum policy should explicitly name and valorise the semiotic repertoires of emergent multilinguals as valuable meaning-making resources. Decolonial theory helps to make visible the meaning-making capabilities of racialised bodies as loc(i) of enunciation which have been marginalised in colonial education. Students' processes of register meshing (Gibbons, 2006) and identity meshing (Tyler, 2022) as exemplified by Khethiwe and Mbulelo need to be seen as productive actions for decolonial learning. Teachers should be supported to recognise and valorise all semiotic resources in their classroom, as they emerge, or even if they are hidden within the coloniality of language. Support should come from the applied linguistic research community providing examples of these resources as well as from teacher educators and government officials. Serving racialised speakers of non-dominant languages requires an understanding of 'dynamic bilingualism'– an acknowledgement at all levels of educational planning and implementation that 'the language practices of bilinguals are complex and interrelated' (García & Li, 2014: 14). Powerful language ideologies such as those revealed in the interviews at Success High need to be tackled in pre-service and in-service teacher education alongside the teaching of skills for multilingual classrooms as these will not take hold if language ideologies which make teachers resistant to the use of students' full semiotic repertoire in learning are not addressed (bua-lit, 2018). These ideologies are also held by parents, school managers and students as was revealed in the linguistic landscapes of Success High and the students' resistance to using African languages for learning. Drawing attention to the use of different registers in exploratory discourses would be a prudent place to start, especially if teachers are resistant to presentational discourse in anything other than English. Language in education policies, whether at a national, provincial or school level, need to be leveraged more strategically if they are to be forces to support quality teaching and learning as well as institutional transformation.

Language policies in schools can address the domains of language in learning, language as subject and language for community life. Extending the language policy to account for students' meaning-making in modes apart from the spoken and written mode would do much to legitimise these modes for learning as well as to make educators aware that these are pedagogic tools. Also important is the acknowledgement in policy of the bilingual reality of most schools, and students in particular, and an acknowledgement of the key role that different registers play in learning. Language in the broader community life of the school is an important aspect of any language policy not only because it incorporates members' self-esteem related to whether they feel their languages are valued at school, but also because the use of language outside the classroom affects learning as has been shown in the present study. All language policies pertaining to education should be more rigorous and detailed at the national and school level, especially with respect to language in learning across the curriculum beyond just naming languages to be used as subjects or as the official medium of instruction. Working with and understanding language policy should be a key part of staff development and school community stakeholders should be included in language policy development.

Second, the goal of language and literacy in schooling should be clearly articulated throughout the system as being the development of an *expanded repertoire* (Lin, 2015) in the students. Following García *et al*. (2021), to realise this goal requires reimagining the existing cultural, linguistic (and I add, embodied) knowledge not as a barrier, not as merely a bridge to the dominant language, but as the bedrock of academic learning throughout the lifetime. Then, new knowledge and new academic registers are added to and meshed with the students' existing repertoires. The semantic relations between terms used in Science such as those outlined in Chapter 4 require many languaging activities using familiar and new registers in order for appropriation to occur for students. A prime example of appropriation was presented by the students during the translation exercise in Chapter 6. Students drew upon features of English and isiXhosa in their existing repertoires in order to prepare glosses of science definitions in a meshed register. Translingual coinages such as 'ihayidrojini' can form part of a new register for Science, thereby revitalising African languages for academic purposes. Students at school can be part of driving the creation of this register within a decolonial borderland. A key consequence of this is that the students' African languages are shown to be useful for learning Science and students take up agency in creating the new register. Instead of only employing professional translators to translate English materials into African languages for use beyond Grade 3 – one solution that has been proposed – the Department of Basic

Education should tap into the languaging of students who are already using African languages for learning Science.

Another way in which African languages were revitalised and students' repertoires expanded was through the translated research tools which enabled Thandile to learn the 'deep Xhosa' phrase 'udliwanondlebe' for 'interview'. This and other formal isiXhosa phrases to which the students were exposed during the research were resisted due to the coloniality of language which renders the language of the colonised invisible. The students have normalised the abnormal use of a foreign language for Science learning. Positioning African languages as resources for meaning-making in Science can contribute to a 'virtuous cycle' (Mohanty, 2019) of language revitalisation in academic contexts. A clearer understanding of how the expanded repertoire can be developed throughout the schooling career of emergent bilingual students needs to be teased out. Within this goal, both dialogic meaning-making via translanguaging and trans-semiotising and chances for students to practice currently dominant academic genres in English (Lin, 2019) are important. Translanguaging and trans-semiotising using students' full semiotic repertoire can become the basis for developing new academic registers in African languages. A focus on metalinguistic awareness (Gibbons, 2006) is important for developing the expanded repertoire so that students understand the differences between registers in their repertoires. In advocating for metalinguistic awareness here, I would add that it needs to be *critical* metalinguistic awareness to avoid developing the ideology in students that what counts as 'academic discourse' is a neutral, static and universally adhered to construct (Flores & Rosa, 2015).

In making recommendations about the use of students' full semiotic repertoires in teaching and learning, the biggest challenge is mounted by assessment practices. However, these need to be tackled as assessments have a powerful washback effect on classroom practices. As the example of the class test in my case showed, summative written assessments such as tests and examinations in multilingual settings have been highly restrictive in terms of condoned registers and the kinds of questions asked. Studies of the use of African languages in school assessments have shown promising results (Charamba, 2021; Heugh et al., 2017). These took the form of side-by-side bi/multilingual texts, and in the case of Charamba's study, students were also allowed to respond in any language, or a mixture of languages. Multilingual formative assessments can serve as a testing ground for this novel approach (see Appendix 2 for an example). This kind of assessment is more likely to be decentralised and locally relevant and can incorporate the registers familiar to the group of children being assessed. Assessment activities that require students to reflect on their learning can draw upon an expanded repertoire and flexible wordings, showcasing what they know rather than what they don't know.

Assessments should include meshed registers as well as more restricted and boundaried scientific registers.

Third, pedagogical cracks should be opened and extended through planned critical language awareness activities and *pedagogical translanguaging* within academic subjects. These cracks should be opened in every subject area and consolidated across subjects through whole-school language-across-the-curriculum foci. Both pre- and in-service teacher education should incorporate pedagogical translanguaging strategies (Hattingh *et al.*, 2021) such as enabling translanguaging in group work, using translation exercises and performing cross-linguistic grammatical analysis. Not only in general education courses but within subject specialisations in order to develop strategies that suit the particular discipline. While overarching principles and models are needed, as far as possible, these decolonial pedagogies should be designed from the bottom-up at the school level as each school has a unique linguistic context.

This study has explored a dominant context in South Africa where an African language and English are both necessary resources for epistemic access and transformation. There is a strong need too for pedagogical translanguaging to find a home in elite school contexts such as private schools and ex-whites-only schools in South Africa. These schools are now racially and linguistically more diverse but have not undergone a sufficient expansion or transformation of ethos, language hierarchies or pedagogy (Christie & McKinney, 2017; Molate & Tyler, 2020). In a country such as South Africa with a bimodal education system, with one tier catering to largely monolingual English, privileged children and one catering to the multilingual minoritised majority, research that cuts across these tiers is rare. Future work that seeks common processes at work in these divergent contexts would do much to reduce the exceptionalism of bilingual education and the deficit ideologies which constrain translanguaging approaches to teaching and learning.

The intervention of a translation activity in the study group showed that resources that include multilingual activities and multilingual text will aid student comprehension and validate the linguistic resources which they have. Resource packs for teachers of content subjects guiding them through translanguaging activities and activities where students can generate their own questions about a topic are, in the short-term, less costly than textbooks and I recommend starting with these. The lack of use of the multilingual glossaries in Ms B's classroom is a reminder of the importance of combining the access to multilingual resources with interventions which are planned with teachers. Teachers need to experience the benefit of multilingual resources in teaching and learning first-hand and be supported in implementing this in their classrooms. The analysis of the identity work and conceptual explorations involved in grassroots decolonial practice in the study has underscored the importance of teachers providing opportunities for the kinds of spontaneous meaning-making students engage in (such as side-talk and seat-talk) and harnessing this towards discourse appropriation. In Chapter 5, we saw Mbulelo, Mthobeli and others engaged in this kind of talk with each other which Ms B allowed. It could be taken further, however, and be made visible by the teacher in the whole-class discussion.

Lastly, decolonial cracks in applied linguistics research methodologies need to be widened (Despagne, 2020; Ndhlovu & Makalela, 2021; Pennycook & Makoni, 2020; Phipps, 2019). I have proposed the comic strip as transvisual in this study as a possible decolonial crack in research which enables a foregrounding of participants' agencies, voices and bodies. Furthermore, the reflections offered on researcher positionality are equally important in presenting the partiality of the analyses and my entanglement in coloniality (Andreotti & Stein, 2022). To date, South African classroom discourse research has been focused on plenary, teacher-controlled settings. In a busy, noisy environment such as a classroom, it is easier and more efficient to capture data from plenary discussions than student discourse in groups, but we need to know more about student-to-student meaning-making. I have made a case in this book for the importance of the meaning-making which takes place through discourse between students, especially between teenagers for whom the peer group is highly significant. It is likely that for the foreseeable future, research into the use of bilingual students' semiotic repertoires for meaning-making will take place predominantly in intervention situations as the language policy environments in schools are not conducive to teachers employing students' full repertoires as meaning-making resources in the classroom. Further, I recommend extending the study of Science meaning-making beyond school into the home and community as these contexts shape the kinds of meanings made at school.

Widening the Cracks in Pedagogical Approach

Current decolonial approaches to education have older roots and intersections with other reform approaches. As educationalists have picked up decolonial theories to apply them to contexts of learning, the resulting propositions have at times merged with pre-existing programmes of social and epistemic justice in education. In this section, I outline the links with decolonial propositions for content learning made in this book and broader and older projects of redress, reform and transformation in education. Below I discuss links to anti-racist education, rich literacies, inquiry-based learning and education for depth.

Race remains a powerful organiser of society and the education system in which Success High is positioned. Indeed, race was a topic that was openly discussed by the students in this study. It also implicitly structured the relationship between myself and the teacher and her students. The tradition of *anti-racist education* is well-known. The work of Paulo Freire

(1996) and his problem-posing education was born out of anti-racist and anti-colonial struggle in 1960s Brazil. An equally strong tradition of anti-racist education exists in the US where thinkers such as bell hooks built on the work of Paulo Freire. In *Teaching to Transgress* (1994), hooks describes education as the practice of freedom and emphasises the importance of this understanding for racialised black Americans. Also in the US, culturally sustaining pedagogy (Paris & Alim, 2014) has built on the work of Gloria Ladson-Billings and seeks to foster connections within school to racialised students' out-of-school-lives in order to develop richer academic identities in these students. Taking language in education as a focus, the study of raciolinguistic ideologies (Flores & Rosa, 2015; García *et al.*, 2021; Kubota, 2021) has sought to expose how speakers of non-dominant language varieties are always positioned as deficient in the eyes of the white listening subject. Scholars using raciolinguistic ideologies as a lens have called for the dismantling of the hegemonic position of the white listening subject.

In South Africa, anti-racist education has been powerfully advocated for by social justice intellectual Neville Alexander. Alexander linked anti-racism and a democratic language policy which seeks to deconstruct the barriers between languages and raise the status of indigenous languages in his writings (see Alexander, 1989, 2000, 2001, 2009). Alexander was an early pioneer of a political project in South Africa to deracialise language in education and to centre the black child in an egalitarian education system. Alexander and colleagues' call for Mother Tongue-Based Bilingual Education (MTBBE) to be an organising approach in South Africa is supported by the present study and is gaining support in the current government. Key to this is a transformative, rather than merely affirmative, approach to multilingualism (Stroud & Kerfoot, 2013) which has to be a cornerstone of any anti-racist education programme. Ignoring the language question in anti-racist education reforms is an impossibility.

Recently, the bua-lit language and literacy collective (2018) has articulated an alternative '*rich literacies*' approach to language and literacy education in South Africa. Rich literacies resists a narrow, colonial, skills-based approach to literacy learning which results in an anaemic experience of reading and writing. A rich literacies approach requires new and alternative texts for children to read, new ways of working with texts and new dispositions by teachers and policymakers towards non-dominant children's repertoires. In terms of new and alternative texts for content subjects such as Science, urgent tasks include:

- creating new non-fiction texts in non-dominant languages for young children to read independently. These texts could highlight local discipline-specific work, such as blogs on new archaeological finds in local areas and could be created by high school students for younger children;

- creating bilingual and translingual learning materials for children throughout the school system which can be used alongside monolingual resources (for examples, see Appendix 1). Enlisting older students in the work of creating these resources, along the lines of the translations made by the Success High students, would benefit both the authors and the readers.

The third aligned educational approach is *inquiry-based learning* (Freire, 1996; Weber & Dyasi, 1985) which has long been advocated in disciplines such as Science (Rosebery *et al.*, 1992; Yager, 2004). Learning as active inquiry positions the student as agentive, as a questioner and as inherently interested in the world (Alvermann, 2004). The Success High students were able to grapple with concepts at a greater conceptual depth when they posed questions and initiated an investigation themselves in the study group. Inquiry-based approaches to education of non-dominant children align with decoloniality in re-centring silenced voices and epistemologies (Ndhlovu & Makalela, 2021). Beginning with students' questions about the world means centring local or indigenous knowledge, languages and local concerns. For examples of South African Science educators drawing on local knowledge in classrooms, see Hattingh (2022) and Ngcoza (2019).

The last and most recent broad educational reform project with which decolonial education aligns is the proposition of *education for depth* made by Andreotti and Stein (2022). This is a future-focused proposition which links the aspirations of educational reform with the need to reform our global modern/colonial economic system to avoid the destruction of our environment and our species. The authors juxtapose education for mastery (a colonial construct, they argue) with education for depth:

> Education for depth invites students, as well as teachers, to dive into the complexities, contradictions, and complicities that characterize the modern/colonial system as we know it so that we might begin to sense the limits of this system alongside its gifts and confront the difficulties of imagining and enacting something otherwise. (Andreotti & Stein, 2022: 213)

In terms of language in education, one way in which students, teachers – and I add policymakers and researchers – engage complexity, contradiction and complicity is by grappling with the place of named languages (Turner & Lin, 2020). Somehow, and for some time to come, these stakeholders need to balance the understanding that students bring diverse semiotic repertoires which are deployed fluidly with the powerful place that nomolanguages occupy in education. Nomolanguages become particularly important in a process of strategic essentialism (Spivak, 1985) when arguing for the use of non-dominant language resources, for example, African languages, in school.

The relationship between a complex perspective on language in learning and these briefly reviewed pedagogical approaches is reciprocal. As the understanding of languaging broadens and deepens, so other learner-centred pedagogies become desirable. As learner-centred pedagogies are explored, so the exploration of more meaningful uses of language in learning occurs naturally. Synchronicity between these approaches will hasten decolonial futures in education.

Conclusion

At the start of this book, I drew attention to the current social movements calling for free, decolonised education in South Africa. The project of envisioning the character and substance of decolonised education is pressing and intertwined with a vision of decoloniality in society more broadly. As Christie and McKinney suggest, 'shifts in the language policies and practices of schooling are an essential starting point for a programme of delinking' from coloniality (Christie & McKinney, 2017: 18). As part of this delinking, let us embrace a vision of young people learning Science that is different from the status quo where non-dominant language students achieve at worst *parroting* and at best *acquisition* of academic discourse in the colonial language. We need a vision of *decolonial learning* – where students draw on their full semiotic repertoires to confidently make their voices heard in the borderlands and lend these to shape future knowledge creation. The decolonial cracks described in the Success High study offer some insights into how to realise this vision.

The work of widening decolonial cracks is complex and difficult, as Andreotti and Stein (2022) quoted above remind us. It is work that requires courage and stamina. Ultimately, it is also hopeful work. Onke, Khethiwe, Thandile and Mbulelo give me hope. And I join all those working for social justice through language in education who have hope for a better schooling experience for our children.

Appendix 1: A Multilingual Science Resources List

This list comprises examples of online and print resources for school-level Science content in indigenous South African languages or in African languages and English.

Science content in African languages online

1. SciBraai: https://scibraai.co.za
   This site includes local South African Science journalism. Some articles are in African languages, such as the isiZulu piece on the discovery of a new dinosaur species in South Africa in 2018: https://scibraai.co.za/ososayensi-bathole-isilwane-sasemandulo-esandisa-umlando-wohlu-lwezilwane/
2. Science Spaza: http://www.sciencespaza.org/
   This Science education site has worksheets, resources for Science clubs, Science-content HipHop songs, many of which are multilingual.
3. iSayensi Yethu: https://bua-lit.org.za/project/isayensi-yethu-grade-4-version-1/
   These are bilingual Science learning materials for the Grade 4 South African curriculum written in English and isiXhosa. They are free to download and distribute via CC-BY attribution.

Science content in African languages in books: fiction and non-fiction

1. Hawking, L. and Hawking, S. (2007) *George's Secret Key to the Universe*. London: Random House Children's Publishers.
   Translated as: Iqhosha eliyimfihlelo kaGeorge kuzungezo lwendalo (isiXhosa)/UJoji nemfihlakalo kakhiye wakhe wendalo yonke (isiZulu).
   This well-known children's book includes a mix of fiction and non-fiction to inspire older children about cosmology and astronomy.
2. Magona, S. and Jablonski, N. (2018) *The Skin We Are In*. Cape Town: David Philip Publishers.

Translated as: Isikhumba esikuso (isiXhosa, translation by Sindiwe Magona). Also translated into isiZulu, Afrikaans and Sepedi.
This mixed-genre children's picture book has text boxes with scientific information about genetics and anatomy.
3. Apps, P. (2008) *My First Book of Southern African Mammals*. Cape Town: Random House Struik.
This children's reference book has information about commonly found mammals in English, isiZulu, Afrikaans and isiXhosa. There are 12 multilingual books in the series including Birds, Insects and Snakes.
4. Trok, L. (2020) *The Forgotten Scientist: The Story of Saul Sithole*. Cape Town: Jacana Media.
The biography of Saul Sithole, a black South African scientist who was never recognised as a scientist, is available in isiXhosa, isiZulu, Sesotho, Sepedi, English and Afrikaans.

Science and Mathematics multilingual glossaries

1. Fricke, I., Hundermark, A., Williams, L. and Translation Team. (2015) *Understand Maths, Natural Science & Technology Grades 4-7 Using Your Language, English-isiXhosa*. Cape Town: Ithutha Books.
2. Fricke, I. and van Lingen, N. (2014) *Understand Science Grades 8-12 Using Your Language, English-isiXhosa*. Cape Town: Ithutha Books. These bilingual books are available in Sesotho sa Leboa (Sepedi), Setswana, isiZulu, Tshivenda, Sesotho and isiXhosa alongside English.
3. Deyi, S., Mzi, M. and Ngcoza, K. (2007) *Multilingual Science Dictionary for South African Schools*. Cape Town: Maskew Miller Longman.
4. Wababa, Z. (ed.) (2013) *Isichazi-magama semathematika nenzululwazi, ibanga 4-9: The Official English-isiXhosa Maths & Natural Science Dictionary*. Alice: IsiXhosa National Lexicography Unit and the University of Fort Hare.
5. Young, D., Van Der Vlugt, J. and Qanya, S. (2005) *Understanding Concepts in Mathematics and Science: A Multilingual Learning and Teaching Resource Book in English, isiXhosa, isiZulu and Afrikaans*. Cape Town: Maskew Miller Longman.
6. The Open Educational Resource Term Bank: http://oertb.tlterm.com/ This online glossary in all 11 official languages of South Africa allows searching for an academic term in any language and includes translations. It is suitable for secondary and tertiary levels.
7. Feza, N., Letsekha, T., Madolo, Y. and Meyiwa, T. (2021) *HSRC Illustrated English-isiXhosa Maths Dictionary Grade R-9*. Cape Town: Human Science Research Council Press.
This bilingual dictionary includes colour pictures of Mathematical terms with local examples.

Appendix 2: Grade 9 Chemical Reactions Tests and Worksheets: English, isiXhosa and Translingual

The first test in English was used by Ms B to assess the Success High students at the end of the topic. The second test in isiXhosa was translated by Babalwayashe Molate for research purposes in order to contrast Science language in English and isiXhosa. The third multilingual test was created by myself and Lara Krause as a thought experiment, and it informed the creation of the iSayensi Yethu materials referenced in Appendix 1.

Grade 9 Natural Sciences Test in English

Question 1

1.1 Write down a word/term that describes each of the following statements:
    1.1.1   The only metal that is a liquid at room temperature.
    1.1.2   A pure substance that is made up of only one type of atom that cannot be split up into simpler substances.
    1.1.3   The common name for ethanoic acid.
    1.1.4   The larger number in the block of an element in the Periodic Table.
    1.1.5   The scientific name for water.   5×1=5
1.2 Write down question numbers 1.2.1 to 1.2.6 in your answer sheet, and next to each, write down the appropriate information for that position in the table below.

Name of element	Number of electrons	Number of protons	Number of neutrons	$_{z}^{A}X$
Potassium	19	1.2.1	1.2.2	$^{39}_{19}K$
Oxygen	1.2.3	8	8	1.2.4
1.2.5	17	17	19	1.2.6

1.3 Write the chemical formulae for the following compounds:
    1.3.1 Aluminium Oxide
    1.3.2 Copper Nitrate
    1.3.3 Potassium Sulphate   2×3=6

Question 2

Helium is an unreactive gas used to fill up balloons and to power air ships.
2.1.1   Draw the atomic (Bohr) diagram showing the electron structure of an atom of Helium.
                                                                                        (4)
2.1.2   By referring to your diagram, explain why Helium is unreactive.
                                                                                       (2)
2.1.3   Neon is also an unreactive gas. How is the arrangement of electrons in Neon:
       a) similar to the arrangement in Helium? And   (1)
       b) different from the arrangement in Helium?   (1)
                                                                                           [8]

Question 3

Key: o-Lithium   •-Sulphur   ▲-Oxygen   ◊-Hydrogen

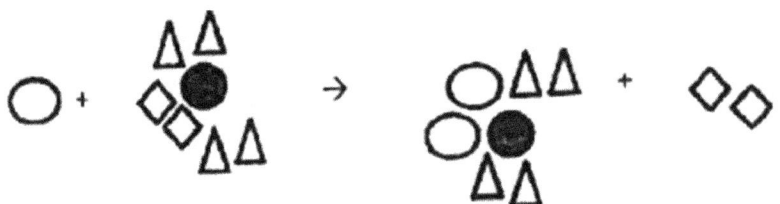

3.1. The drawings above represent a chemical reaction and each shape represents an atom.
For the chemical reaction above, write down:
    3.1.1   A word equation for the reaction.   (2)
    3.1.2   A chemical equation for the reaction.   (3)

END OF TEST

TOTAL MARKS: 35

Grade 9 Natural Science test in isiXhosa

IBANGA LE - 9

EZENZULULWAZI ZOMHLABA

IKOTA YESI – 2: UVAVANYO LWAPHAKATHI KWEKOTA

UMBUZO 1

1.4 Bhala phantsi igama elichaza enye yezinkcazelo zilandelayo:
   1.4.1 Intsimbi ekukuphela kwayo ebangamanzi kwiqondo lobushushu legumbi.
   1.4.2 Into esulungekileyo eyenziwe ngohlobo olunye lwe-athom engenokwazi ukuzahlula ibengamaqhekezana alula.
   1.4.3 Igama eliqhelekileyo ebizwa ngayo i-ethanoic acid.
   1.4.4 Elona nani likhulu kwibhokisi yesiqalelo esikuludwe lwexesha
   1.4.5 Igama amanzi abizwa ngalo kwezenzululwazi   5×1=5

1.5 Bhala phantsi la manani:1.2.1 ukuya ku 1.2.6 kwiphepha lakho leempendulo uze ecaleni kwawo, ubhale inkcazelo efanelekileyo njengoko kubhaliwe kule tafile ingezantsi.

Igama lesiqalelo	Ubuninzi bee-elektroni	Ubuninzi beeprotoni	Ubuninzi beenutroni	$_z^AX$
Potassium	19	1.2.1	1.2.2	$^{39}_{19}K$
Oxygen	1.2.3	8	8	1.2.4
1.2.5	17	17	19	1.2.6

                                                                                                               6×1=6

1.6 Bhala ifomyula yemichiza yezi mbumba zilandelayo:
   1.3.1 I- Aluminium Oxide
   1.3.2 I-Copper Nitrate
   1.3.3 I-Potassium Sulphate   2×3=6

UMBUZO 2

I-Helium yigesi emo ingaguqukiyo esetyenziswa ekugcwaliseni iibhaluni ngomoya nasekupheni inqanawa ngamandla okuduma.

2.1.1 Zoba umfanekiso we-athom iBohr ebonakalisa ubume be-elektroni be-athom ye-Helium.   (4)
2.1.2 Ngokubhekisela kumfanekiso, cacisa unobangela wokuba i-Helium ingaguquki   (2)
2.1.3 I-Neon yigesi engaguqukiyo nayo. Zibekwe njani ii-elektroni kwi-Neon:
      a) ngokufanayo nohlobo ezibekwe ngayo kwi-Helium? Kwaye
                                                                                                        (1)
      b) zahlukile kwindlela ezibekwe ngayo kwi-Helium?
                                                                                                           (1)
                                                                                                              [8]

UMBUZO 3

Key: ○-Lithium ●-Sulphur ▲-Oxygen ◊-Hydrogen

3.1. Le mizobo ingentla imele intshukumo yemichiza kwaye umilo ngalunye lumele i-athom.
Ngale ntshukumo yemichiza ingentla, bhala:
3.1.1 Igama lolinganiso lwale ntshukumo (2)
3.1.2 Ulinganiso-michiza lwale ntshukumo (3)
[5]

ISIPHELO SOVAVANYO

AMANQAKU APHELELEYO: 35

Translingual (with isiXhosa and English) Grade 9 Chemical Reactions worksheet

iWorksheet yeChemical Reactions
Ibanga le-9

Namkelekile kwi-worksheet yenu. Khethani iilwimi zenu freely xa niya-phendula. Ninga-mixa!

Question 1.

1.1 Bhala phantsi i-term echaza enye yee-statements ezilandelayo:
    1.1.1   The only metal eyi-liquid kwi-room temperature.
    1.1.2   I-substance e-pure eyenziwe ngohlobo olunye lwe-athomi engenokwazi ukusplita into simpler substances/into iisubstances ezilula kunayo.
    1.1.3   Igama eliqhelekileyo for i-ethanoic acid.
    1.1.4   The larger number kwi-box ye-element kwi-Periodic Table.
    1.1.5   Igama amanzi abizwa ngalo kwi-Science.

Question 2

    2.1.1   Draw the atomic (Bohr) diagram showing the electron structure of an atom of Helium.
    2.1.2   By referring to your diagram, explain why Helium is unreactive.
    2.1.3   iNeon yigesi e-ngareactivekanga (unreactive gas) nayo. Injani i-arrangement ye-electrons kwi-Neon (zibekwe njani ii-electrons?):
        a) ngokufanayo ne-arrangement yazo kwi-Helium? Kwaye
        b) ngendlela ehlukene ne-arrangement yazo kwi-Helium?

Question 3

Translate the following definition into standard English.
i-Molecule yeyona part encinci kuyo yonke into esingongqileyo enokwazi ukuzimela yodwa and ngeyi-one or more ntlobo ze athomi. One molecule yametsi is H2O kwaye kuzosoloko kukho ihydrogen ezimbini in nature.

Question 4

Jonga kwi-Periodic Table yenu. Write about how the elements are arranged. Make two points.

Appendix 3: Transcription Convention

Symbol	Meaning
…	A pause, each dot indicating a second
(indistinct)	The speech was indistinct and so is not transcribed
/	Speech has been omitted, next relevant clause continues after the /
L	Student
L1	Specific student
Ls	More than one student speaking simultaneously
T	Teacher
I	Interviewer
(1)	Number given to a speaking turn in a long extract
//	Overlapping speech
superscript	Rising intonation
subscript	Falling intonation
<u>Underlined</u>	Syllable emphasised
<fast> </fast>	Faster than normal speech begins and ends
:	Follows a lengthened sound
bold	Significantly higher volume speech than surrounding speech
italics	Significantly lower volume speech than surrounding speech

References

Adendorff, R. (1993) Codeswitching amongst Zulu-speaking teachers and their pupils: Its functions and implications for teacher education. *Language and Education* 7 (3), 141–162.
Agha, A. (2006) *Language and Social Relations*. Cambridge: Cambridge University Press.
Alexander, N. (1989) *Language Policy and National Unity in South Africa/Azania*. Cape Town: Buchu Books.
Alexander, N. (2000) *English Unassailable but Unattainable: The Dilemma of Language Policy in South African Education* (PRAESA: Occasional Papers No. 3). Cape Town: PRAESA.
Alexander, N. (2001) Majority and minority languages in South Africa. In G. Extra and D. Gorter (eds) *The Other Languages of Europe: Demographic, Sociolinguistic and Educational Perspectives* (pp. 355–370). Clevedon: Multilingual Matters.
Alexander, N. (2009) Mother tongue based bilingual education in Africa: A cultural and intellectual imperative. In I. Gogolin and U. Neumann (eds) *Streitfall Zweisprachigkeit – The Bilingualism Controversy* (pp. 199–214). Wiesbaden: VS Verlag für Sozialwissenschaften.
Alvermann, D.E. (2004) Multiliteracies and self-questioning in the service of science learning. In E.W. Saul (ed.) *Crossing Borders in Literacy and Science Instruction: Perspectives on Theory and Practice* (pp. 226–238). Newark, DE: International Reading Association.
Andreotti, V. and Stein, S. (2022) Education for depth: An invitation to engage with the complexities and challenges of decolonial work. In C. McKinney and P. Christie (eds) *Decoloniality, Language and Literacy: Conversations with Teacher Educators* (pp. 207–214). Bristol: Multilingual Matters.
Antia, B. (2017) Shh, hushed multilingualism! Accounting for the discreet genre of translanguaged siding in lecture halls at a South African university. *International Journal of the Sociology of Language* 2017 (243), 183–198.
Antia, B.E. and Dyers, C. (2019) De-alienating the academy: Multilingual teaching as decolonial pedagogy. *Linguistics and Education* 51, 91–100.
Anzaldúa, G. (1987) *Borderlands/La frontera: The New Mestiza*. San Francisco: Aunt Lute Books.
Anzaldúa, G. (2015) *Light in the Dark, Luz en lo Oscuro: Rewriting Identity, Spirituality, Reality* (ed. A. Keating). Durham, NC: Duke University Press.
Archer, A. (2014) Designing multimodal classrooms for social justice. *Classroom Discourse* 5 (1), 106–116.
Baker, C. (2011) *Foundations of Bilingual Education and Bilingualism (5th edn)*. Bristol: Multilingual Matters.
Bakhtin, M.M. (1981) Discourse in the novel. In M. Holquist (ed.) *The Dialogic Imagination: Four Essays* (pp. 259–422). Austin, TX: University of Texas Press.
Ballenger, C. (1997) Social identities, moral narratives, scientific argumentation: Science talk in a bilingual classroom. *Language and Education* 11 (1), 1–14.
Bamgbose, A. (2000) *Language and Exclusion: The Consequences of Language Policies in Africa*. Münster: LIT Verlag.

Banda, F. (2010) Defying monolingual education: Alternative bilingual discourse practices in selected coloured schools in Cape Town. *Journal of Multilingual and Multicultural Development* 31 (3), 221–235.

Barnes, D. (1992) The role of talk in learning. In K. Norman (ed.) *Thinking Voices: The Work of the National Oracy Project* (pp. 123–128). London: Hodder and Stoughton.

Baynham, M. and Tong King Lee. (2019) *Translation and Translanguaging*. New York: Routledge.

Bester, M., Bezuidenhout, M., Clacherty, A., Cohen, S., Doubell, S., Erasmus, J., Joannides, A., Lombard, G., Nkosi, E., Paarman, S., Padayachee, K., Sadie, R. and Schreuder, L. (2013) *Platinum Natural Sciences: Student's Book 9*. Cape Town: Maskew Miller Longman.

Bhabha, H. (1990) The Third Space (Interview with Homi Bhabha). In J. Rutherford (ed.) *Identity: Community, Culture, Difference* (pp. 207–221). London: Lawrence & Wishart.

Bhatt, R.M. and Bolonyai, A. (2019) On the theoretical and empirical bases of translanguaging. *Working Papers in Urban Language & Literacies* 254, 1–22.

Blackledge, A. and Creese, A. (2017) Translanguaging and the body. *International Journal of Multilingualism* 14 (3), 250–268.

Blackledge, A. and Creese, A. (2019) *Voices of a City Market: An Ethnography*. Bristol: Multilingual Matters.

Blommaert, J. (2010) *The Sociolinguistics of Globalization*. Cambridge: Cambridge University Press.

Blommaert, J. (2017) Ludic membership and orthopractic mobilization: on slacktivism and all that. Tilburg Papers in Culture Studies Paper 193. See https://www.tilburguniversity.edu/upload/6cfbdfee-2f05-40c6-9617-d6930a811edf_TPCS_193_Blommaert.pdf

Blommaert, J. and Dong, J. (2010) *Ethnographic Fieldwork* (1st edn). Bristol: Multilingual Matters.

Blommaert, J. and Backus, A. (2011) Repertoires revisited: "Knowing language" in superdiversity. Working papers in Urban Language and Literacies WP67. See https://www.academia.edu/6365319/WP67_Blommaert_and_Backus_2011._Repertoires_revisited_Knowing_language_in_superdiversity

Blommaert, J. and De Fina, A. (2016) Chronotopic identities: On the timespace organization of who we are. Tilburg Papers in Culture Studies Paper 153. See https://www.tilburguniversity.edu/upload/ba249987-6ece-44d2-b96b-3fc329713d59_TPCS_153_Blommaert-DeFina.pdf

Bock, Z. and Stroud, C. (eds) (2021) *Language and Decoloniality in Higher Education: Reclaiming Voices from the South*. London: Bloomsbury.

Botha, L. (2012) Discourses of language acquisition and identity in the life histories of four white South African men, fluent in isiXhosa. Unpublished doctoral dissertation, University of the Western Cape, Cape Town.

Brown, B.A. (2006) "It isn't no slang that can be said about this stuff": Language, identity, and appropriating science discourse. *Journal of Research in Science Teaching* 43 (1), 96–126.

bua-lit collective (2018) How are we failing our children? Reconceptualising language and literacy education. See https://bua-lit.org.za/wp-content/uploads/2019/02/bua-lit-FINAL051218-2.pdf

Bucholtz, M. (2000) The politics of transcription. *Journal of Pragmatics* 32 (10), 1439–1465.

Canagarajah, S. (2011) Codemeshing in academic writing: Identifying teachable strategies of translanguaging. *Modern Language Journal* 95 (3), 401–417.

Canagarajah, S. (2021) Materialising semiotic repertoires: Challenges in the interactional analysis of multilingual communication. *International Journal of Multilingualism* 18 (2), 206–225.

Carlone, H.B., Johnson, A. and Scott, C.M. (2015) Agency amidst formidable structures: How girls perform gender in science class. *Journal of Research in Science Teaching* 52 (4), 474–488.

Cenoz, J. and Gorter, D. (2017) Minority languages and sustainable translanguaging: Threat or opportunity? *Journal of Multilingual and Multicultural Development* 38 (10), 901–912.

Cenoz, J. and Gorter, D. (2021) *Pedagogical Translanguaging*. Cambridge: Cambridge University Press.

Charamba, E. (2021) Exploring the efficacy of bilingual assessments in Science and Technology education: A case of a rural primary school. *Journal of African Films & Diaspora Studies* 4 (1), 15–34.

Charamba, E. and Zano, K. (2019) Effects of translanguaging as an intervention strategy in a South African Chemistry classroom. *Bilingual Research Journal* 42 (3), 291–307.

Chick, J.K. (1996) Safe-talk: Collusion in apartheid education. In H. Coleman (ed.) *Society and the Language Classroom* (pp. 21–39). Cambridge: Cambridge University Press.

Chimbutane, F. (2013) Codeswitching in L1 and L2 learning contexts: Insights from a study of teacher beliefs and practices in Mozambican bilingual education programmes. *Language and Education* 27 (4), 314–328.

Christie, P. (2020) *Decolonising Schools in South Africa: The Impossible Dream?* Abingdon: Routledge.

Christie, P. (2021) Colonial palimpsests in schooling: Tracing continuity and change in South Africa. *Postcolonial Directions in Education* 10 (1), 51–79.

Christie, P. and McKinney, C. (2017) Decoloniality and 'Model C' schools: Ethos, language and the protests of 2016. *Education as Change* 21 (3), 160–180.

Cleghorn, A. and Rollnick, M. (2002) The role of English in individual and societal development: A view from African Classrooms. *TESOL Quarterly* 36 (3), 347–372.

Copland, F. and Creese, A. (2015) *Linguistic Ethnography: Collecting, Analysing and Presenting Data*. London: Sage.

Cummins, J. (2008) Teaching for transfer: Challenging the two solitudes assumption in bilingual education. In N. Hornberger (ed.) *Encyclopedia of Language and Education* (pp. 65–75). New York: Springer.

Davies, B. and Harré, R. (1990) Positioning: The discursive production of selves. *Journal for the Theory of Social Behaviour* 20 (1), 43–63.

de Sousa Santos, B. (2012) Public sphere and epistemologies of the South. *Africa Development* 37 (1), 43–67.

Department of Education (1997) Language in education policy. See https://www.education.gov.za/Portals/0/Documents/Policies/GET/LanguageEducationPolicy1997.pdf?ver=2007-08-22-083918-000

Department of Basic Education (2011) Foundation phase curriculum and assessment policy statement: English additional language. See https://www.education.gov.za/Portals/0/CD/National%20Curriculum%20Statements%20and%20Vocational/CAPS%20ENGLISH%20FAL%20GR%201-3%20FS.pdf?ver=2015-01-27-155321-957

Despagne, C. (2020) *Decolonizing Language Learning, Decolonizing Research: A Critical Ethnography Study in a Mexican University*. New York: Routledge.

Dörnyei, Z. (2007) *Research Methods in Applied Linguistics*. Oxford: Oxford University Press.

Dowling, T., McCormick, K. and Dyers, C. (2019) Language contact in Cape Town. In R. Hickey (ed.) *English in Multilingual South Africa: The Linguistics of Contact and Change* (pp. 129–150). Cambridge: Cambridge University Press.

Fanon, F. (1961/1990) *The Wretched of the Earth*. London: Penguin Books.

Flores, N. and Rosa, J. (2015) Undoing appropriateness: Raciolinguistic ideologies and language diversity in education. *Harvard Educational Review* 85 (2), 149–171.

Freire, P. (1996) *Pedagogy of the Oppressed*. New York: Continuum.
García, O. (2009) Emergent bilinguals and TESOL: What's in a name? *Tesol Quarterly* 43 (2), 322–326.
García, O. and Li, W. (2014) *Translanguaging: Language, Bilingualism and Education*. Basingstoke: Palgrave Macmillan.
García, O., Johnson, S.I., Seltzer, K. and Valdés, G. (2017) *The Translanguaging Classroom: Leveraging Student Bilingualism for Learning*. Philadelphia, PA: Caslon.
García, O., Flores, N., Seltzer, K., Wei, L., Otheguy, R. and Rosa, J. (2021) Rejecting abyssal thinking in the language and education of racialized bilinguals: A manifesto. *Critical Inquiry in Language Studies* 18 (3), 203–228.
Gebhard, M., Chen, I. and Britton, L. (2014) 'Miss, nominalization is a nominalization:' English language students' use of SFL metalanguage and their literacy practices. *Linguistics and Education* 26, 106–125.
Gee, J.P. (2002) Literacies, identities, and discourses. In M. Schleppegrell and M. Colombi (eds) *Developing Advanced Literacy in First and Second Languages: Meaning with Power* (pp. 159–175). New York: Lawrence Erlbaum.
Gee, J.P. (2004) Language in the Science classroom: Academic social languages as the heart of school-based literacy. In E.W. Saul (ed.) *Crossing Borders in Literacy and Science Instruction: Perspectives on Theory and Practice* (pp. 13–32). Newark: International Reading Association.
Gee, J.P. (2008) *Social Linguistics and Literacies* (3rd edn). London: Routledge.
Genishi, C. and Dyson, A. (2009) *Children, Language and Literacy: Diverse Students in Diverse Times*. New York: Teachers College Press.
Gibbons, P. (2006) *Bridging Discourses in the ESL Classroom*. London: Continuum.
Goffman, E. (1975) Role distance. In D. Brissett and C. Edgley (eds) *Life as Theatre* (pp. 123–133). New York: Aldine de Gruyter.
Goffman, E. (1981) *Forms of Talk*. Philadelphia, PA: University of Pennsylvania Press.
Gononda. (2013) Xhosa live dictionary. See http://www.gononda.com/xhosa/
Grosfoguel, R. (2007) The epistemic decolonial turn: Beyond political-economy paradigms. *Cultural Studies* 21 (2–3), 211–223.
Gumperz, J.J. and Hymes, D. (eds) (1972) *Directions in Sociolinguistics: The Ethnography of Communication*. New York: Holt, Rinehart & Winston.
Gutierrez, K., Rymes, B. and Larson, J. (1995) Script, counterscript and underlife in the classroom: James Brown versus Brown v. Board of Education. *Harvard Educational Review* 65 (3), 445–471.
Guzula, X. (2022) De/coloniality in South African language in education policy: Resisting the marginalisation of African language speaking children. In P. Christie and C. McKinney (eds) *Decoloniality, Language and Literacy: Conversations with Teacher Educators* (pp. 23–45). Bristol: Multilingual Matters.
Guzula, X., McKinney, C. and Tyler, R. (2016) Languaging-for-learning: Legitimising translanguaging and enabling multimodal practices in third spaces. *Southern African Linguistics and Applied Language Studies* 34 (3), 211–226.
Halliday, M.A.K. (1978) *Language as Social Semiotic*. London: Arnold.
Halliday, M.A.K. and Martin, J.R. (1993) *Writing Science: Literacy and Discursive Power*. London: The Falmer Press.
Hammersley, M. and Atkinson, P. (1995) *Ethnography: Principles in Practice* (2nd edn). New York: Routledge.
Harré, R. (1991) *Physical Being: A Theory for a Corporeal Psychology*. Oxford: Wiley Blackwell.
Hattingh, A. (2022) Learning Science from uma Gogo: The value of teaching practice in semi-rural school contexts. In P. Christie and C. McKinney (eds) *Decoloniality, Language and Literacy: Conversations with Teacher Educators* (pp. 98–116). Bristol: Multilingual Matters.

Hattingh, A., McKinney, C., Msimanga, A., Probyn, M. and Tyler, R. (2021) Translanguaging in science education in South African classrooms: Challenging constraining ideologies for science teacher education. In A. Jakobsson, P. Nygard Larsson and A. Karlsson (eds) *Translanguaging in Science Education* (pp. 231–256). Berlin: Springer.

Hanrahan, M. (2006) Highlighting hybridity: A critical discourse analysis of teacher talk in science classrooms. *Science Education* 90 (1), 8–43.

He, P., Lai, H. and Lin, A. (2017) Translanguaging in a Multimodal Mathematics presentation. In C.M. Mazak and K.S. Carroll (eds) *Translanguaging in Higher Education: Beyond Monolingual Ideologies* (pp. 91–120). Bristol: Multilingual Matters.

Heugh, K. (2002) The case against bilingual and multilingual education in South Africa: Laying bare the myths. *Perspectives in Education* 20 (1), 171–196.

Heugh, K., Prinsloo, C., Makgamatha, M., Diedericks, G. and Winnaar, L. (2017) Multilingualism (s) and system-wide assessment: A southern perspective. *Language and Education* 31 (3), 197–216.

hooks, b. (1994) *Teaching to Transgress*. New York: Routledge.

Hornberger, N.H. and Link, H. (2012) Translanguaging and transnational literacies in multilingual classrooms: A biliteracy lens. *International Journal of Bilingual Education and Bilingualism* 15 (3), 261–278.

Janks, H. (2010) *Literacy and Power*. New York: Routledge.

Jaspers, J. (2017) The transformative limits of translanguaging. *Language and Communication* 58, 1–10.

Jørgensen, J.N., Karrebæk, M.S., Madsen, L.M. and Møller, J.S. (2011) Polylanguaging in superdiversity. *Diversities* 13 (2), 22–37.

Kapp, R. (2004) 'Reading on the line': An analysis of literacy practices in ESL classes in a South African township school. *Language and Education* 18 (3), 246–263.

Kell, C. (2006) *Moment by moment: Contexts and crossings in the study of literacy in social practice*. Open University. EThos: e-theses online service (uk.bl.ethos. 434278).

Kell, C. (2010) Ethnographic studies and adult literacy policy in South Africa. In C. Coffin, T. Lillis and K. O'Halloran (eds) *Applied Linguistics Methods: A Reader* (pp. 216–233). New York: Routledge.

Krause, L.S. (2022) *Relanguaging Language from a South African Township School*. Bristol: Multilingual Matters.

Kress, G., Jewitt, C., Ogborn, J. and Tsatsarelis, C. (2014) *Multimodal Teaching and Learning: The Rhetorics of the Science Classroom* (2nd edn). London: Continuum.

Kubota, R. (2022) Critical antiracist pedagogy in ELT. *ELT Journal* 75 (3), 237–246.

Kusters, A., Spotti, M., Swanwick, R. and Tapio, E. (2017) Beyond languages, beyond modalities: Transforming the study of semiotic repertoires. *International Journal of Multilingualism* 14 (3), 219–232.

Kyratzis, A. and Johnson, S. (2017) Multimodal and multilingual resources in children's framing of situated learning activities: An introduction. *Linguistics and Education* 41 (2017), 1–6.

Lemke, J. (1990) *Talking Science: Language, Learning and Values*. Norwood, NJ: Ablex Publishing Corporation.

Lemke, J. (2004) The literacies of Science. In E.W. Saul (ed.) *Crossing Borders in Literacy and Science Instruction: Perspectives on Theory and Practice* (pp. 33–47). Newark: International Reading Association.

Li, W. (2017) Translanguaging as a practical theory of language. *Applied Linguistics* 39 (2), 1–23. https://doi.org/10.1093/applin/amx044.

Li, W. (2011) Moment analysis and translanguaging space: Discursive construction of identities by multilingual Chinese youth in Britain. *Journal of Pragmatics* 43 (5), 1222–1235.

Lin, A.M.Y. (2007) What's the use of 'triadic dialogue'? Activity theory, conversation analysis, and analysis of pedagogical practices. *Pedagogies: An International Journal* 2 (2), 77–94.

Lin, A.M.Y (2008) *Problematizing Identity: Everyday Struggles in Language, Culture and Education*. New York: Lawrence Erlbaum.

Lin, A.M.Y. (2015) Egalitarian bi/multilingualism and trans-semiotizing in a global world. In W.E. Wright, S. Boun and O. García (eds) *Handbook of Bilingual and Multilingual Education* (pp. 19–37). Hoboken, N J: Wiley-Blackwell.

Lin, A.M.Y. (2016) *Language Across the Curriculum and CLIL in English as an Additional Language Contexts: Theory and Practice*. New York: Springer.

Lin, A.M.Y. (2019) Theories of trans/languaging and trans-semiotizing: Implications for content-based education classrooms. *International Journal of Bilingual Education and Bilingualism* 22 (1), 5–16.

Lin, A.M.Y. and Wu, Y. (2014) 'May I speak Cantonese?' – Co-constructing a scientific proof in an EFL junior secondary science classroom. *International Journal of Bilingual Education and Bilingualism* 18 (3), 289–305.

Lin, A.M.Y., Wu, Y. and Lemke, J.L. (2020) 'It takes a village to research a village': Conversations between Angel Lin and Jay Lemke on contemporary issues in translanguaging. In S.M.C. Lau and S. Van Viegen (eds) *Critical Plurilingual Pedagogies: Struggling Toward Equity Rather than Equality* (pp. 47–74). New York: Springer.

Lo Bianco, J. (1996) *Language as an Economic Resource*. Pretoria: CTP Book Printers.

Macdonald, C. (1990) *Crossing the Threshold into Standard Three in Black Education: The Consolidated Main Report of the Threshold Project*. Pretoria: Human Sciences Research Council.

Machin, D. and Mayr, A. (2012) *How to Do Critical Discourse Analysis: A Multimodal Introduction*. Thousand Oaks: Sage.

Makalela, L. (2014) Fluid identity construction in language contact zones: Metacognitive reflections on Kasi-taal languaging practices. *International Journal of Bilingual Education and Bilingualism* 2014, 1–15.

Makalela, L. (2015) Translanguaging as a vehicle for epistemic access: Cases for reading comprehension and multilingual interactions. *Per Linguam* 31 (1), 15–29.

Makalela, L. (2016) Ubuntu translanguaging: An alternative framework for complex multilingual encounters. *Southern African Linguistics and Applied Language Studies* 34 (3), 187–196.

Makalela, L. (2018) Community elders' narrative accounts of ubuntu translanguaging: Learning and teaching in African education. *International Review of Education* 64 (6), 823–843.

Makoe, P. and McKinney, C. (2009) Hybrid discursive practices in a South African multilingual primary classroom: A case study. *English Teaching* 8 (2), 80–95.

Makoe, P. and McKinney, C. (2014) Linguistic ideologies in multilingual South African suburban schools. *Journal of Multilingual and Multicultural Development* 35 (7), 658–673.

Makoni, S. and Pennycook, A. (2005) Disinventing and (re)constituting languages. *Critical Inquiry in Language Studies: An International Journal* 2 (3), 137–156.

Makoni, S., Makoni, B. and Rosenberg, A. (2010) The wordy worlds of popular music in eastern and southern Africa: Possible implications for language-in-education policy. *Journal of Language, Identity and Education* 9 (1), 1–16.

Maldonado-Torres, N. (2007) On the coloniality of being: Contributions to the development of a concept. *Cultural Studies* 21 (2–3), 240.

Malherbe, E.G. (1946) *The Bilingual School: A Study of Bilingualism in South Africa*. Johannesburg: Central News Agency.

Masola, A. (2020) Journeying home, exile and transnationalism in Noni Jabavu and Sisonke Msimang's memoires. Unpublished thesis, Rhodes University.

Maturana, H.R. (1990) *Emociones y lenguaje en educación y política*. Santiago de Chile: Centro de Estudios de Desarrollo.

May, S. (2014) *The Multilingual Turn: Implications for SLA, TESOL and Bilingual Education* (2nd edn). New York: Routledge.

Mayaba, N., Otterup, T. and Webb, P. (2013) Writing in science classrooms: A case study in South African and Swedish second-language classrooms. *African Journal of Research in Mathematics, Science and Technology Education* 17 (1–2), 74–82.

Mbude, N. (2019) IsiXhosa as the language of teaching and learning Mathematics in Grade Six: Investigating the mother tongue based bilingual education Mathematics pilot in the Eastern Cape Province, South Africa. Unpublished doctoral thesis, Rhodes University.

McKinney, C. (2007) 'If I speak English, does it make me less black anyway?' 'Race' and English in South African desegregated schools. *English Academy Review* 24 (2), 6–24.

McKinney, C. (2010) Schooling in black and white: Assimilationist discourses and subversive identity performances in a desegregated South African girls' school. *Race Ethnicity and Education* 13 (2), 191–207.

McKinney, C. (2017) *Language and Power in Post-colonial Schooling: Ideologies in Practice*. New York: Routledge.

McKinney, C. (2020) Decoloniality and language in education: Transgressing language boundaries in South Africa. In J.A Windle, D. de Jesus and L. Bartlett (eds) *The Dynamics of Language and Inequality in Education: Social and Symbolic Boundaries in the Global South* (pp. 115–132). Bristol: Multilingual Matters.

McKinney, C. (2022) Delinking from coloniality and increasing participation in early literacy teacher education. In C. McKinney and P. Christie (eds) *Decoloniality, Language and Literacy: Conversations with Teacher Educators* (pp. 155–172). Bristol: Multilingual Matters.

McKinney, C. and Norton, B. (2008) Identity in language and literacy education. In B. Spolsky and F.M. Hult (eds) *The Handbook of Educational Linguistics* (pp. 192–205). Oxford: Blackwell Publishing.

McKinney, C. and Tyler, R. (2018) Disinventing and reconstituting language for learning in school Science. *Language and Education* 33 (2), 141–158.

McKinney, C. and Christie, P. (eds) (2022) *Decoloniality, Language and Literacy: Conversations with Teacher Educators*. Bristol: Multilingual Matters.

McKinney, C., Carrim, H., Marshall, A. and Layton, L. (2015) What counts as language in South African schooling? Monoglossic ideologies and children's participation. *AILA Review* 28, 103–126.

Menezes de Souza, L.M.T. (2019) Glocal languages, coloniality and globalization from below. In M. Guilherme and L.M. Menezes de Souza (eds) *Glocal Languages and Critical Intercultural Awareness: The South Answers Back* (pp. 17–41). New York: Routledge.

Menezes de Souza, L.M.T. (2021) Foreword. In Z. Bock and C. Stroud (eds) *Language and Decoloniality in Higher Education: Reclaiming Voices from the South* (pp. 6–19). London: Bloomsbury.

Mercer, N. (1995) *The Guided Construction of Knowledge: Talk Amongst Teachers and Students*. Clevedon: Multilingual Matters.

Merriam, S.B. (1991) *Case Study Research in Education*. Oxford: Jossey-Bass Publishers.

Mesthrie, R. (2010) Sociophonetics and social change: Deracialisation of the GOOSE vowel in South African English. *Journal of Sociolinguistics* 14 (1), 3–33.

Mignolo, W. (2000) *Local Histories/Global Designs: Coloniality, Subaltern Knowledges and Border Thinking*. Princeton, NJ: Princeton University Press.

Mignolo, W. (2009) Epistemic disobedience, independent thought and de-colonial freedom. *Theory, Culture and Society* 26 (7–6), 1–23.

Mignolo, W. (2011) *The Darker Side of Western Modernity: Global Futures, Decolonial Options*. Durham, NC: Duke University Press.

Mignolo, W.D. and Walsh, C.E. (2018) *On Decoloniality*. Durham, NC: Duke University Press.

Milligan, L.O., Clegg, J. and Tikly, L. (2016) Exploring the potential for language supportive learning in English medium instruction: A Rwandan case study. *Comparative Education* 52 (3), 328–342.

Mjoli, N. (2015) How I envision a decolonised UCT to be like. In M. Jones and L. Naidoo (eds) *The Johannesburg Salon* (Vol 9). Johannesburg: The Johannesburg Workshop in Theory and Criticism.

Mohanty, A.K. (2019) *The Multilingual Reality: Living with Languages*. Bristol: Multilingual Matters.

Molate, B. and Tyler, R. (2020) The status of African languages in previously white schools. *Daily Maverick*, 19 February. See https://www.dailymaverick.co.za/article/2020-02-19-the-status-of-african-languages-in-previously-white-schools/

Mortimer, E.F. and Scott, P.H. (2003) *Meaning Making in Secondary Science Classrooms*. Maidenhead: Open University Press.

Msimanga, A. and Lelliott, A. (2014) Talking Science in multilingual contexts in South Africa: Possibilities and challenges for engagement in students' home languages in high school classrooms. *International Journal of Science Education* 36 (7), 1159–1183.

Myers-Scotton C. (1993) *Duelling Languages: Grammatical Structure in Code-switching*. Oxford: Clarendon.

Nabe, H., Dreyer, P. and Kakana, G. (1976) *Xhosa Dictionary* (2nd edn). Johannesburg: Educum Publishers.

Ndhlovu, F. and Makalela, L. (2021) *Decolonising Multilingualism in Africa: Recentering Silenced Voices from the Global South*. Bristol: Multilingual Matters.

Ndlovu-Gatsheni, S.J. (2015) Decoloniality as the Future of Africa. *History Compass* 13 (10), 485–496.

Ngcoza, K.M. (2019) Education for sustainable development at the problem-posing nexus of re-appropriated heritage practices and the science curriculum. *Southern African Journal of Environmental Education* 35, 1–10.

Ngũgĩ wa Thiong'o (1986) *Decolonising the Mind: The Politics of Language in African Literature*. London: James Currey.

Ngũgĩ wa Thiong'o (2018) The politics of translation: Notes towards an African language policy. *Journal of African Cultural Studies* 30 (2), 124–132.

Nomlomo, V.S. (2007) Science teaching and learning through the medium of English and IsiXhosa: A comparative study in two primary schools in the Western Cape. Unpublished doctoral dissertation, University of the Western Cape, Cape Town.

Nomlomo, V.S. (2010) Classroom interaction: Turn-taking as a pedagogical strategy. *Per Linguam* 26 (2), 50–66.

Norton, B. (2013) *Identity and Language Learning: Extending the Conversation* (2nd edn). Bristol: Multilingual Matters.

Ochs, E. (1979) Transcription as theory. In E. Ochs and B. Schieffelin (eds) *Developmental Pragmatics* (pp. 43–73). New York: Academic Press.

Otheguy, R., García, O. and Reid, W. (2015) Clarifying translanguaging and deconstructing named languages: A perspective from linguistics. *Applied Linguistics Review* 6 (3), 281–307.

Paris, D. and Alim, H.S. (2014) What are we seeking to sustain through culturally sustaining pedagogy? A loving critique forward. *Harvard Educational Review* 84 (1), 85–100.

Paxton, M. and Tyam, N. (2010) Xhosalising English? Negotiating meaning and identity in Economics. *Southern African Linguistics and Applied Language Studies* 28 (3), 247–257.

Pennycook, A. and Makoni, S. (2020) *Innovations and Challenges in Applied Linguistics from the Global South*. New York: Routledge.

Phillipson, R. (2009) English in globalisation, a lingua franca or a lingua Frankensteinia? *TESOL Quarterly* 43 (2), 335–339.

Phipps, A. (2019) *Decolonising Multilingualism: Struggles to Decreate*. Bristol: Multilingual Matters.
Prah, K.K. (2017) The intellectualisation of African languages for higher education. *Alternation* 24 (2), 215–225.
Pratt, M.L. (2019) Decolonization. *Language, Culture and Society* 1 (1), 120–125.
Probyn, M. (2001) Teachers' voices: Teacher reflections on learning and teaching through the medium of English as an additional language in South Africa. *International Journal of Bilingual Education and Bilingualism* 4 (4), 249–266.
Probyn, M. (2006) Language and learning Science in South Africa. *Language and Education* 20 (5), 391–414.
Probyn, M. (2009) 'Smuggling the vernacular into the classroom': Conflicts and tensions in classroom codeswitching in township/rural schools in South Africa. *International Journal of Bilingual Education and Bilingualism* 12 (2), 123–136.
Probyn, M. (2015) Pedagogical translanguaging: Bridging discourses in South African science classrooms. *Language and Education* 29 (3), 218–234.
Probyn, M. (2019) Pedagogical translanguaging and the construction of science knowledge in a multilingual South African classroom: Challenging monoglossic/post-colonial orthodoxies. *Classroom Discourse* 10 (3–4), 216–236.
Probyn, M. (2021) Translanguaging for learning in EMI classrooms in South Africa: An overview of selected research. In B. Paulsrud, Z. Tian and J. Toth (eds) *English-Medium Instruction and Translanguaging* (pp. 158–172). Bristol: Multilingual Matters.
Probyn, M., Murray, S., Botha, L., Botya, P., Brooks, M. and Westphal, V. (2002) Minding the gaps – An investigation into language policy and practice in four Eastern Cape districts. *Perspectives in Education* 20 (1), 29–46.
Quijano, A. (2000) Coloniality of power and Eurocentrism in Latin America. *International Sociology* 15 (2), 215–232.
Quijano, A. (2017) 'Good living': Between 'development' and the de/coloniality of power. In W. Raussert (ed.) *The Routledge Companion to Inter-American Studies* (pp. 379–387). New York: Routledge.
Rampton, B. (1995) *Crossing: Language and Identity Among Adolescents*. London: Longman.
Rosebery, A.S., Warren, B. and Conant, F.R. (1992) Appropriating scientific discourse: Findings from language minority classrooms scientific discourse. *The Journal of the Learning Sciences* 2 (1), 61–94.
Roth, W.M. (2004) Gestures: The leading edge in literacy development. In E.W. Saul (ed.) *Crossing Borders in Literacy and Science Instruction: Perspectives on Theory and Practice* (pp. 48–67). Arlington, VA: NSTA Press.
Set, B. (2020) Using semiotic resources to teach and assess scientific concepts in a bilingual Namibian primary school: A social cultural discourse analysis. Unpublished doctoral thesis, University of Cape Town.
Setati, M. and Adler, J. (2000) Between languages and discourses: Language practices in primary multilingual mathematics classrooms in South Africa. *Educational Studies in Mathematics* 43, 243–269.
Setati, M., Adler, J., Reed, Y. and Bapoo, A. (2002) Incomplete journeys: Code-switching and other language practices in Mathematics, Science and English language classrooms in South Africa. *Language and Education* 16 (2), 128–149.
Shohamy, E. (2004) Assessment in multicultural societies. In B. Norton and K. Toohey (eds) *Critical Pedagogies and Language Learning* (pp. 72–92). Cambridge: Cambridge University Press.
Sinclair, J. and Coulthard, M. (1975) *Towards an Analysis of Discourse*. Oxford: Oxford University Press.
Soudien, C. (2012) *Realising the Dream: Unlearning the Logic of Race in the South African School*. Pretoria: HSRC Press.

Soudien, C. (2015) Curriculum, knowledge, and the idea of South Africa. *International Journal of Development Education and Global Learning* 7 (2), 26–45.
Spivak, G. (1985) Can the subaltern speak? In C. Nelson and L. Grossberg (eds) *Marxism and the Interpretation of Culture* (pp. 271–317). Chicago, IL: Illinois University Press.
Stake, R.E. (1995) *The Art of Case Study Research*. Thousand Oaks, CA: Sage.
Statistics South Africa (2012) *Census 2011: Census in brief*. See http://www.statssa.gov.za/census/census_2011/census_products/Census_2011_Census_in_brief.pdf
Stein, P. (2000) Rethinking resources: Multimodal pedagogies in the ESL classroom. *TESOL Quarterly* 34 (2), 333–336.
Stroud, C. and Mpendukana, S. (2009) Towards a material ethnography of linguistic landscape: Multilingualism, mobility and space in a South African township. *Journal of Sociolinguistics* 13 (3), 363–386.
Stroud, C. and Kerfoot, C. (2013) Towards rethinking multilingualism and language policy for academic literacies. *Linguistics and Education* 24 (4), 396–405.
Swain, M. and Lapkin, S. (2013) A Vygotskian sociocultural perspective on immersion education: The L1/L2 debate. *Journal of Immersion and Content-based Language Education* 1 (1), 101–129.
Taylor, D.L. and Cameron, A. (2016) Valuing IKS in successive South African physical sciences curricula. *African Journal of Research in Mathematics, Science and Technology Education* 20 (2), 35–44.
Thibault, P.J. (2011) First-order languaging dynamics and second-order language: The distributed language view. *Ecological Psychology* 23 (3), 210–245.
Thomas, W.P. and Collier, V. (1997) *School Effectiveness for Language Minority Students*. Washington, DC: National Clearinghouse for Bilingual Education.
Tolentino, H. (2007) Race: Some teachable – and uncomfortable – moments. *Rethinking Schools* 22 (1), 46–50.
Turner, M. and Lin, A.M. (2020) Translanguaging and named languages: Productive tension and desire. *International Journal of Bilingual Education and Bilingualism* 23 (4), 423–433.
Tyler, R. (2016) Discourse-shifting practices of a teacher and learning facilitator in a bilingual mathematics classroom. *Per Linguam* 32 (3), 13–27.
Tyler, R. (2021) Transcribing whole-body sense-making by non-dominant students in multilingual classrooms. *Classroom Discourse* 12 (4), 386–402. https://doi.org/10.1080/19463014.2021.1896563
Tyler, R. (2022) Identity meshing in learning Science bilingually: Tales of a 'coconuty nerd' In C. McKinney and P. Christie (eds) *Decoloniality, Language and Literacy: Conversations with Teacher Educators* (pp. 63–77). Bristol: Multilingual Matters.
UNESCO (1953) *The Use of Vernacular Languages in Education*. Paris: UNESCO.
Veronelli, G.A. (2015) The coloniality of language: Race, expressivity, power, and the darker side of modernity. *Wagadu: A Journal of Transnational Women's & Gender Studies* 13, 108–134.
Walsh, C. (2014) Pedagogical notes from the decolonial cracks. *Decolonial Gesture* 11 (4). See https://hemisphericinstitute.org/en/emisferica-11-1-decolonial-gesture/11-1-dossier/pedagogical-notes-from-the-decolonial-cracks.html
Weber, L. and Dyasi, H. (1985) Language development and observation of the local environment: First steps in providing primary-school science education for non-dominant groups. *Prospects* 15 (4), 565–576.
Western Cape Education Department (2017a) WCED minute DCG 00002.2017: Incremental introduction of African languages (IIAL) in 2017. See https://wcedonline.westerncape.gov.za/circulars/minutes17/CMminutes/edcg2_17.html
Western Cape Education Department (2017b) Curriculum minute DCF 0016/2017. Retention of language compensation until 2022. See https://wcedonline.westerncape.gov.za/circulars/minutes17/CMminutes/edcf16_17.html

Williams, C. (1996) Secondary education: Teaching in the bilingual situation. In C. Williams, G. Lewis, and C. Baker (eds) *The Language Policy: Taking Stock* (pp. 39–78). Llangefni: CAI.

Wu, Y. and Lin, A.M. (2019) Translanguaging and trans-semiotising in a CLIL biology class in Hong Kong: Whole-body sense-making in the flow of knowledge co-making. *Classroom Discourse* 10 (3–4), 252–273.

Yager, R.E. (2004) Science is not written but it can be written about. In E.W. Saul (ed.) *Crossing Borders in Literacy and Science Instruction. Perspectives on Theory and Practice* (pp. 95–107). Arlington, VA: NSTA Press.

Yin, R.K. (2009) *Case Study Research: Design and Methods* (4th edn). Thousand Oaks, CA: Sage.

Young, D., Van Der Vlugt, J. and Qanya, S. (2005) *Understanding Concepts in Mathematics and Science: A Multilingual Learning and Teaching Resource Book in English, isiXhosa, isiZulu and Afrikaans*. Cape Town: Maskew Miller Longman.

Zuma, S. (2006) Some strategies used by isiZulu-speaking students when answering TIMMS 2003 Science questions. Unpublished Masters Dissertation, University of Kwazulu-Natal.

Index

activity type 70, 72–74, 77, 80, 84, 86, 99, 107, 109–110, 136
Anglonormativity 5, 19, 24, 41, 49, 67, 78, 110, 112, 116, 135–136
Apartheid 5–6, 8, 10, 14, 21, 41, 110
appropriation/appropriate 34, 37, 70, 100, 103, 107, 109, 114, 116, 127, 130, 136, 140, 143
assessment 8, 13, 25, 33, 44, 66–71, 73, 75, 77, 79, 80–81, 83, 116, 132–133, 136, 138, 141–142

Bakhtin 27, 37–38, 67, 103, 130
Bantu education 6–7
bilingual education 4, 21, 26, 28, 52, 142, 144
body 3, 11–12, 19–23, 25, 27, 29–33, 35, 37, 39–40, 42–43, 51, 77, 85, 89, 95, 100, 102, 104, 106–107, 118, 124, 136–138
border 11–12, 21–22, 28, 40, 84, 100, 103, 107, 124, 136, 138, 140, 146

chemical reaction 1, 13, 17, 69, 70, 71, 72, 78, 107, 119, 121, 123–126, 128, 136
code-switch 9, 22–23, 28, 40, 54–55, 57, 62, 63, 136, 137
coloniality 1–6, 8–12, 18–20, 22, 24, 26–27, 32, 41, 45, 58, 61, 67–68, 70, 82, 84, 107, 109–110, 114, 116–118, 125, 133–139, 141, 143, 146
curriculum 6, 8–9, 13, 44, 68, 69, 70, 82, 88, 102, 107, 109, 118, 136, 139, 140, 142

de/coloniality 1–2, 19–21, 135
decolonial cracks 2, 10, 12–13, 18–22, 32, 39, 41, 67, 74, 83–84, 86, 107, 109, 118, 124, 133–139, 143, 146
dialogic 36, 39, 141

embodied 11–12, 19, 39, 107, 140
English-dominant 26, 55, 58–59, 86, 123
Ethnography 28, 36, 41, 105, 113
exploratory talk 35, 75, 82, 87–88, 93, 115, 120, 123

fixed 5, 37–38, 63, 75, 126
flexible 7, 23, 27, 35, 63, 85, 109, 127, 132–133, 141

gesture 11, 30, 71, 74, 77–78, 85, 89, 97, 100, 102, 120, 124, 133, 137

heteroglossic 21, 46, 48, 51, 64, 67, 114, 133, 137, 136, 138
home language 4–5, 7–9, 14–15, 23–25, 43–44, 50–52, 57–58, 63–65, 105–106, 110, 112, 124, 125, 132, 136

identity 51, 61, 85, 95, 97, 100–104, 107, 112–113, 118, 134
 identity meshing 21, 37, 39, 85, 95, 101, 103–104, 107, 136–139
inquiry 13, 39, 118–119, 123, 143, 145
IRE discourse 72–75, 82, 136
isiXhosa-dominant 42, 57

Khayelitsha 1, 17, 41–42, 48–49, 57, 102

language ideology 4–5, 41, 44, 64, 67, 106, 139
language policy 6–7, 9, 13, 19, 41–45, 48, 53–54, 56, 61, 64–65, 67, 69,

82, 84, 102, 106, 109, 124, 128, 136, 138, 104, 143, 144
languaging-for-learning 10, 28, 35
Lemke 20, 31–36, 38, 63, 70–72, 74, 77–78, 84, 86, 95–97, 99, 102, 105, 107, 109–110, 120, 123–124, 126–127, 133, 136
Lin 11–12, 21, 27–31, 34–37, 74, 77–78, 85, 93, 99, 103, 104, 107, 125, 140–141, 145
linguistic landscape 5, 13, 19, 40–41, 45, 48, 67, 139

McKinney 4–5, 7–10, 14, 27–29, 31, 36, 38–39, 44–45, 56, 61, 67, 75, 102, 136, 138, 142, 146
meaning-making 12–13, 17–18, 21, 25–28, 33, 36, 65, 72, 74, 77–78, 80–82, 85, 88, 102–106, 110, 114, 120, 126, 127, 131, 136–143
media 7–8, 32, 58, 139
metalinguistic 23, 63, 67, 81, 118, 141
mignolo 2, 10–12, 14, 20, 32, 40, 107, 109, 138, 139
monoglossic 5, 26, 28, 45, 61, 106, 133
monolingual 4–5, 8, 13, 18, 21, 24–25, 27, 29, 32–33, 35, 44, 50–52, 69, 78, 82, 84–85, 107, 116, 127, 132–134, 142, 145,
mother tongue 7, 26, 52–54, 60–61, 144
multilingual 2, 4–5, 7–9, 11–14, 18–23, 25–32, 35–36, 38–41, 43–44, 50–52, 55, 57–58, 63–64, 67, 72, 78, 82, 84–85, 109, 124, 126–128, 136, 139, 141–142, 144
multimodal 1, 6, 14, 19, 21, 25, 30, 33, 37, 72, 89, 126, 136

plenary 69, 72, 84, 97–98, 143
positioning 14, 21, 30, 38–39, 43–44, 52, 61, 100, 103, 110, 141
power 2–3, 5, 12–14, 34, 36–37, 44–45, 51, 55, 57, 59, 78, 88, 100, 107, 110, 112, 117, 138–139, 141, 143–144, 145
principal 13, 19, 23, 41–44, 50–57, 79, 136

race 3, 8, 21, 61, 112–113, 118, 143
racialised 2, 4–5, 9, 61, 63, 107, 113, 139, 144

register 18, 20, 32–36, 38–39, 46–47, 56–57, 72, 75, 77–79, 81–83, 85, 88–89, 93, 97–98, 100, 102–104, 106–107, 114, 116–118, 124–133, 136, 138–140
trans-registering 32, 35–36, 40, 136
familiar register 47, 56, 82, 97–98, 102–103, 136, 138–140
register meshing 32, 35–36, 39, 106–107, 139
scientific register 20, 33–34, 77, 81–82, 117, 125, 127, 131
repertoire 20, 21, 25–27, 30–33, 36, 44, 50, 51, 57–58, 65, 72, 85, 105–107, 123–125, 127–128, 131, 136, 139–141
semiotic repertoire 26, 30, 72, 85, 105, 127, 131, 137, 139, 141
resource 4, 6, 25–26, 31–32, 55, 84–85, 88, 104, 107, 109, 117, 119, 125, 127–129, 133–134, 136, 142, 148

safe-talk 23, 75, 82
seatwork 19–20, 72–74, 77–79, 81, 84, 88–90, 104, 107, 110, 118, 128, 132–133, 136
semantic relation 71, 120, 133, 140
siding 20, 29, 72, 78, 84, 95–97, 107, 109, 137
spontaneous 19–20, 29, 39, 80, 83–84, 86, 104, 106–107, 125, 137, 139–140
standard 6, 26, 32, 44–45, 51, 57, 63, 69, 88, 117, 125, 133, 153

teacher education 8, 20, 22, 56, 63, 70, 136, 139, 142
test 20, 23–25, 38, 42, 69–71, 77, 80–82, 88, 132–133, 137, 141, 149–151
textbook 14, 29, 69–71, 73, 77–81, 88–89, 102, 104, 117–118
transgressive 12, 14, 27–28, 65, 106, 109, 127–128
translanguaging
translanguaging space 9, 13, 30, 84, 109–110, 133–134, 139
pedagogical translanguaging 20, 29, 40, 62, 84, 109, 128, 137, 142
translation 12, 18, 20, 24, 28, 30, 40, 48–49, 85–86, 109, 116–117, 126–130, 132, 140, 142

translingual 9, 57, 63–64, 107, 109, 118, 132–133, 140, 145, 149, 153

ukuzilanda 39

Walsh 2, 12, 20, 107, 109, 138–139
whiteness 5, 44
whole-body sense-making 20–21, 27, 31, 44, 85, 89, 95, 100, 107, 118, 124, 136, 137

For Product Safety Concerns and Information please contact our EU Authorised Representative:

Easy Access System Europe

Mustamäe tee 50

10621 Tallinn

Estonia

gpsr.requests@easproject.com

www.ingramcontent.com/pod-product-compliance
Lightning Source LLC
Chambersburg PA
CBHW070616300426
44113CB00010B/1554